Subaru
Impreza
Turbo

First published in November 2001 as *You & Your Subaru Impreza Turbo*
This revised and expanded edition published July 2010

British Library cataloguing-in-publication data:
A catalogue record for this book is available from the British Library.

ISBN 978 1 84425 956 4

Library of Congress catalog card number 2010921833

Published by Haynes Publishing, Sparkford, Yeovil, Somerset BA22 7JJ, UK

Tel: 01963 442030 Fax: 01963 440001
Int. tel: +44 1963 442030 Fax: +44 1963 440001
E-mail: sales@haynes.co.uk
Website: www.haynes.co.uk

Haynes North America Inc.
861 Lawrence Drive, Newbury Park, California 91320, USA

Printed and bound in the USA

Haynes Enthusiast Guide

Subaru
Impreza
Turbo

PRO 200

Chris Rees

SUBARU IMPREZA TURBO
CONTENTS

ACKNOWLEDGEMENTS

Writing any book can be a solitary experience. At times, when you have been staring at a screen for hours, it comes as welcome relief to be able to speak with helpful souls who are prepared to spend their time and energy to assist. I would like to express my gratitude to everyone who has helped along the way.

At Subaru UK I would like to thank Arthur Fairley and Kate Bishop in the press department for their continued support. At Subaru in Japan, I would like to acknowledge the help of Keiko Sato for furnishing so much material so readily, and to Impreza project leader Takeshi Ito for answering my questions so fully and thoughtfully.

At Prodrive, I would like to thank Steve Webb and Liam Clogger in the press department, and within the company I appreciate the time and effort given to me out of very busy schedules by David Lapworth, Richard Taylor and Mike Wood.

In piecing together the worldwide story of the Impreza I would like to thank Kelly Stennick in the USA, Nicholas Senior and Linda Lord in Australia and Dominik Hurter at Subaru Switzerland.

At Scoobysport, Pete Croney was both extremely helpful, very knowledgeable and fast to turn around chapters for reading. Passionate Subaru enthusiast Nino Morelli kindly agreed to read the manuscript too.

For photographic contributions, I must acknowledge the assistance of David Finch in Subaru UK's photographic department: many of David's pictures appear in this book, as well as those of his colleague Darren James. I must also thank Steve Webb at Prodrive, Dan Pullen, Jonathan Dredge, Martin Vincent, Simon Fox at Haymarket, Kathy Agar and Tim Wright at LAT, the staff at Lancaster of Pangbourne, Zoë Harrison and Dave Wigmore.

Further photographic contributions were gratefully received from Ken Honda and Yoko Izumi in Subaru's Marketing Division in Japan. I also acknowledge the comments and reminiscences of Ed Swatman, Chief Executive at Subaru UK, after he read the first printing of this book.

Chris Rees
December 2009

INTRODUCTION
THE PERFECT ALL-ROUNDER

Some cars are alluring because of their styling. Some have the right badge. Others boast high levels of equipment. The Subaru Impreza appeals across many fronts, but its strengths do not lie in any of the aforementioned fields. One thing above all sets it apart: the drive. Approach anyone after their maiden voyage in an Impreza and you will get the same result every time – a look of astonishment, a gentle shake of the head and a broad smile.

No other car at anywhere near the Impreza's price level offers such a convincingly tantalising sweep of abilities on the road. A family sized saloon (or indeed a five-door estate) should not be able to travel quite this fast, should it? Whooshes from the turbo catapult the Impreza forwards at supercar-slaying pace. And then a tight bend approaches. The all-wheel-drive Subaru eats it up with such breathtaking composure that you think it must be tearing up Newton's physics rulebook. Even in the wet and in snow, its handling remains sublimely sure-footed and safe.

I can certainly vouch for this. I vividly remember, in my road testing capacity, my first experience of the Impreza Turbo at the Millbrook test track in Bedfordshire. Around the handling circuit it was simply astounding, and on the Alpine hill circuit it tackled the deep, high-g curves with contemptuous ease. I have had the good fortune to test drive almost every Impreza variant since, not only UK-specification Turbos, but as editor of *Carbuyer* and *Japanese Performance* magazines, many Japanese imports too, as well as tuned cars. The most memorable first-generation variants were undoubtedly the brilliant RB5 with the Prodrive Performance Pack fitted, and the sublime P1. As for Japanese cars, while every STi variant gets the adrenaline flowing, none does it better than the 22B – virtually a rally car.

As for the second-generation Impreza, I think I've driven every example of that, too. I had many memorable journeys in a 'New Age' WRX Sports

Wagon company car, which doubled up as a practical load-lugger. Then I ran a 2006 STi 2.5-litre PPP as a long-term test car – probably the best Impreza yet, although the run-out RB320 probably marked the zenith of the New Age Impreza.

When the all-new third-generation arrived in 2007, I shared many enthusiasts' dismay at the styling of the hatchback. But when I drove the new STi at its launch around Fuji Raceway in October 2007, I had to concede that Subaru had done it yet again – this was another great car. At the time of writing, I've just spent a year running an STi 330S and in my view it's the best all-round Impreza ever: very fast and superb around corners – as ever – yet far more practical for everyday use. Yes, other manufacturers have caught up with Subaru, so the gap between Imprezas and regular GTIs is not as great as it once was, but a gap there certainly remains.

However, the Impreza is not just about travelling more quickly across twisty back roads than virtually any other car. It boasts many other strengths as well. The Impreza is well-built and reliable, as its Number 1 slot in the JD Power customer satisfaction survey in Britain two years running amply demonstrates. It is also practical, understated and charismatic. Above all, it offers unparalleled value.

↑ The Impreza is all about driving but it's also perfect practical family transport and one of the most reliable cars ever made.

Few cars can boast such an extraordinarily accomplished range of abilities as the Subaru Impreza – at any price. A whole generation of performance car enthusiasts came to adulate the Impreza's intoxicating blend of speed, cornering prowess and durability.

Of course, it was the Impreza's rally prowess that sealed its reputation. The Impreza turned its first wheel in anger mid-way through the 1993 season on the World Rally Championship circus, showing instant promise. Colin McRae became synonymous with the Impreza, especially after he won the World Rally Championship in 1995. Further manufacturers' titles in 1996 and 1997 secured legendary status for the Prodrive-prepared rally champ, while drivers' titles in 2001 (Richard Burns) and 2003 (Petter Solberg) cemented the Impreza's impeccable rally credentials..

The thought that drivers with real world incomes could step into a road car and be rewarded with a driving experience that really wasn't far off what McRae, Sainz and Burns were doing has been just too deliciously tempting for a whole generation of enthusiasts. If ever a car with supercar performance levels made sense, it is the turbocharged Impreza, being reliable, durable and fairly easy to maintain. Moreover, it is a car that lends itself perfectly to tuning and modification. Even modest changes can bring about satisfying improvements in the way the car performs, handles and stops. Small wonder that a burgeoning industry has built up around modifying the Impreza.

I have enjoyed writing this book immensely. The raw appeal of the Impreza constantly inspires enthusiasm, and it has been impossible for me not to share it. Personally speaking, there is something satisfying in making sense of the perplexingly varied versions of the WRX, for example, as well as disentangling all the changes to a car that has been with us for so long. I hope that I have done justice to what is a complicated but inspiring story, and trust that if this book delivers even a fraction of the pleasure you get from driving your Impreza, it will have succeeded.

MODEL YEARS

Throughout this book I have made reference to Model Years (MY). Almost without exception, the Impreza was uprated in the autumn of each year, creating a 'Model Year' that ran through to the following autumn. So a 1997 Model Year Impreza, for example, was launched in September or October 1996 (depending on market) and usually ran for the next 12 months. In Japan, the STi was upgraded annually with the name Version II, Version III and so on up to Version VI. In the USA, Model Years typically run from much earlier the preceding year. For example, the 1998 Model Year Impreza was launched in the USA as early as April 1997.

→ The new WRC2008 car based on the hatchback shell scored second place in its first event at the Acropolis Rally, with Petter Solberg at the helm.

↓ Spanning the generations. This Subaru press photo marked 15 years of the Imreza Turbo.

CHAPTER I
GENESIS AND EVOLUTION

World Rally Championship conqueror, practical everyday transport, blistering performance road car icon – the Subaru Impreza Turbo really does have it all. It is an utterly unique car, with its four-wheel-drive transmission, flat-four turbocharged engine and unpretentious appearance. Very few cars of any description can match its cross-country pace and it has an uncanny ability to go around corners at absurd speeds in safety and equally to amaze passengers in a straight line.

Yet the legend that is the Impreza arrived virtually through the back door. Before Colin McRae and the World Rally title, very few people really knew what to make of the turbocharged version of the rather ordinary Subaru Impreza. A handful of enthusiasts immediately recognised it as a towering, almost sublime, performance tool, but it took a few years and many hard-won rally stages for the Impreza Turbo to impress itself on the wider motoring public.

The 1992 Impreza was a fresh departure for Subaru yet it marked the culmination of an engineering progression that is unique among car manufacturers. Subaru was a relative latecomer in Japan's post-war automotive rebirth. Fuji Heavy Industries was formed in 1953 out of six ventures that had been split apart following the Second World War. It produced scooters, bus bodies and engines, but its first-ever car did not arrive until 1958, when it launched the very odd 'jelly-mould' 360 microcar. Here was a car designed to exploit Japan's newly created economy car class, but at least the bug-like machine showed early signs of Subaru's unconventional bent.

Subaru's first boxer engine – a format that would always single out the Japanese car maker – came in the FF-1 of 1966. Although hardly a driver's car, its front-wheel-drive layout was well ahead of the game, especially for a Japanese company. Easily the most significant event in Subaru's early years was its bold and early

flirtation with four-wheel-drive. The Leone saloon had made its debut in 1971, and with the Leone 4WD Estate in September 1972, Subaru broke entirely new ground. Previously four-wheel-drive had been the exclusive domain of off-road vehicles (with the sole exception of the 1966 Jensen FF supercar). The Leone 4WD was the world's first-ever mass-market 4x4 car, launched years in advance of any other rival and offering a distinctive advantage for the maverick Japanese company.

The Leone offered car-like comfort and unbeatable traction for far less money than most purpose-built off-roaders in the Land Rover class. When it was first marketed, demand centred around its abilities in niche areas. It became the darling of hill farmers and anyone who had to deal with mud and snow regularly. Steadily, other people cottoned on to it, such as skiers and anglers. Very quickly it became the world's top-selling 4x4 passenger car.

Subaru never flinched in its pursuit of the four-wheel-drive ideal. It began offering 4x4 on vehicles that had never before enjoyed such engineering, including the Japanese microcar class from 1983. Subaru also pioneered electronic variable torque split 4x4, as well as marketing the world's first ECVT car.

However it was left to others to exploit the sporting potential of four-wheel drive at first. Audi provided the beacon with the 1980 Quattro, combining turbocharging and four-wheel-drive in one devastating package. The Quattro became the dominant force in rallying and paved the way for the next generation of homologation rally cars.

In 1982, Subaru created its first turbocharged four-wheel-drive car in the Leone 4WD Turbo but this was hardly a sporting tool. Its 1.8-litre boxer engine boasted only 120bhp and the only transmission choice was a three-speed automatic! The first car that Subaru could truly claim to be a performance machine was the curious Alcyone

← The first-generation Impreza Turbo single-handedly transformed Subaru from a manuafacturer of useful but unexciting 4x4s into a truly iconic performance car brand..

← This is the car that the Impreza nominally replaced: the L-Series range that consolidated Subaru's credentials as the leading supplier of 4WD cars. But it was very long-in-the-tooth by the end of its production life.

of 1985. This was the domestic market name for the model, after a particularly bright star in the Pleiades (which star cluster provides the origin of the six-star badge used by Subaru). In the United States and Europe the Alcyone was simply called the Subaru XT. Supposedly evoking 'the aerodynamic shape of a hawk or eagle', it was very aerodynamic (it had the world's lowest coefficient of drag at 0.29) but ultimately it looked gawky and its interior was an exercise in pure gimmickry. And while it did have full-time 4WD transmission and reasonably powerful engines (up to 150bhp on the flat-six version), its floorpan was basically a humble Subaru Leone saloon and could never be properly described as a sports car, or even as the ancestor of the Impreza.

Indeed, the car that really sired the Impreza was the Subaru Legacy (also badged Liberty in some markets), launched in 1989. This large saloon was an absolutely crucial car for Subaru. For a start, it was a statement of the company's internationalisation after an unusually inward-looking history for a Japanese car company. Part of this process was the involvement of so many Europeans in its development. For example, Giorgetto Giugiaro produced the early concepts and Dave Richards' Prodrive was hired to prepare it for world rallying.

The Legacy was the brainchild of Masaru Katsurada, a highly talented engineer who was absolutely committed to Subaru's unconventional approach. Katsurada would go on to sire further

generations of Legacy and would eventually become vice president in charge of product planning at Fuji Heavy Industries. By this stage, his reputation was legendary. Katsurada disdained the usual oriental modesty, happily admitting that the latest Legacy was 'the best'. His team members called the car the 'Katsurada Legacy' which was notable because such personalisation is rare indeed in Japan.

The Legacy platform would serve for ten years in two generations of Legacy, while it also formed the basis for the Impreza, as we shall see, and later still for the Forester. The Legacy was an entirely new type of car for Subaru. For a start it was much larger, competing in the Mercedes 190 class. The trademark Subaru boxer four-cylinder engine was there, slung out ahead of the front transaxle, in

↑ The closest Subaru got to a 4x4 sports car in the 1980s was the curious XT (called Alcyone in the Japanese market). But it was based on the decidedly unsporting L-Series floorpan and its engine (120bhp in the UK) was hardly breathtaking in its performance.

← Pioneering Subaru was the world's first company to mass-produce a true 4x4 car. This was the Leone 4WD launched in 1972, rapidly becoming the simultaneous darling of hill farmers in Wales and skiers in Calgary.

↑ **The Impreza owes more than a little to the first-generation Subaru Legacy, launched in 1989. The general layout of the suspension, four-wheel-drive and EJ20 alloy flat-four engine was crystallised in the Legacy and applied to the smaller Impreza.**

Subaru's trademark boxer unit. Masaru Katsurada said: 'We are trying both. My own opinion and that of the company are different. It depends on the car but for me, with an engine bigger than, say, 1.8 litres, the horizontally opposed engine is better for its smoothness and lack of vibration. Below that, cost is very important so I think an in-line or cheaper engine would be appropriate.'

The Impreza project leader was Hideshige Gomi (who at the time of writing is now senior vice president and chief general manager of Subaru Engineering Division). The project sub-leader was Takeshi Ito, who co-ordinated the whole engineering team.

Prodrive was also consulted as early as 1990 for its ideas on how to make the forthcoming Impreza more suitable as a rally car. Prodrive suggested lightweight panels and advised on air inlets and turbo intercooler size. And it was Prodrive that tested the relative merits of air-to-water and air-to-air intercooling and recommended the latter.

But the Impreza was always a road car first. As Takeshi Ito told the author: 'It is our understanding that a good road car should have any potential. The Impreza road car was not developed with the intention of it being the basis for a rally car. Therefore the original Impreza road car would have happened exactly as it did even if the rally car had never been developed.'

It was therefore the primary role of the new Impreza to replace the creakingly aged L-Series, well and truly outdated by the early 1990s. Subaru took its time to get the new car right. As Peter Nunn in *Car* magazine put it: 'Nobody could ever accuse Subaru of rushing the gestation of the Impreza … Since 1979, the L-Series has been at the heart of Subaru's line-up … The Impreza consigns it to history.'

The engineering team drew directly on the Legacy's chassis to create the smaller, sportier Impreza. The floorpan was adapted to suit the Impreza's role as Subaru's crucial mid-size family car. As Ito put it, the Legacy was used for its 'core technologies, horizontally opposed engine with lower centre of gravity and symmetrical AWD powertrain.'

A stiffer bodyshell, larger diameter MacPherson struts front and rear and lighter L-shaped transverse link struts all helped provide sharper

1.8 and 2.2-litre sizes, both entirely new, normally-aspirated units. Turbocharged RS versions also appeared, perfect for Subaru's rally effort and resulting in absolutely storming road cars.

Katsurada was passionate about the light alloy flat-four engine: 'Light weight, a low centre of gravity and longitudinal location with a short overhang make it an ideal powertrain for the all-wheel-drive configuration.' No less than three different types of 4x4 system were fitted. A simple selectable type was standard on entry-level cars; high-performance models like the RS Turbo had a centre differential with viscous coupling; and automatic versions had the computer-controlled multi-plate variable torque split system from the XT. The suspension by independent coil spring struts all round with wishbones up front and trailing arms and twin lateral links to the rear was a clear precursor to the Impreza.

With the Legacy in production and gaining accolades around the world, already by 1990 the Impreza project was in train. Indeed, there was already discussion, aired in public, about the possibility of the future Impreza getting a conventional in-line four-cylinder engine instead of handling. Longer wheel travel, better damping and more negative camber for the rear suspension also played their part.

Of course, an in-line engine was never used in the Impreza: the flat-four powerhouse was retained, based on the EJ20 four-cam, four-cylinder boxer unit used in the Legacy. Compact and bursting with high technology, its two banks of two cylinders sprouted in opposite directions to each other.

Crucial to the overall dynamics of the Impreza was its all-wheel-drive system. With 25 years of experience with 4x4, Subaru was in a perfect position to adapt its experience to suit a high-performance setting. The system featured a central viscous coupling that, in normal conditions, split the torque evenly between the front and rear axles. In slippery conditions, it sensed which axle had the better grip and distributed the torque to minimise wheelspin, all enhanced by a limited slip differential. The five-speed manual transmission had close-set ratios, which as a later road test put it, resulted in faster in-gear times than a Porsche Boxster.

The all-around independent strut suspension from the standard Impreza needed little

↑ The first drawings for the Impreza show alternative ideas for the five-door version. Conventional hatchback, curved rear glass and high-tail fastback treatments were considered, but the final choice was a highly distinctive look claimed to evoke the silhouette of a bird in flight.

← One of the leading lights in the development of the Impreza was Takeshi Ito. The Impreza became his 'baby' over a full decade, such that he was the natural choice to head up development of the second-generation Impreza.

modification for the turbocharged Impreza. Uprated springs and dampers and thicker anti-roll bars front and rear gave it a stiff sports feel. Rally-sized brake discs (vented at the front, solid to the rear) were supplemented by a four-sensor, four-channel anti-lock braking system.

The Impreza's relatively sober shape was set at a fairly early stage. The earliest sketches already showed both four-door saloon and five-door estate forms, the latter presented in a number of different styles, including fastback hatch and bustle-back hatch – although the distinctive five-door form that ultimately made it into production was already a proposal in the early stages. And I bet you never knew what the inspiration for the Impreza's shape was. Subaru explains it thus: 'The silhouette of a waterfowl in flight was taken as a motif and used to bring a swift and active styling to the design. It is attractive yet soft.' Now you know.

The shape was modelled in clay to 1/5th scale and aerodynamically tested (the Impreza eventually achieved a Cd factor of 0.35). A more detailed plastic model was then created, including

transparent windows so that the designers could get a more realistic impression of its final appearance. Then a full-scale clay model was created using computer-aided modelling machinery, fettled by hand to achieve the correct and extremely precise shape (including the full interior in clay). Finally a full-size mock-up was created in plastic to evaluate design elements such as visibility, functionality and the final details of the styling.

The standard car's styling was tweaked in the turbocharged versions, gaining a deep front spoiler with very large integral spotlights, air-gulping vents and scoops in the bonnet, side skirts and a rear spoiler. This was a highly practical car, although with plenty of space for passengers and luggage.

The Impreza was launched in Japan on 1 November 1992 as a medium-range contender with a broad spread of models, starting with a (rather boring) 1.5-litre front-wheel-drive saloon and extending up to the phenomenal 2.0-litre turbo WRX. Perhaps, because it was launched at the same time as the rest of the line-up, the top-

↓ Computer-aided modelling machines created a full-scale clay model, which then had to be finished by hand to end up with the final finished shape.

of-the-range WRX did not get the sort of billing it deserved from the outset. But this situation would not last long, for the turbocharged, four-wheel-drive version had greatness stamped on it. This was a car designed from scratch as a tough, durable and extraordinarily competent machine, and one that could handle extraordinary power outputs and rally stage abuse.

All Imprezas were manufactured at the Fuji Heavy Industries Yajima Factory in Ota City in Japan (the sole exception being an assembly line created to build Imprezas from knock-down packs in Taiwan from 1997). The same Yajima production line also made the Forester in due course.

Europe had its first taste of the Impreza at the March 1993 Geneva Motor Show but the roadgoing Impreza Turbo did not arrive in Europe until March 1994, and then only in Britain and Switzerland to start with. And this was not to be the hot 240bhp WRX sold in Japan but a detuned version with a still-healthy 211PS (208bhp). Launched in the UK at a bargain £17,499 for the saloon and £500 more for the quirkily styled but very practical five-door estate, the Impreza represented incredible value. The

press raved about it. *Autocar* said: 'There's no doubting the rally car in its blood, not least because it can leave a Cossie or Integrale standing.' It added: 'An enthusiast with less than £18,000 could never hope to find himself behind the wheel of a sophisticated four-wheel-drive chassis backed by Cosworth levels of performance. Not until the Impreza Turbo 2000, that is.' Very quickly a waiting list developed for the limited number of imports Subaru could bring in under the quota system then in force – and that waiting list has never gone away.

Crucially for the marketing effort, the Impreza could never be dissociated from rallying. This was a role that the Impreza had been groomed to fulfil. The famous '555' rally Impreza arrived well into the 1993 season with immediate impact. For example, Colin McRae led the 1993 RAC Rally in the Impreza at one point. It took until 1995 for the Impreza to fulfil its promise completely, when McRae and Subaru took both World Rally titles, followed by manufacturers' titles in 1996 and 1997.

The European Turbo stayed essentially unchanged for three years. While there was a

↑ **Once the full-size clay model was signed off, Subaru created a mock-up in plastic for final evaluation of detail elements.**

Sports Wagon wins popularity contest
Overall, Impreza buyers preferred the five-door Sports Wagon to the
four-door saloon. Of the 729,471 first-generation Imprezas built, only
306,680 (or 42 per cent) were saloons, whereas 422,791 (or 58 per cent)
were five-doors. The ratio was swung by the domestic Japanese popularity
of the five-door, which sold more than twice as well as the saloon. In
export markets, the saloon was narrowly more popular than the estate.
As no separate production figures are available for the turbocharged
Imprezas, we cannot say for sure what the split of sales was, but I think we
can be pretty confident that in this form the four-door was much more
popular than the five-door.

↑ **The finished article
was given extra tweaks in
the turbocharged version,
including a deep front
spoiler with big integral
spotlights, vents and scoops
in the bonnet, side skirts
and a rear spoiler.**

minor facelift for the 1997 Model Year, the 1998
Model Year saw the first really major revisions,
with a much better interior and increased
engine torque. The first increase in power came
for the 1999 Model Year, when output rose to
218PS (215bhp).

In Japan, the WRX range flowered into a
profusion of different variants, reaching a peak
of 12 distinct models in the most prolific model
year (1998). The full story is told in the chapter
on the WRX and STi, but the succession of

zeniths was unceasing. The rally-style STi version
was always the one to have, with its extra
power, blueprinted engine, close-ratio quick-shift
gearbox, better suspension and stronger brakes.

Even more extreme was the STi Type R,
a two-door coupé that also boasted a pukka
Group N gearbox, rally-type differentials, quicker
steering and an intercooler water spray. Yet
the Type R was not the ultimate Scooby. That
honour went to the phenomenal 22B, a limited
edition made in 1998 only. Bolstered bodywork
hid wide-track forged aluminium suspension
arms, ultra-firm springing and a bigger, 2.2-litre
four engine.

Although the American market never
received a turbo version of the original Impreza,
its own RS (launched for the 1998 Model Year)
sparked interest in the rally-conquering Subaru:
so much so that the all-new turbocharged
Impreza WRX was launched in the USA for the
2002 Model Year.

The 'New Age' Impreza marked a fresh
chapter for Subaru's performance legend.
Launched in August 2000 in Japan, it was bigger,
stronger and more refined than before. It was

aesthetically a clear evolution of the Impreza's well-known profile, but its bug-eye front-end styling proved very controversial and was frankly never accepted by enthusiasts. Subaru finally bowed to opinion and came up with a fresh face for the 2003 Model Year. With the worldwide availability of the STi version, Subaru fully exploited the potential of what was acknowledged to be one of the world's greatest performance cars – all aided by Subaru returning to World Rally Championship-winning form, when Richard Burns won the title in 2001 and Petter Solberg did the same in 2003.

Popular opinion has it that the all-new Impreza presented in 2007 is an ugly, ill-conceived flop. That's very far from the case. The new model's intended goal was to broaden its appeal and in that it's been very successful, with sales boosted significantly. The Impreza's strong presence in global markets is proven by the fact that 2007 and 2008 were the two best sales years the Impreza has ever enjoyed in its entire lifespan.

While the current WRX may be a shadow of its former self, the STi is arguably the best Impreza that's ever been built: not only fast but far more practical and comfortable too – and just as reliable and capable of being modified. Many Impreza tuners expound the viewpoint that the Impreza has never been better.

At the time of writing, the Impreza remains very much alive. Not only is it Subaru's best-selling model which, more than any other, defines the brand, but it also continues to be a big hitter on the world stage – one of the planet's most potent and enduring icons.

Impreza milestones

1992 – The Impreza range is launched in Japan in November, of which the undoubted star is the turbocharged 240bhp WRX.

1993 – The first non-turbo Imprezas arrive in Europe. Meanwhile Subaru's new rally tool makes its debut mid-season and McRae starts a legendary relationship at the RAC Rally.

1994 – The first roadgoing turbocharged cars are sold in UK (as the Turbo), Australia (as the WRX) and Europe (as the GT). In Japan the rally-inspired STi is launched in January. Colin McRae wins two World Rally events in 1994, coming fourth in the title race.

1995 – In the UK, the first limited-edition Impreza, the Series McRae is launched. It is well timed, as McRae takes the WRC drivers' title and Subaru takes the manufacturers' crown.

1996 – Subaru wins the manufacturers' title in the World Rally Championship for the second time in succession.

1997 – Subaru celebrates its third successive World Rally manufacturers' victory. In Japan the STi Type R is launched, and in the USA a 'warm' 2.5 RS model ignites Impreza interest for the '98 MY.

1998 – Revisions to the engine increase torque and the interior is made sportier. The 'ultimate' 2.2-litre 22B is launched as a near-rally spec machine.

1999 – Prodrive and Subaru finally address latent UK demand for hotter Imprezas with the RB5 special edition and the phenomenal P1. The final STi incarnation (Version VI) appears in September.

2000 – In Japan a wild bodykitted S201 bids farewell to the first-generation Impreza, for in August the 'New Age' Impreza is launched, followed by the new STi in October.

2001 – A 227bhp WRX is launched for the US market at the Detroit Motor Show. The UK300 special edition is launched in the UK. Minor Type B changes are applied across the range, and STi Prodrive Style and Spec C versions are launched in Japan. Meanwhile, Richard Burns takes the WRC drivers' title.

2002 – The limited-edition S202 goes on sale in Japan. A facelifted Impreza previewed at the September Paris Motor Show gets new nose and tail styling.

2003 – The 2.5-litre 300bhp STi is launched in the USA and a restyled Impreza goes on sale in Europe. Petter Solberg wins the drivers' title in the SWRT Impreza.

2004 – The UK gets a 320PS WR1 limited edition. Major chassis revisions alter the STi's wheelbase and add a yaw sensor, while the WRX gets inverted strut suspension. S203 launched in Japan.

2005 – Major 'Hawkeye' facelift. All European and US WRX and STi models receive 2.5-litre engine. S204 launched in Japan.

2006 – STi Spec D launched in UK, followed by similar A-Line in Japan. Prodrive Performance Packs launched for 2.5-litre engines. Spec C Type RA-R launched in Japan, RB320 launched in UK.

2007 – Run-out GB270 special editions in UK. All-new Impreza saloon and hatch launched at the New York Auto Show, STi launched at Tokyo Motor Show.

2008 – 2.5-litre STi goes on sale in Europe. WRX-S and STi 330S launched in UK. Boxer Diesel Impreza arrives. Subaru announces its withdrawal from WRC rallying.

2009 – STi A-Line launched in Japan with 2.5 engine and auto gearbox. 308PS Spec C launched in Japan. Impreza-powered Toyota FT86 concept displayed at Tokyo Motor Show.

CHAPTER 2
THE TURBO

Some of the greatest trees in the automotive forest started as the most modest of acorns. The VW Beetle was branded as inferior in 1945, the Mini was woefully unpopular in its first six months of existence, and the Toyota Corolla was unknown in the West for many years. It took time for them to realise their potential.

So it was with the Subaru Impreza. What would become one of the greatest icons for enthusiasts in the 1990s was greeted more with a distant parp than a great fanfare when it first appeared. The Impreza range, launched in Japan in November 1992, slipped in virtually unnoticed by most western audiences. In journals which had a Japanese correspondent, an occasional footnote remarked on how fast and grippy the WRX version was, and didn't the five-door version look odd?

No, in Europe the Impreza started life as an oddity so far on the sidelines that it was a no-hope sub sitting on the bench watching a game played by Escorts and Astras. It took until 17 May 1993 for the non-turbo Subaru Impreza to arrive in Europe. What would become one of the greatest of all car icons was presented in utterly prosaic tones as an 'interesting' rival in the Escort/Astra class. At that time, Subaru UK viewed the Impreza as a useful new model in its strictly limited artillery, for at this time all Japanese manufacturers were working to a strict quota system limiting the number of cars they were allowed to import. The Impreza filled a gaping void between the Justy and the Legacy and was hoped to lower the average age of Subaru buyers in Britain by ten years.

Given the furore awaiting the Impreza in years to come, it all seemed a pretty downbeat launch. Only two engine options were available in Europe initially, an 88bhp 1.6 and a 101bhp 1.8. Hardly the stuff of dreams, although four-wheel-drive was standard across the range. In the motoring press it was hardly an auspicious start, with *Top Gear* magazine rating the Mazda 323 as more impressive,

and *Performance Car* magazine relegating the Subaru below the Ford Mondeo.

Paul Horrell in *Car* magazine (August 1993) proclaimed: 'I can't help wishing they did a more sporting variant, with a few more ponies and a tauter chassis. They wouldn't need big changes, but I reckon they'd make a healthy difference.' Quite.

In fact there was already plenty of speculation about the possible arrival of a hotter Impreza in Europe. After all, Japan had had the 240bhp WRX since launch. At the time of the 'ordinary' Impreza's launch in Europe, Subaru told the press that the WRX was unlikely to come to Europe during 1993. Subaru had hoped to homologate the WRX by April 1993, in which case a European version of the turbocharged Impreza could have arrived by the end of the year, but in practice Europe was forced to wait until 1994.

Indeed, there had been plenty of talk that the Japanese-market WRX could be transplanted directly over to Europe, complete with its 240bhp engine. It was also reported that, in addition to the WRX, there might be an extra model with the 197bhp EJ20 turbocharged 2.0-litre engine taken straight from the Legacy Quad Cam Turbo. In the event, neither of these scenarios happened.

It transpired that the WRX – fully described in the following chapter – was deemed unsuitable for export outside Japan, at least to begin with. Mostly because of emissions and noise regulations, the WRX never made it officially to Europe. Japanese fuel quality was much higher than in other parts of the world, with octane ratings significantly

DID YOU KNOW?
In 1993, Subaru UK imported six WRX Imprezas from Japan (in fact these were all RS prototypes, the development cars that sired the RA). Due to type approval regulations, the cars had to be registered as 1.8GLs! Three cars went to Prodrive but the other three were later sold by Subaru as used cars, of which at least one is known to survive.

↑ Dancing girls and smoke for the UK launch of the Impreza range in May 1993 could not hide the rather downbeat birth of Subaru's new mid-range car. The real fireworks were still to come – the Impreza Turbo arrived in Britain some 10 months later.

above Europe and Australia, for example. The engine would require considerable modification to make it suitable for other markets. So Subaru developed a specially engineered Turbo model for export markets. Project sub-leader Takeshi Ito recalled: 'We had no choice but to use just 95RON fuel despite the availability of 100RON for the Japanese market. In this condition, our first priority was that we should keep higher performance while complying with emissions standards and acceleration noise standards.'

The turbocharged export versions would go out to Europe, Australasia, South Africa and South America. The European version received its debut at the Geneva Motor Show in March 1994, initially going on sale in only two European markets the same week: the UK and Switzerland.

There was more than a twinge of disappointment that the export turbo model did not have 240PS but a mere 211PS. But this was nevertheless one of the healthiest power outputs of any 2.0-litre engine at the time, and certainly on a par with direct rivals such as the Lancia Integrale and Ford Escort Cosworth. The export version of the EJ20 turbocharged engine boasted 14bhp more

power than its Legacy brother, at 211PS (208bhp/ 155kW) at 6,000rpm. However the torque curve was peakier than the Legacy's: while maximum torque of 201lb ft (270Nm) was better than the larger car, it arrived at 4,800rpm – compared with the Legacy's 193lb ft (262Nm) at 3,600rpm.

The main differences between the Impreza and Legacy engines were improved fuel injection, direct valve actuation and a different turbocharger and intercooler. In contrast to the Legacy's water-to-air unit, the Impreza used an air-to-air intercooler. The Legacy RS engine used a combination of hydraulic lash adjuster and rocker valve actuation, which had proved problematic in service. So the Impreza switched to direct actuation of the valves by the camshaft. Compared with the WRX, the Turbo had a physically smaller turbocharger and different engine management too.

The engine was one of the great Impreza hallmarks from day one. In layout, it was 'flat-four' or 'boxer' four-cylinder engine of two banks of two horizontally opposed cylinders, mounted longitudinally up front. This was a classic 16-valve, single overhead camshaft-per-bank Subaru engine with an alloy block and heads, plus cast-iron cylinder liners. The spark plugs were centrally mounted and the engine boasted very efficient pent-roof combustion chambers. The pistons themselves were cast aluminium, as was the inlet manifold, although the exhaust manifolds were a combination of cast iron and stainless steel. The camshafts were driven by a toothed rubber belt acting on plastic cam pulleys, with automatic belt tension adjustment.

The turbocharger installation was made a little awkward because of the low-down, far-forward engine position. The turbo itself was mounted on the right-hand side of the engine. The intake tubes sat on the upper side of the engine, while the exhaust tubes lay partly on the lower part. The exhaust tubes being of significantly different lengths, it was relatively difficult to ensure constant charging of the compressor wheel. Due to packaging and cost restrictions, the intercooler was sited above the engine towards the back, which was generally agreed to be a less than ideal location as far as cooling was concerned. The Nissan Pulsar GTi-R had a similar layout and its positioning led to the intercooler being nicknamed 'interwarmer'! The problems were not perhaps as great in the Impreza, but it still had to deal with intake air temperatures of around 50°C, to the detriment of engine efficiency. Tellingly, rally Imprezas relocated the intercooler to the front bumper.

The turbocharger used in European Turbo/GT cars was made by the Japanese manufacturer Hitachi (IHI). This was a relatively small unit compared with the truck-sized turbo of the Escort Cosworth, and it was also smaller than that of the Japanese WRX. The chosen turbocharger favoured low-end torque with as little turbo lag as possible. The trade-off was a drop-off in output at high engine speeds. In Australia the turbocharger was a Mitsubishi TD05 unit.

One of the major advantages of positioning the engine low-down (a layout ideally suited to boxer engines) was to give the Impreza a very low centre of gravity. Additionally, the longitudinal layout made the gearbox and transmission much easier to fit and service than a transversely mounted engine configuration such as the Integrale or Celica GT-Four.

The Impreza's transmission was one if its most impressive features. Permanent four-wheel-drive elevated grip and balance far above most other

performance cars, and matched the systems in the Escort Cosworth, Integrale, Celica GT-Four and Lancer Evolution.

Like most 4x4 turbocharged cars, there was a free differential in the front axle that had no wheelspin limiting mechanism. Because of the north–south engine layout, the front differential was sited in front of the gearbox. The centre epicyclic differential was sited at the rear of the gearbox to regulate the torque split between the front and rear axles. This was a viscous coupling device, that is, it used a special silicone fluid to transfer torque. In normal circumstances, it split the torque 50–50 front–rear. There was some comment that it was 'detuned' so as not to interfere with the ABS system that was standard in most markets. A second viscous coupler was fitted in the rear differential, elevating it above more 'normal' AWD Imprezas, and providing torque split to each of the rear wheels.

The gearbox was a very robust unit with five forward speeds, derived from the 'box used in the Legacy RS. Compared with the Japanese WRX unit, it had wider-spaced ratios and a more long-

↓ With its big foglamps, deep front spoiler, gulping bonnet vents, alloy wheels and rear spoiler, the Turbo looked much more purposeful than the ordinary members of the Impreza family.

↓ ↓ Opinion was divided about the five-door Turbo's styling, ranging from 'individual' to 'ugly'. Whatever your view, there was no denying that, in Autocar's words, this was 'a sports car disguised as an estate'.

↑ In a straight line the Impreza Turbo was devastatingly fast, as road tests confirmed. Autocar magazine recorded a 0–60mph (0–96kph) time of just 5.8 seconds, which it described as 'scarcely believable.'

legged final drive ratio, suiting European driving conditions better.

The suspension was classical, too, consisting of MacPherson struts front and rear. At the front there was an L-shaped lower wishbone (or lower control arm) anchored to the front crossmember at one end and the chassis at the other end, both

DID YOU KNOW?
The 'AWD' Impreza

Subaru signified its permanent 4x4 transmission in typically idiosyncratic syntax. Rather than call it 4x4 or 4WD, Subaru always referred to its four-wheel-drive system as AWD, for All Wheel Drive. Subaru sought to highlight the differences between its sophisticated system and the more usual off-road 4x4 systems. It explained: 'With All Wheel Drive, engine power is transferred to all four wheels, not just the front two or rear two as is the case with many of today's cars. This means the Impreza WRX has around twice the traction of ordinary cars and that makes for better roadholding, handling, stability and braking.' Certainly the Impreza made its reputation to a large extent because of its brilliantly conceived all-wheel-drive system.

ends being rubber-bushed. There was of course an anti-roll bar as standard.

At the rear end, there were four lateral links, plus two links anchored to the wheel hub assemblies at one end and the chassis at the other end. The lower arms were linked by a rubber-bushed anti-roll bar.

Uprated springs and dampers, plus anti-roll bars front and rear distinguished the Turbo chassis from lesser Impreza family members (the anti-roll bars were linked to the wishbones via rather flimsy moulded plastic links). Compared with the Japanese WRX, export versions had smaller anti-roll bars and different springs, although the double-acting gas pressurised hydraulic dampers were identical to cars from Japan.

Braking was by rally-sized ventilated 276mm discs at the front with plain 230mm discs and floating callipers at the rear. In the UK and most northern European markets, there was a standard sophisticated four-sensor, four-channel ABS system (some markets had Turbo models without ABS, mirroring the specification of some WRX models in Japan).

The bodywork was essentially the same as the Japanese WRX. Compared to the 'normal' Impreza, it gained a deep front spoiler with a gaping maw (inside which the registration plate was fixed). To either side were very large 'dentist's chair' spotlights encased in vents that fed air to the brakes.

Dominating the bonnet was an air scoop that was split 75/25, the larger part feeding the

→ Easily the most remarkable facet of the Impreza Turbo was the handling engendered by its all-wheel-drive system. Grip levels were astonishing but there was also an uncanny degree of driver involvement and feedback.

intercooler, the smaller part channelling air to the turbocharger. (Incidentally the flat straked air intakes set into the bonnet served no practical purpose in the road car, but they had to be there for homologation purposes, as in the rally car they were essential.)

There were also deformable dark-coloured side skirts and rear under-valance extensions. On the saloon version the boomerang-shaped rear spoiler sat atop the boot. For the five-door, there were two spoilers, one at roof level and one waist level. The early Turbo had 6 x 15-inch wheels (identical to the Japanese WRX except they were always finished in silver, never dark grey). The chosen tyre type was Michelin Pilot HX 205/55 R15, with

a space saver spare (the intercooler sat in the underbonnet area where the spare wheel went on non-turbo Imprezas).

From launch there were four and five-door Turbo models with almost identical specifications, although the five-door had a rear wash/wipe that the European four-door lacked, plus a luggage cover for the rear. In either form the Impreza was a highly practical car, with plenty of space for passengers and folding rear seats in both the saloon and estate versions. As for which body style was best, opinions were very divided. *Autocar*'s James Thomas argued: 'We'd pick the five-door alternative every time. The saloon is a far less appealing car to look at.' However some sources suggested it actually had less luggage room with the rear seats raised and cargo cover in place than the four-door, although other official documents describe the relative VDA volumes as 353 litres for the saloon (later revised to 374 litres) and 356

litres for the five-door (later revised to 376 litres). Obviously the estate was more capacious with the rear seats folded, up to 1,275 litres being liberated. The five-door had 60/40 split folding rear seats but then so did the four-door, which also boasted a ski hatch in the rear seat.

Equipment was fairly impressive too. UK market cars came as standard with a driver's airbag and an insurance industry approved

↑ In most export markets outside Japan, the turbocharged Impreza got a detuned version of the WRX EJ20 2.0-litre engine: 28PS less at 211PS (208bhp). This was mainly down to a smaller turbocharger and different engine management, both of which were designed to cope with lower octane fuel than Japan.

← The dashboard of the Turbo differed little from other members of the Impreza family, which suffered somewhat from scattered switchgear. British market Turbos had a driver's airbag. Note the early-type black-faced gauges. One of the most criticised areas of the early Impreza was its interior. Padded bolsters were not enough to disguise the inadequacies of the seats, while much of the plastic used was downright unpleasant. It is hardly surprising that this became the number one area of modification among owners.

↘ Boot space in the estate was impressive, especially with the rear seats folded. Until the advent of the Impreza, drivers had no right to expect supercar performance at this level of practicality.

↑ ↑ While the Impreza Turbo was astoundingly complete straight out of the showroom, Prodrive and others proved how modifications could squeeze even more out of a remarkable package. This is a Prodrive car on test with Autocar magazine.

↑ Spurred on by rally successes, it did not take long for drivers – especially in rally-mad Britain – to cotton on to the dynamic delights of the Impreza, including McRae-style excursions on to the rough stuff.

immobiliser. In many other countries a passenger airbag was also standard. Other standard equipment included central locking, electric windows and mirrors, heated rear window, headlamp washers, headlamps levelling, height-adjustable driver's seat, tilt adjustable leather-trimmed steering wheel, leather Nardi gear knob, sports seats, quartz digital clock, stereo radio/cassette and side-impact protection beams. Another feature unique to export Imprezas was the curious 'bright switch' placed with delightfully inexplicable prominence in the centre of the dashboard. Its sole function was to override the dimming of the clock when the lights were turned on …

However, the cabin was often criticised for being rather sombre and cheap in feel, with uninspiring cloth seats in early cars and rather low-rent plastics in evidence. Paint colours available at launch were White, Flame Red, Light Silver metallic, Deep Green metallic and Black Mica (metallic and mica colours optional at £219 extra). The interior trim in all Turbo models was called 'Rallyweave'.

As if Ford and Lancia were not quaking in their boots at the Subaru's on-paper specification and road test adulation, the Impreza offered up one more sting in the tail for its rivals. The launch price in the UK was a dauntingly low £17,499 (or £500 more for the five-door), at a time when the Escort Cosworth cost £22,500 and the Integrale was £25,000. Insurance was fittingly stiff for such a high performance machine, in Britain being placed in a high, Group 17.

In the right-hand-drive UK and Irish markets the turbocharged version was called the Impreza Turbo 2000 AWD while in most of the rest of Europe and other markets the left-hand-drive car was known as either the Impreza GT or GT Turbo.

The press raved about the new Turbo. Colin Goodwin in Car magazine (June 1994), driving a five-door Turbo across Ireland, praised the suspension: 'The Impreza has the most amazing damping. Yumps, pot-holes, cracks and ruts fail to disturb it, evidence no doubt that Subaru's rallying experience is paying off.'

Impreza GT in Europe

While the right-hand-drive model was marketed as the Impreza Turbo 2000 AWD in the UK and Eire, mainland (left-hand-drive) European markets generally referred to the turbocharged version as the GT or GT Turbo. The five-door was also commonly known as the Compact Wagon in Europe.

At the international launch of the top-of-the-range turbocharged Impreza at the Geneva Motor Show in March 1994, it was presented as the 'transcendent' GT Turbo. The Swiss-market press release described the car as 'a mechanical force in sexy clothing, boasting super-equipment levels. A saloon with a sporting character, or as Subaru adverts say, a veritable 'Tour-beau'.' The latter statement demonstrates that corny puns are not alien to French-speaking people.

The performance claims did not really reflect the results achieved in independent tests: a top speed of 143mph (230kph) was higher than most testers achieved, while in contrast the 0–100kph (0–62mph) time of 6.6 seconds was an understatement.

The GT Turbo arrived sporadically across Europe. Indeed, it was only available in Switzerland initially. It did not make it to France until April 1995 for the four-door, and one month later for the five-door, while the GT remained out of the German market until 1996.

Specifications differed across Europe too. In France, the four-door lacked ABS, an airbag and anti-theft protection, while the five-door had them as standard, as well as a sunroof. The estate had gained twin airbags by 1997, in contrast to the four-door, which could however be ordered with these items fitted for an extra 10,000Ff. In fact, in many European markets such as Holland and France, there were eventually two versions of the GT: one with a stripped-down spec excluding airbags and ABS, and a higher-spec version with these items added. In France, the Year 2000 base model had twin front airbags as standard (four-door only); an ABS-equipped model was also available in both body types.

The GT Turbo never took off in Continental Europe in the same way as it did in Britain, which was always the Impreza's best market within the EU. In some cases (such as Belgium), this was down to higher taxes for more powerful cars and in others (like Italy) it was due to tough import quotas for Japanese cars, but even in markets where one might have expected a good following, the Impreza was always viewed as rather marginal.

It took a while for the Impreza to filter through to European markets (as the GT), but the effort was helped by Kenneth Eriksson, seen here demonstrating the road car's tenacious abilities to a journalist in his home country, Sweden.

He continued: 'I didn't think of this car as a serious rival to the Lancia Delta or the Ford Escort Cosworth, but now I'm changing my mind. Driving an Intergrowler this fast [across Irish roads] … would be terrifying, if not impossible … Sure, I'll bet an expert rally driver could blast the Delta at enormous speed across here but I'd wager that a normal person would be faster in the Impreza.'

Car magazine again: 'If you're really ham-fisted and throw the Impreza into a sharp corner with unreasonable brutality, then it will understeer straight on until you lift off and allow it to tuck back in. Drive sensibly and the levels of grip will amaze you.'

Road tests confirmed the abilities of the Impreza in objective terms. *Autocar* recorded a top speed of 137mph (220kph) and a remarkable 0–60mph (96.5kph) time of just 5.8 seconds, which the magazine described as 'scarcely believable.' It also recorded a 30–70mph (48–113kph) sprint time of 6.6 seconds, matching the Integrale and Escort Cosworth. *Autocar* continued: 'The Impreza behaves a little like its brother, the Legacy, with turbo lag evident at low revs and less electric throttle response than its high-torque competitors. From about 3,500 up to its 7,000rpm red line the Impreza delivers a smoothly consistent rush of turbo thrust. It is an addictive sensation and one that will soon have you forgiving the engine for its somewhat coarse, unrefined manners.'

Mirroring the limited edition Imprezas offered in Britain, many Continental markets received their own special editions. Generally speaking, these were marketed under the name 555 with Rally Blue colouring and gold alloy wheels.

In France in 1996, the 555 included black WRX seats in grey Alcantara, a black facia and Nardi leather steering wheel and gear knob, all for 10,000Ff (around £1,250) above the standard price. The following year there was a WRX limited edition in France with stickers on the boot lid, front wings and interior. The 1998 WRX was painted black rather than the usual Rally Blue, while a WRX3 version was later launched in silver.

The Dutch (who also had the 555 edition) produced something very similar to the RB5 in January 1999 to celebrate 25 years of Subaru in Holland. The oddly named Stars 25 was available in Black Mica (40 produced) or Blue Steel (120 made), both with gold wheels and Alcantara-trimmed seats. Other European countries had similar special editions in 1999, although Germany struck out on its own with a 'Classic' edition which was a five-door in Black Mica with wood and leather interior trim.

As for the handling, *Autocar* enthused: 'Steam into a corner too quickly and the Impreza will start to run wide, with gentle and predictable understeer sending an early warning of relinquishing grip. Raising your right foot a shade

tightens the line accurately and effortlessly, though. Simply put, the Impreza feels confidently neutral, benign even, in most situations.'

Criticisms were few. The gearchange was described as baulky and rubbery, the pillarless doors produced wind noise and the steering was 'a touch too light for a car of the Impreza's meaty aspirations'. And there was the inevitable criticism of the dull grey cabin: 'an unrelenting grey cocoon of nastily textured cloth and indifferent quality plastics.' Also, fuel economy was not great, as *Autocar* recorded a measly 18.7mpg (15.1 litres/ 100km) over the duration of the test. However, more light-footed progress would yield better results, as the EC's official figures confirmed: 24.8mpg (11.4 litres/100km) in the urban cycle, 39.8mpg (7.1 litres/100km) at a constant 56mph (90kph) and 30.1mpg (9.4 litres/ 100km) at 75mph (120kph).

1995 – McRae's year

It did not take long for a waiting list to develop for the limited number of imports Subaru could bring in under the European quota system – and that waiting list never went away. In 1995, Subaru

→ European markets gained their own special editions. This is the 'Collection' edition launched in Switzerland in 1998, but many were actually badged WRX to acknowledge the Japanese Impreza and its World Rally impact.

(UK) announced that the Turbo accounted for no less than 45 per cent of all domestic Impreza sales – a phenomenal percentage for such a high-performance machine. At its peak, the Turbo would account for an incredible 65 per cent of Impreza sales. No doubting it, the Impreza Turbo had caught on like wildfire.

The reason for this can be attributed to one factor – British driver Colin McRae's phenomenal success in world rallying. Having won the RAC Rally on home soil in November 1994 to huge celebration, followed by even greater successes in the 1995 season, Subaru decided to produce the first of a string of limited edition road cars based on the Turbo.

The first of these special editions was the Series McRae, launched in June 1995, which unlike most other editions had the huge distinction of being prepared by Oxfordshire-based Prodrive. The distinctive WRC-inspired colour scheme was Rally Blue Mica with gold 6.5 x 16-inch Speedline Safari eight-spoke alloy wheels with Pirelli P Zero 205/50 ZR16 tyres, plus special Series McRae decals on the flanks and boot of the car. The interior was treated to McRae-signature Recaro open-headrest front seats with the seats and side panels trimmed in matching speckled Le Mans/ Avus material. Curiously for a car inspired by rally success, Subaru factory-fitted an electric tilt/slide sunroof. An individually numbered dash plaque was provided too. Only 200 cars were produced (numbered 1 to 201 as there was no number 13) at an on-the-road price of £22,999 (some £5,000 more than the standard car). The Series McRae is

still very much regarded as 'one to have' by British Impreza enthusiasts.

1996 – everyone wants a Turbo

In February 1996, a Turbo-lookalike version of the Impreza was launched to capitalise on the huge popularity of the Impreza in Britain. Frankly, the Turbo's popularity had been at the expense of models further down the scale and Subaru saw an opportunity for the Turbo kudos to rub off on a cheaper, non-turbocharged model. So enter the 2.0 Sport. Under the skin it may have been the same as a 2.0GL (115PS/113bhp non-turbo engine but still all-wheel-drive), but it did its best to look like a Turbo. It had the front airdam and giant foglamps, the dark skirts and rear under-valance

↑ That's more like it! The Series McRae had specially monogrammed Recaro open-headrest seats and speckled Le Mans/Avus trim (Prodrive offered the same seats but non-monogrammed). A numbered plaque told you that your car was one of only 200 produced.

← Subaru exploited Colin McRae's success in the World Rally Championship with the Series McRae special edition of 1995. Special paint, Speedline Safari 16-inch gold wheels, decals and a sunroof identified this very special car.

and the boot spoiler (twin spoilers on the five-door). But the Sport's denuded spec included smaller wheels with higher-profile tyres, and no bonnet scoops or vents. Its price was some £4,000 less than the Turbo.

Underscoring a new regime in the UK, the 1.6, 1.8 and front-wheel-drive derivatives were dropped from the range in September 1996. That left a completely AWD line-up consisting of the 2.0 GL (first seen in December 1995), 2.0 Sport and 2000 Turbo. Subaru stated: 'The reason is to concentrate on the sporty dynamics and lively performance of the Impreza, which is still enjoying the connection with Colin McRae's World Rally Championship-winning car.' The bottom line was that Turbo sales were 50 per cent up on 1996 thanks to the McRae effect. The 2.0 Sport would prove to be a successful addition in Britain. And

that's the way things remained, although the last few examples of the 1996 Model Year Turbo model received the revised brake callipers of the '97 model.

1997 – facelift and torque lift

Shortly after the 1997 Model Year Impreza was released in Japan, Subaru UK presented the new-look 1997 Impreza range at the October 1996 Birmingham NEC Motor Show. The significantly revised Impreza featured a sportier exterior, a plusher interior and a major torque boost for the Turbo, enhancing its flexibility.

The new exterior was an in-house design exercise. A lower and more deeply contoured bonnet line was joined by a new front grille, no longer a split item but boasting a body-coloured insert encasing black mesh. To either side the headlights were squarer too. The rear bumpers were more rounded and 'cleaner' in profile than before. Unique to the Turbo was a neater bonnet air scoop, while the new bonnet included mesh covers for new-shape twin louvres. All Imprezas now featured high-level rear stop lamps, in the case of the Turbo and Sport saloons mounted in the boot spoiler. The Sport and Turbo continued to boast their own distinct alloy five-spoke wheels.

The manual gearbox was now slicker-acting thanks to double synchromesh cones, which

↘ For the 1997 Model Year, the Impreza had a facelift and a much-needed boost in the interior. The Turbo at last had some decent seats in the form of a high-backed winged sports design, with matching door trims.

↓ A significant boost in torque for the 1997 Model Year across a wider rev band produced even more startling test results: some magazines recorded just over five seconds 0–60mph. Mid-range thrust was notably improved.

made a dramatic improvement in first-to-second gear changes, a well-known weakness of early Imprezas. Reverse gear also now had synchromesh. The suspension was also uprated, benefiting from a thicker rear anti-roll bar. Brake callipers were also revised.

Inside, all Imprezas had new cloth interior trim. The GL and Sport featured more deeply contoured front seats while the Turbo benefited from high-backed winged sports front seats, at last getting rid of the decidedly unappealing seats of yore. Other changes included simplified heating and ventilation controls and a larger load area for the five-door. The rear suspension towers took up less space and the jack and radio speakers were moved to maximise luggage room. The audio system was also changed from a Subaru-badged Panasonic radio/cassette to a Philips unit with a removable front. Impreza five-door models also gained standard roof rails. All Imprezas gained factory-fitted transponder immobilisers using the normal ignition key to unlock the engine management system. Some different exterior colour choices also arrived at this time.

Perhaps the most significant changes happened under the bonnet. Certainly the modifications in the engine department were the most significant to date, producing very noticeable performance enhancements. First among the changes, the compression ratio was raised from 8.0 to 9.7:1. Also, new, low-friction molybdenum-coated pistons were introduced for better power delivery and fuel consumption, with improved cylinder head cooling via ceramic coating for the piston crowns. More advanced ignition for more power consisted of wasted-spark ignition instead of coil-on-plug (double-ended coil bolted to top of inlet manifold, firing spark plugs via high-tension cables in groups of two). Solid valve lifters with shim adjustable tappets improved reliability at sustained high revs and allowed more aggressive and efficient cam profiles. There was now also an improved turbo intake system to boost torque: air entered the turbo directly from under, rather than behind, the inlet manifold. The manifold itself was revised with longer intake runners for improved torque, and to deliver the necessary clearance for a new near-straight turbo inlet port. This had previously been snorkel-shaped and the

← **Part of the facelift announced for 1997 was a lower, deeply contoured new bonnet. The Turbo gained a new bonnet air scoop, while new-shape twin louvres echoed those of the World Rally Car.**

new, straighter design reduced lag. There was also an improved exhaust manifold cover to reduce noise levels. The engine management system was revised and the turbocharger itself was smaller, while the intercooler grew in size and was not offset as before. Maximum turbo boost pressure was now up to 13.05psi.

The most notable result of these changes was an increase in torque which Subaru described as 'massive'. In fact maximum torque rose by five per cent, from 201lb ft (270Nm) to 214lb ft (290Nm) at 4,000rpm, which was some 800rpm lower than before. Maximum power remained at 211PS (208bhp) but was developed at a more accessible 5,600rpm, 400rpm less than before.

Mid-range and in-gear acceleration was greatly improved, while Subaru claimed that off-boost lethargy was 'all but eliminated'

↑ The second UK special edition was the Catalunya or 'Cat' of 1997. Black Mica paint was complemented by 15-inch gold-coloured alloy wheels and Catalunya badging to the sides and on the rear.

↗ The best feature of the Catalunya was its startling red-trimmed seats and interior, plus carbon-fibre gauge surrounds. Air conditioning, badged floor mats and a numbered plaque completed the picture.

– certainly turbo lag was vastly improved. The official figures recorded marginally improved performance: top speed for the saloon was now 143.5mph (231kph)(1.5mph/2.4kph higher) while the five-door at 142mph (228.5kph) was identical to the old model. The Turbo's claimed 0–62mph (100kph) time was improved too, at 6.4 seconds for the saloon and 6.5 for the five-door. This was in fact a gross understatement of the car's true abilities. *Performance Car* magazine tested the new model over the 1/4-mile drag strip at Santa Pod Raceway in the November 1997 issue. Admittedly, these times were taken on a grippy drag strip with very little fuel on board, but a 0–60mph time of 5.03 seconds is supercar material in anyone's book. *Top*

Gear magazine of the same month produced a 0–60mph time of 5.2 seconds, a maximum of 140mph (225kph).

There was good news on the fuel consumption front too. Using the EC's more rigorous Urban/ Extra Urban and Combined system revealed figures of 20.5/34.9 (13.8/8.1 litres/100km) and 29.7mpg (9.5 litres/100km). By comparison, the 185bhp Saab 900 Turbo returned 18.7/37.2 and 27.2mpg (10.4 litres/100km).

The press seemed convinced. John Barker in *Car* magazine said: 'There's much more mid-range thrust than the original had, and thus a much wider power band to play with. Better still, its handling has an almost Prodrive feel to it, with much less dive and squat … It helps that the brakes are among the best of any road car I've tried.'

Some of the Turbo's engine changes were also applied to the non-turbo Impreza GL/Sport powerplant, including the low-friction pistons, narrower and straighter inlet ports to boost mid-range pulling power, compression ratio raised from 9.5:1 to 9.7:1, improved head cooling and advanced ignition, and a new 5.2-litre auxiliary chamber added to the air cleaner. There were also changes to the non-turbo exhaust system. Enhanced torque response and economy were claimed: torque was marginally up at 127.4lb ft (172Nm) but at 4,000rpm instead of 4,400rpm. The top speed for the Sport manual was now 118mph (190kph) (116mph/187kph for the five-door), with 0–62mph times of 9.7 and 10.0 seconds respectively.

The whole 1997 Impreza range was more refined, not only thanks to the engine revisions but also because of extra sound deadening, underbonnet shields, new exhausts, reinforced body and dual door seals, and roof trim in unwoven cloth instead of vinyl, all helping to dampen road noise.

Prices rose only by a marginal amount, to £18,499 for the Turbo four-door and £18,999 for the five-door. British Impreza owners were so impressed with the overall ownership package that the car secured the Number 1 spot in the renowned JD Power customer satisfaction survey in the UK in 1998. This feat would be repeated again in 1999, while in 2000 the Impreza came second – it was beaten by the Subaru Legacy!

Police Imprezas

Imagine you were a bank robber. Which car would you choose as a getaway vehicle? Right – an Impreza. As many police forces around the world discovered, the combination of turbo power and four-wheel-drive handling gave the Subaru cult status in the rarefied world of getaway drivers in those markets where the Impreza had gained a following, such as Britain, Australia, Japan and New Zealand.

In Britain, six forces – Nottinghamshire, North Yorkshire, Cumbria, Humberside, Surrey and Hampshire constabularies – all used Impreza Turbos for pursuit and serious crime response. They said the Impreza acted as a deterrent, making criminals think twice before entering into a pursuit if they knew the police car chasing them would be an Impreza Turbo.

Cumbria traffic police's Sgt Steve Lambert said: 'With no motorway sections and a lot of rural roads, the Impreza is ideal for us because it is relatively small and incredibly agile. From a safety point of view, the police officer is not having to put himself under pressure when driving at speed. Officers only need to push the Impreza Turbo about 70 per cent of the extent to which they need to drive other, larger patrol cars, to exceed their performance capabilities. What is also important is that the car gives us real credibility. We find that people having seen it tend not to want to get involved in a pursuit in the first place.'

In Australia, police forces in New South Wales, Queensland, Canberra and Victoria all evaluated the Impreza as a pursuit vehicle to replace their Commodores and Falcons.

↑ Among the modifications on the police Impreza were a base radio station and headset, video camera and screen and pursuit lighting switches.

← While the Impreza made the perfect choice as a getaway car for criminals, the corollary was that it made the perfect police pursuit vehicle. This is an Impreza Turbo in use with the Humberside police in Britain.

Catalunya Celebration

Although Colin McRae failed to clinch the 1996 World Rally Championship, Subaru succeeded in retaining the manufacturers' title at the Catalunya Rally. Predictably, to celebrate this victory Subaru UK launched its second limited edition Impreza Turbo, called the Catalunya, in March 1997.

This time the paint finish was a unique black mica with colour-matched door mirrors complemented by 15-inch alloy wheels (identical to those on the 2.0 Sport but painted gold). There was Catalunya badging to the sides and on the rear.

The interior was retrimmed in black with red highlights on the seats and interior trim, while the instrument dials had a carbon-fibre surround. The gear knob was a short rally-type stick (although

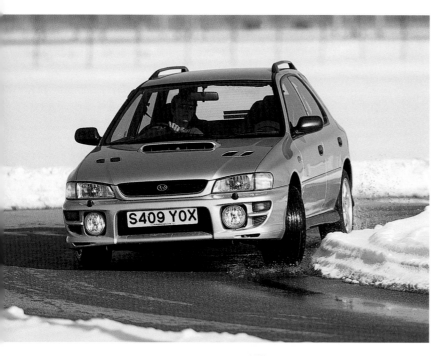

and saw a major overhaul of the interior. A completely new dashboard, based on the Forester's, featured white dials that turned black at night with glowing gold numbering, rearranged dials (the speedo was now central), a computerised odometer/tripmeter, and a low-fuel light. The clock moved to the instrument pod rather than the centre console as before. Some of the switchgear moved around too. A new centre console now incorporated a lidded box and the inevitable cupholders, while revised cloth-covered inner door panels were of a different design. Twin airbags were now standard in the UK, as well as a new Momo four-spoke leather steering wheel, leather-covered handbrake lever and a shorter throw gear lever. And what looked like a standard tweeter kit was actually only a grille with no tweeters behind.

↑ Perhaps the Impreza's most impressive dynamic advantage was its grip in wet and icy conditions. Permanent four-wheel-drive dispatched the dangers of driving in such weather with an ease that other performance cars could never hope to match.

↗ White dials, a new dashboard with a lidded centre box, new centre console and new type door panels distinguished the 1998 Model Year Impreza Turbo, as well as a new Momo four-spoke leather steering wheel.

→ ↗ A curious 'Bright' button kept dashboard lighting up when the lights were switched on (this is a later car with the different-style dashboard). Air conditioning was optional in most of Europe but was standard in Australia.

not a quick-shift), and there was standard air conditioning, Catalunya badged black-and-red mats, and of course

an individually numbered plaque on the dash. Again only 200 were built at an on-the-road price of £21,610. Some UK dealers cashed in on the huge demand for the 'Cat' (as it was nicknamed), fitting expensive options such as leather seats and a sunroof. It boosted their profits but made the purchase price higher.

1998 – insider dealing

Following a September 1997 debut in Japan, the 1998 Model Year Impreza was presented in October 1997 at the London Motor Show

The only external change was a new, WRX-style larger alloy wheel set. Previously the Turbo had standard 6 x 15-inch wheels, with 16-inch wheels strictly optional. However in Europe the standard wheel size now grew to 7 x 16-inchers shod with lower-profile 205/50 VR16 Bridgestone Potenza tyres. In Australia the wheel size was 6.5 x 16 inches. The switch to 16-inchers occurred three full years after the WRX in Japan had switched to 16-inch wheels as standard. The engine was also very slightly modified to make it smoother. The new specification included a bigger turbo dump valve, revamped turbo inlet and a re-routed air intake.

In the UK, the price went up to compensate, by just over £600. Not that it dented sales at all: indeed, the Impreza continued its unstoppable march, in Britain at least. In the UK it was in such demand that the Turbo had a waiting list of close on one year by 1998.

Such demand had been fuelled by ever more glowing press tributes. *Car* magazine said: 'The Subaru has similar power to the Boxster. It lapped faster. It's a four-door saloon. And if it had been wet or bumpy the difference would almost certainly have been greater. An amazing car … Buy one.'

Autocar's February 1998 test of a five-door returned a five-star result, a very rare occurrence (only two cars did so in 1997) and described the Impreza as: 'The best affordable performance car yet … We can think of no other car that is quicker over the ground which also competes on price.' It recorded a remarkable 0–60mph time of only 5.5 seconds, with 0–100mph in 15.8, and the 30–70mph increment took a mere 5.6 seconds, a full second faster than the Porsche Boxster, while its 50–70mph top gear time of 8.5 seconds was fully five seconds faster than the old Impreza.

In its end-of-year round in December 1997, *Auto Express* placed the Impreza five-door ahead of the Honda Integra Type-R, Fiat Coupé Turbo and Nissan 200SX, saying that 'many cars trying to corner at similar speeds would end up in the scenery.'

In February 1998, *Performance Car* pitched the Impreza against rally/turbo rivals such as the original Audi Quattro 20V, Lancia Integrale Evo, Escort RS Cosworth and Nissan Skyline GT-R. 'The Impreza does without the luxury of gorgeous looks, winning you over with its honesty and awesome ability. Any half-decent driver will cover ground at a stormingly fast pace, whatever the conditions. And if very little can live with it on the road, no new car can touch it on value for money. It's not perfect, but after two days in Wales it won by the slimmest of margins.'

Terzo edition

April 1998 saw the launch of the third special edition Turbo in the UK, rather unimaginatively called the Terzo (Italian for 'third'), to celebrate the Impreza's third successive victory in the World Rally Championship manufacturers' title.

↓ **The UK's third special edition was the 1998 Terzo, with its attractive blue paint scheme, gold alloy wheels, special decals and Alcantara-trimmed STi-type seats.**

In a poetic touch, 333 cars were built at a price of £22,995 each. The paint scheme was once again unique to these cars, a blue that was similar (but not identical) to the WRC cars. There were gold-coloured 16-inch alloy wheels and special 'Terzo' badging on the sides and rear. Inside, the seats and panels were trimmed in grey Alcantara with black 'Jersey' surrounds on the seats (the rear seats did not split/fold in this edition), the front seats incidentally being based on the Japanese STi seat. Carpets embossed with the Terzo logo, a numbered plaque and air conditioning were all standard, as was a Cobra 6422 Thatcham Grade 1 remote alarm/immobiliser system.

Very similar special editions were also marketed in other countries under various different names. For example, in Switzerland it was called the 'Collection' (see separate panel on European special editions).

1999 – STi influence

Subaru's European offshoots began to turn increasingly to the developments being made in Japan at Subaru Tecnica International when it came to ideas for updating the Impreza. The 1999 Model Year Turbo therefore incorporated several items taken more or less directly from the Japanese STi. The 1999 model was officially revealed in the UK at the October 1998 Birmingham Motor Show, but the car actually first appeared in Australia in August 1998. This was historic in a way, as it was the first time that a new model from Subaru had been unveiled outside of Japan.

The STi-type improvements included four-pot front brake callipers, ventilated rear discs, the trademark STi tall rear wing and height-adjustable front seats (although they gained more padding for Europe). The brakes were probably the most significant of these: bigger, 294mm rally-bred ventilated front discs and ventilated rear discs were a big advance, and the STi Version IV four-pot front callipers looked great and worked brilliantly. The suspension was also made considerably firmer.

Cosmetically the 1999 MY front bumper was slightly modified, being a little deeper and with just one vane (instead of two) and rather odd orange plastic wedges next to the fog lights. The fog lights and headlights also gained multifaceted reflectors

and clear lenses, making for much brighter night-time illumination, while there was a new honeycomb front grille (shared with the Sport). The colour palette changed again, with reddish blue deleted and Dark Blue Mica and Dark Silver added. Inside, the car benefited from the new STi seats already mentioned, extra sound-deadening, a facia-mounted cupholder and a slightly different Momo steering wheel. At long last a Sigma Thatcham 'Category 1' alarm and immobiliser became standard in the fight-back against the Impreza's image as one of the most 'nickable' cars on the road.

Apart from the new STi-style touches, the other important news was the arrival of the new Phase 2 version of the EJ20 engine (already seen in the Legacy) that yielded an extra 7bhp. The main changes were a different blow-off valve and an internal modification to the heads, which now had roller rockers. The net result was a higher power output of 218PS (215bhp/160kW) at the same 5,600rpm, although the quoted torque remained at 290Nm (214lb ft) at 4,000rpm.

Subaru also referred to a revised gearbox to overcome a 'reluctance to engage second gear' – a rather mystifying statement given that the second gear problem had been sorted on 1997 Model Year cars. In fact, the major change for the gearbox for 1999 was a stiffer casing, bolted to the engine in seven places.

The price in the UK went up by £1,185, taking the Impreza over the £20,000 mark for the first time but still positioned deep within bargain territory compared with rivals. The Impreza continued to pile up rave reviews. *Evo* magazine even called it 'a semi-STi Impreza'. In a May 1999 *Auto Express* giant test of best-driving cars, it pitched the 1999 Impreza against the Honda Accord Type R. It glowed that the Subaru's 'Lightning-quick acceleration, competition-developed engines and brakes powerful enough to stop a runaway train were once the sole preserve of supercars,' adding that it was 'best in value for money performance cars.' Compared with the Honda, 'Getting the best out of the rally-inspired Impreza is an altogether easier task … The car's flat-four turbocharged engine delivers thrust further down in the rev range and although you have to wait momentarily for the turbo to spool up to speed, acceleration is savage in every gear.' It concluded: 'The Impreza's crushing ability, both as a track car and a road car, is so impressive it's hard not to write off rivals such as the Accord as also rans. The Accord is certainly a well-balanced car but it just can't deliver the kind of fun the Impreza supplies as standard.'

Evo magazine did the same test in its December 1998 issue. The five-star rated Impreza won. 'The Impreza gives so much for so little effort, in both performance and handling, it makes any driver like Colin McRae. The moment you drive off, you know your in something special, and everything just happens from there just endorses that feeling … there isn't another saloon for less than £30,000, possibly £40,000 that satisfies like an Impreza.'

As much was confirmed by *Car* magazine, which put the much more expensive Audi TT coupé up against it in the January 1999 issue, with the Impreza winning. 'No wonder this car is considered one the greatest of the '90s,' it opined. 'Character is the Subaru's ace card – the extraordinary flat-four that's like nothing else on the road, the prominent turbo whistle, the deep, race-derived seats, the Momo wheel … Neither the front nor the rear of this car are in control; it moves all of a piece, all four tyres gripping or slipping according to your strict instructions.' It concluded: 'Being close to an Impreza means being close to a car enthusiast's idea of perfection, an automotive immortal. The Impreza is that high a benchmark.' *Autocar* said the same of the Impreza as it trounced Audi's S3 in March 1999: 'For sheer driving pleasure it is still at the very top of the heap,' and it also put the Impreza top in its 100 Best Cars list.

Evo also gave fourth place to the Impreza as its Car of the Year in January 1999, behind the Porsche 911, Lotus Elise and Ferrari F355. 'It's a cult, a craze, a supercar for "ordinary blokes",' it said. It praised the 'storm of torque,' the 'incredible traction' and the 'stupid performance', while adding that it 'defies physics'. If there was a criticism, it was that the ride had gone 'a bit fidgety' compared with 1998's car, but all was forgiven: 'This car makes every driver feel like a hero, makes every cross-country charge feel like a tarmac stage.'

UK gets the 22B

The October 1998 British Motor Show also saw the UK debut of what would be the most extreme Impreza of all. The 22B-STi had already been

Britain's Subaru importer managed to persuade Fuji Heavy Industries to release 16 examples of the spectacular wide-bodied 22B for the UK market, specially modified for local conditions. All were snapped up immediately.

↑ Richard Burns and his racing number (5) lent his name to the RB5 edition, which boasted cloth-and-Alcantara seats, graphite console trim, air conditioning, Prodrive quickshift, and special RB5 mats, decals and plaques.

seen in Japan but, following plenty of rumours in the British press, this was the point of public confirmation that Subaru was going to sell the car officially in Britain.

The full 22B story is recounted in the chapter on the WRX and STi. Originally a strictly limited run of only 400 cars, all for Japan, had been envisaged. Subaru UK managed to persuade Subaru Tecnica International and Fuji Heavy Industries to

Perhaps the most desirable of all Impreza special editions was the 1999 RB5, especially when fitted with Prodrive's Performance Package. Prodrive had huge input into the RB5 project.

release a further 16 cars for the UK market (in fact the total production run would be 424, as a few more cars were built for other markets).

A special 22B-STi Type UK had to be created because the Japanese-market 22B as it was could not pass the UK Single Vehicle Approval test (for example, it needed a rear fog light, a narrower fuel filler for unleaded pumps, and an mph speedometer). Prodrive modified the cars to pass the SVA test, while at the same time it took the opportunity to add some features to distinguish it from the gamut of grey import 22Bs that had filtered into the UK unofficially during 1998.

The full list of changes over the Japanese 22B were a longer final drive ratio (in Japan it was 4.444:1, in the UK 3.900:1), the electronic speed limiter restricting top speed to 112mph (180kph) was removed, the new 1999 Model Year height-adjustable multi-reflector headlamps were fitted, as were high-power driving lamps (STi covers were also supplied loose in the boot), UK-spec rear lights (i.e. orange rather than clear indicator lenses), a Thatcham Grade 1 remote alarm/immobiliser, a facia modified to accept a European DIN hi-fi, four speakers and special interior mats. There was also

extra anti-corrosion treatment. Official Type UK specification cars had three different 'Type UK' and 'Prodrive' badges and logos on the boot to identify them from the 408 non-UK cars.

Subaru UK described the 22B as 'the road version of the Impreza World Rally Car '97'. It was keen to mark a notch up against grey importers: 'Good low to medium-speed pulling power were key design goals, making this engine far more flexible than the Japanese-market 2.0STi, yet with genuine "Supercar-like" performance.'

The press praised and damned the 22B in equal measure. *Autocar* stated that, 'The 22B comes to life over a good road like no other car we've driven,' but the driving experience was raw and the car didn't deliver its best unless you were really wringing it. Full press comment is covered in the following chapter on Japanese market cars.

Subaru placed a Motor Show price tag of £39,950 on the 22B-STi Type UK (roughly the same sort of level as grey imports). Hundreds of potential owners applied to buy one of the strictly limited cars. Certain terms and conditions had to be met, including the fact that you had to prove you were a current owner of a Subaru, guarantee that you would not sell the car within a certain period, and adhere to one of a select few dealerships that met certain Subaru UK criteria.

One small stumbling block was that the 22B Type UK could not actually be sold in Britain until January 1999 because the strict SVA import quota system limited the number of imports to 50 of any particular model in one year; 1998's allowance had already been used up by grey imports!

RB5 – Richard Burns's road car

Probably the best 'off-the-shelf' Turbo of all was the March 1999 RB5 special edition, which in its most developed form finally saw the UK-spec Impreza approach the power and performance of the Japanese WRX models. The RB5 was so called because it commem-orated the return of Richard Burns to the Subaru rally camp, and because his rally car was Number 5.

A very impressive specification made this the ultimate special edition. Perhaps the most significant feature was under the skin: unlike ordinary Imprezas with their folding rear seats, the RB5 had a bespoke shell with a rigid rear bulkhead, stiffening up the shell considerably.

The paintwork was called Blue Steel metallic (actually not blue at all – it was the same as Cool Grey on Japanese STis). Everything was fully colour-coded, including the door mirrors, door

handles, side skirts, front and rear under-spoilers, and spot lamp covers (there was a PIAA driving light conversion for the fog lights). The wheel choice was a Speedline 17-inch six-spoke design in pewter colour, fitted with Pirelli P Zero 205/45 ZR17 tyres. RB5 decals adorned the driving light covers, sides and rear end, as well as the interior carpet mats.

Inside the seats were upholstered in black 'Jersey' cloth with blue Alcantara inserts, and there was special graphite trim for the centre console. Standard equipment included air conditioning, a Prodrive quickshift, RB5 mats and roof-mounted map reading lamps. A numbered plaque by the gear lever informed you that you were driving one of only 444 cars produced, at a cost of £24,995.

UK-based Prodrive had been offering performance and cosmetic upgrades officially for years, and for the RB5 Subaru offered Prodrive's WR Sport Performance Package as a £2,550 option. This consisted of a new ECU, exhaust and air filter, new intercooler piping and a Prodrive tall rear wing, resembling the STi Version 5 item but with the brake light on the wing rather than on the boot lid. Power was boosted to 240PS (238bhp) at 6,000rpm for 145mph (233kph) and 0–60mph in 5.2 seconds and much better mid-range torque (maximum 258lb ft at 3,500rpm). Moreover, the Subaru warranty was not affected.

The standard RB5 was essentially an ordinary Impreza Turbo under the skin, the only major

↓ **The Prodrive Performance version of the RB5 had better engine response, a throatier exhaust note, superior ride, steering and braking and of course, it was also much quicker with its 238bhp power output.**

The world may have taken a little while to appreciate the strengths of the Impreza Turbo but when it did, the accolades poured forth. Possibly the most gratifying was the title 'Car of the Decade' from the respected British magazine, *Car*. The Impreza beat legendary contenders such as the McLaren F1, Audi TT, Porsche 911 and Ferrari 360 Modena.

'This is the car that ate the '90s, then came back for seconds,' the magazine enthused. 'Supernatural is the word that springs to mind when trying to account for the Impreza's cornering ability; here was a car that shrugged off the worst you could throw at it. For a Japanese four-door saloon/oddball semi-estate, the Impreza's sheer competence in tough conditions beggared belief. Of course, young, fitter rivals duly arrived to depose the new hero. Happily, though, they were all wearing Impreza badges, too. A raft of interior improvements took care of the Subaru's only real weakness. Cleverly, with only a little guile, then, the Impreza Turbo has wound up in the back half of 1999 in better, more celebrated shape than it was at launch in 1994; the standard bearer for a thriving Subaru sub-culture. In an era strangled by spin, the Impreza Turbo was an underground hit that gradually went overground, unhindered by hype – not the '90s way. The antithesis of the period it dominated, the Subaru Impreza Turbo is our Car of the Decade.' Other magazines concurred. *Evo* magazine described the Impreza Turbo as 'the performance car bargain of the decade,' while *Performance Car* magazine also named it 'Performance Car of the Decade'.

difference being 17-inch wheels. Many road testers felt that the RB5 was the best Impreza yet, although most of them were driving the WR Sport Performance version. For example, *Autocar* said: 'It has notably more initial response, the turbo spooling up … from as low as 1,800rpm … and the engine comes on strong again over the last 1,200rpm of its rev range, which is precisely where the standard unit starts to flag … It also sounds better, throatier.' It also praised the superior ride and crisper steering, braking and throttle. It concluded that the RB5 was 'the best Impreza yet to use every day on the road.'

The final fling – Year 2000

The 2000 Model Year Impreza received another dose of improvement in its final year in production. It was first seen in Australia, then in left-hand-drive European guise before finally being presented at the London Motor Show at Earl's Court in October 1999.

Some small cosmetic alterations saw body-colour door mirrors and door handles, new design slender six-spoke alloy wheels and, inside, a graphite finish metallic centre console and facia panel, map reading lights and a new gear knob. The Turbo also gained variable-speed intermittent windscreen wipers. A new locking device for the easy fitment of child safety seats reduced the movement of the child seat during impact or heavy braking. The very popular Dark Blue Mica colour was replaced by a lighter Deep Blue Mica colour, and Red Mica joined the colour palette.

Despite its advancing years, the Impreza Turbo remained absolutely convincing. The standard Turbo even held up persuassively in *Car* magazine's January 2000 Impreza giant test against the RB5, STi Type R, 22B, Scoobysport and P1: 'At £20,950 from your neighbourhood Subaru dealer, nothing (at the moment) comes close,' said the magazine. 'It's the consummate all rounder.' And at the *What Car?* 2000 Used Car Awards, the Best Used Sports Car prize went to the Impreza Turbo.

The Turbo did not get the special edition farewell treatment reserved, somewhat disingenuously, for many slower-selling departees. However, in June 2000, Subaru UK did celebrate the end of the first generation Impreza with a limited edition Sport Special, 'available in any colour the customer wants as long as it's either Black Mica or Cashmere Yellow,' said Subaru. This was a non-turbo model based on the 2.0 Sport. Its interior featured high-backed Turbo front seats with bright yellow accent panels front and rear, plus standard air conditioning, the current Turbo rear spoiler, leather-covered Momo steering wheel and white-backed instruments. The Sport Special price was £1,000 extra at £16,500 (saloon only) and production was strictly limited to 200 in each of the two colours.

As the first-generation Impreza neared the end of its production life, it was still hugely popular. Subaru's Edward Swatman at a conference in Tokyo, with every Subaru distributor in the world, commented that ever since McRae's and Burns's rally wins, Britain had been going mad over Imprezas.

There was no question that the first generation Impreza Turbo had been a resounding success, especially in Britain, which was, alongside Australia, the largest export market for the turbocharged Impreza. Perhaps the biggest tribute for the original Turbo was that many potential Impreza owners, concerned about the aesthetics of the 'New Age' Impreza, rushed to buy the last of the old Turbos. In all, the Turbo accounted for around half of all Impreza sales in the UK, whereas in France they went one better: the GT Turbo accounted for no less than 50 per cent of all Subaru sales.

Australia and New Zealand

Like virtually every other country outside Japan, Australia and New Zealand received the (rather watered-down) export version of the Impreza Turbo. Slightly misleadingly, the 211PS Impreza was marketed as the WRX in both Australia and New Zealand. For most of the model's existence in these markets, it was certainly not the Japanese-spec WRX.

The Impreza 'WRX' was launched in Australia at the Melbourne Motor Show in March 1994. In virtually every respect it was the same as the European Turbo, although there were some minor regional variations such as standard air conditioning. Both ABS and non-ABS versions were marketed initially, at prices from $38,590 (non ABS) and £39,990 for the ABS version.

The Impreza quickly gained an avid following. As in most markets, the saloon was more popular than the hatch: for instance in its first year (1994), the WRX sold 325 saloons and 213 estates. One peculiarity of Australia was that an automatic gearbox became available in 1997 for the WRX saloon and five-door (self-shifting transmission was also offered in Japan but on the Sports Wagon only). However the take-up was understandably slight: in fact, less than one in five sales were automatics.

Local magazine tests demonstrated the car's performance prowess. After initial disappointment in 1997, when *Wheels* recorded a slightly below-par 6.7 seconds for the 0–100kph dash, the following year the magazine posted a time of 5.8 seconds.

Like most other markets, Australia boasted numerous special editions. The first was the WRX Rallye of 1996, with Blue 555 Prodrive paint and gold alloys (121 sold in 1996, 52 sold in 1997 including 16 automatics). Then came the Black edition of 1997, with black paint, gold wheels and red seats, available in saloon and estate form with manual or automatic transmission (122 sold). The same year saw the Clubspec arrive, with Sonic Blue Mica paint, gold wheels and red seat/door

trim (196 sold). Another Black edition arrived in 1998, fully colour-coded with gold wheels but only available with automatic transmission (97 sold) and a Clubspec Evo 2 followed it with Blue Mica paint, gold wheels, STi Version III Alcantara trim, Nardi steering wheel, quick-shift gear change, leather gear lever gaiter, Tracker security system and Evo 2 stickers and rally badges (229 sold, all manual saloons).

Then in March 1999 came the LE (Limited Edition of 100 units), sold in a choice of WRC Blue Mica, Dark Blue Mica, Dark Green Mica or Black Mica paint with colour coded mirrors and door handles. Inside were a metallic grain instrument panel, beige leather seats, a CD player, Brant alarm, woodgrain Momo airbag steering wheel and a woodgrain gear knob. Manual and automatic transmissions were offered at prices from $42,990. This was followed by the Evo 3 in May 1999, with Blue Steel paint, blue Alcantara and 'Jersey' seats, gold-painted alloy wheels, colour-keyed bodykit, door handles and exterior mirrors, metallic-type instrument panel and keyless entry. All 150 units were manual and priced at £41,690.

Australia and New Zealand were also exceptional in that both received, towards the end of the first production cycle, official versions of the Japanese STi. The full story behind these imports is told in the following chapter.

Australia was the biggest market in the world behind Japan for the WRX, recording year-on-year sales increases pretty much throughout the Impreza's life. By 2000, nearly 10,000 WRX Imprezas had been sold in Australia out of a total of nearly 31,000 Imprezas of all types. The importance of the Australian market was recognised in August 1998 when, in a first for Subaru, the 1999 Model Year Impreza was revealed in Australia before even in Japan.

Other worldwide markets

We have seen how basically the same car was marketed as the Turbo 2000 in Britain, GT in Europe and WRX in the Antipodes. Other markets such as South America and South Africa also called it the Impreza GT. There were many local variations according to market, including standard climate control or air conditioning, cruise control, automatic transmission, heated seats and so on. As for the RS sold in the USA, that is covered in a separate chapter.

CHAPTER 3
WRX AND STi

Sometimes three small letters can make a very powerful statement. Everyone knows how 'GTi' enlivened the rump of the VW Golf and catapulted it into the annals of motoring iconolatry. In their own way, the letters WRX and STi had the same sort of impact as the highest expressions of the turbocharged Impreza cornucopia. And even though they were reserved almost exclusively for the domestic Japanese market, their impact was felt worldwide.

The whole Impreza road car story began in Japan on 1 November 1992 with the launch of Subaru's latest mid-range contender. The quirky saloon and 'sports wagon' range consisted of front-wheel-drive 1.5 and 1.6-litre entry-level models, four-wheel-drive 1.6 and 1.8-litre models and – topping the range – the very first WRX with its 2.0-litre turbocharged engine.

The WRX – so named because it had been in part specifically conceived as the homologation vehicle for the World Rally Championship – may have looked similar to the later European-market Turbo but in many respects it was a different vehicle. And in most respects it was generally viewed as superior.

For starters, its engine was a lot more powerful, rated by the Japanese measuring system at 240PS at 6,000rpm (compared with 211PS in Europe and Australia). The WRX achieved its higher power output by using a bigger IHI turbo and larger intercooler, run by a different engine management set-up. The compression ratio was also slightly higher at 8.5:1 (versus 8.0:1 in Europe).

Power was not the only difference that the Japanese market WRX carried compared with the Turbo in Europe: the suspension was also enhanced, being rather harder thanks to stiffer springs, although the dampers were identical on both the Turbo and WRX. Japanese gearing was different too, with closer-set ratios and a more

frenetic 4.111:1 final drive ratio; Japanese product planners were not concerned with high top speeds as every domestic market car – including the WRX – was electronically limited to a top speed of 180kph (112mph). Also the saloon – which was the only WRX body style available at launch – did not come with the folding rear seat of the European Turbo, having a solid rear bulkhead instead. And while lesser members of the Japanese Impreza family had a 50-litre fuel tank, the WRX always came with a 60-litre tank, like the Turbo in Europe.

The list of standard equipment was also much more complete than European cars would have: climate control was standard, the colour-coded door mirrors were electrically retractable for parking, and there was a standard rear wash/wiper (we're talking about the four-door, remember), twin cup holders, map lights and a superior gear lever gaiter. There was also an electric aerial mounted on the rear three-quarter panel, and the seats were superior. By 1994 the WRX had gained colour-coded door handles, unlike the black items of European cars.

← The secret of the Impreza's handling lay in its chassis balance and its four-wheel-drive system. The boxer engine could be slung out low with the gearbox mounted in-line for perfectly symmetrical balance. Meanwhile, there were three differentials: one right at the front, one behind the gearbox and one for the rear axle.

↓ Japanese WRX engines were always more powerful than export versions: the launch WRX had 240PS compared with 211PS in Europe and Australia. This was down to a larger turbocharger and intercooler, higher compression ratio and different engine management. Note the intercooler sited on top of the engine at an angle.

↑ The Japanese WRX
dashboard was similar
to the UK layout, but it
lacked a driver's airbag and
console-mounted digital
clock. Japanese Imprezas
also did without the
'Bright' dashboard lighting
button fitted to UK cars.

However, four items were missing from the
WRX that European Turbo/GT owners were
familiar with: no tilt adjustable headlamps,
no headlamp washers, no split/fold rear seat
on the saloon and no 'bright' button on the
dashboard.

Japanese-market WRX logo decals were
particularly gruesome. A wide variety of
designs was produced over the years, almost
all of them in large, cartoon-like lettering
and bright colours that seemed out-of-place
to western eyes – looking more suited to a
surfboard than a serious performance machine
– but it all fitted in with the Japanese idiom.

The WRX launch price was 2,298,000 yen
and it was instantly greeted with enthusiasm by
the domestic market.

'Race Altered' RA

Also available from launch was a lightweight WRX
RA (Race Altered) version. It is a quirk of the
Japanese market that specialist lightweight versions
of cars like the Impreza are produced and offered
for sale as part of the general catalogue, in theory
serving as the basis for a customer Group N rally
car. In practice, many people bought this type
of car because they proved to be more focused
performance tools and, it must be said, they were
not as expensive as the normal version.

To save weight, the RA was denied numerous
items of equipment. For example, the first edition
made do without foglamps (it had gaping holes
instead), there was no boot spoiler, underseal
or radio/cassette, no air conditioning or electric

windows and much of the sound-deadening material from the cabin was missing. The total weight saving was 30kg (66lb)(total weight 1,170kg/2,580lb). Later RAs did come with boot spoilers, however.

An RA was easy to spot because it lacked side skirts and rear valance extensions, had black door mirrors (other WRX models were body-coloured) and while later WRX models had body-coloured door handles, the RA stayed with black ones. All RA models were

always available in any colour you liked, as long as it was white.

In fact, many of the items that were deleted on the RA were made available to add on as options, and many roadgoing RAs were in fact refitted with weight-generating 'luxury' items. This would naturally raise the price, which was considerably less than the ordinary WRX. For example, in 1994 the RA was priced at 2,198,000 yen, some 300,000 yen (or 12 per cent) less than the contemporary WRX.

All RA engines prior to 1996 featured a 'closed-deck' block, that is to say, the cylinder liners were not exposed at the cylinder head gasket face. This meant the block was much stiffer and allowed for much improved head gasket sealing. Of course this also made it much more amenable to modification.

The RA's gearing was also shorter with the following gear ratios (ordinary WRX ratios in brackets):

1st	3.454
2nd	2.333 (2.062)
3rd	1.750 (1.448)
4th	1.354 (1.088)
5th	0.972 (0.825)

The RA started off with a 4.111:1 final drive ratio but the 1995 Model Year RA had a taller ratio (3.900:1), then even taller from the 1996 Model Year at 3.545:1. The RA also had an adjustable centre differential.

Unlike later versions of the RA, the 1993 Model Year version did not have a roof-mounted air vent. This rally-type device would be sited immediately above the interior rear view mirror on later versions. Conforming to a Japanese penchant for stripped-out rally-style lightweight models, the RA would make a consistent appearance in Subaru's catalogues in a bewildering array of types for the rest of the Impreza's life.

Unaware of the budding legend on their hands, the press greeted the new Impreza's Japanese launch in rather downbeat terms. Peter Nunn in the British magazine *Car* (January 1993) argued: 'The Impreza doesn't have the space and practicality of the ancient L-Series, or the smart Giugiaro looks of the Legacy. But it's a well developed, capable, interesting car with a lot on its side.' Hardly glowing. However he did reserve a special mention for the qualities of the WRX: 'The definite hot ticket is the WRX. The ride of this rally car rattles your teeth, and the massive intercooler vent blocks your view out over the bonnet. You get stunning acceleration, short and close gear ratios, strong brakes and a neutral 4WD chassis that just hangs on and on. Entertaining? But of course.' Early indications of greatness.

Not even a year after the launch of the original WRX – and still many months before the European Turbo's debut – Subaru expanded and improved its WRX range. The 1994 Model Year WRX (with B-series chassis coding) arrived on 9 October 1993. The range was expanded with the notable addition

← The first WRX was launched in saloon form only in Japan, as early as November 1992. In this unassuming and rather inconspicuous new arrival was the seed of a World Championship-winning rally car, blistering road car and performance icon of the 1990s.

← Seats inside the WRX were vastly superior to the flat-shaped, industrial textile-covered chairs in European cars. These were proper high-backed contoured seats, while the bright colour schemes alleviated what was otherwise a dull grey cabin.

← The RA 'Race Altered' version was always part of the Impreza WRX catalogue. The first version of this stripped-out special did without a rear spoiler or foglamps, as well as sound deadening, air conditioning and many other items of equipment.

→ A five-door WRX 'Sports Wagon' appeared in October 1993 in Japan. This is the SA version, a special lightweight model sold only for the 1994 Model Year.

of a new five-door WRX. General improvements for the B-series were revised spring and damper rates, reprogrammed engine management and much improved electrics.

The five-door version of the WRX – always referred to as the WRX Sports Wagon in Japan – was based on the shell of the normal five-door Impreza that had been offered since the outset in 1992. In WRX guise it sported twin rear spoilers, standard roof rails and an aerial resited from the rear three-quarter panel to the roof.

However, the Sports Wagon was not simply the same WRX mechanical package with a bigger boot. The Sports Wagon was treated initially as a more 'touring' member of the WRX family and came with a detuned engine of 'only' 220PS at 6,000rpm and less torque too at 280Nm (206lb ft) at 3,500rpm. Additionally, the domestic market Sports Wagon was only supplied with ABS as an optional extra. Another peculiarity of the Sports Wagon version was that you could order one with four-speed automatic transmission – a seemingly bizarre option for a rally escapee, but then the Japanese market is full of such contradictions. With automatic specified the usual viscous coupling centre differential was replaced by a Variable Torque Distribution (VTD) set-up. The automatic version could do the 0–100kph (0–62mph) sprint in a claimed 6.9 seconds.

For the 1994 Model Year only, the WRX five-door also came in a cheaper, lightweight version called the SA that skimmed 50kg (110lb) off the overall weight, leaving out items such as the lower rear spoiler. This was several hundred thousand yen cheaper than the standard five-door WRX.

While the early four-door was only available in White, Silver or Black, the five-door could also be ordered in Metallic Blue. The only four-door models sold in blue (which was, after all, the rally livery) were the limited edition models, almost always known as V-Limited in Japan. However, the metallic blue used did not precisely match the shade used on the rally cars.

Birth of a legend: the STi

The really big news for the 1994 season was the arrival of the legendary WRX STi model, launched on 20 January 1994. Seldom have three such innocuous letters had such a powerful effect on any car. They transformed the Impreza WRX into 'the real thing' – a road-going car that was genuinely much closer to Subaru's rally car.

STi is a moniker for Subaru Tecnica International, the company's tuning and competitions wing (see separate panel). Working its magic on the WRX produced a car with more

Subaru Tecnica International

Subaru Tecnica International (or just STi) is the motorsport and high performance wing of Subaru. Founded in 1988 it was set up to promote Subaru products in the international market, founded on a strong base of competition success. In the domestic market it produced numerous STi badged versions of Subaru products and offered tuning parts for Subarus, while in rallying it was pivotal in creating championship-winning formulae.

STi's first success was setting two world records and 13 international records in the 100,000km FIA World Speed Record in January 1989 with the newly launched Legacy. The World Rally Championship project followed and became a full-scale factory effort when, for the 1990 season, STi joined forces with Prodrive in Britain. The Prodrive-engineered Legacy RS proved a fine rally tool.

Of course, some of the patina of the rally success rubbed off on Subaru's mainstream marketing but more practically speaking, many of the lessons learned in competing in the World Rally Championship were directly incorporated into production cars.

STi went on to produce a range of special edition STi-version models in Japan, and more recently in other international markets, specially modified to comply with local laws – and chief among those was the Impreza WRX STi. Remarkably, the STi versions of the Impreza eventually accounted for more than 50 per cent of Impreza WRX saloons sold in Japan.

Today, STi is responsible for the development and control of all Subaru motorsport activities for international and domestic events, overseeing the management of the Subaru World Rally Team. It also conducts research and development for Subaru rally cars and gives technical support to private teams, all of which provides feedback to assist in the development of Subaru's volume production cars. STi also has a large road car research and development wing, not only creating special STi-versions but also STi tuning parts.

power, greater engineering tolerances, many parts that were close to rally-spec, bespoke quality and an enviable level of kudos.

Every car was hand-built in limited numbers. Impreza engineering chief Takeshi Ito recalled: 'In the early stages after the STi's introduction, we had to make the conversions at STi's factory after production.' But that changed: 'Today, every STi Version is assembled at production lines like other Impreza models, which has enabled us to produce more units.'

Each engine was blueprinted (i.e. manufactured and assembled to higher tolerances) and added a closed-deck cylinder block finished in a red crackle finish, forged pistons, steel crankshaft, bigger valves, a better intercooler, a bigger radiator, reset ECU and an uprated turbocharger. The Fujitsubo part-stainless steel exhaust had a much wider bore, a

↑ **The very first STi appeared in January 1994. Unlike later versions, this was taken off the production line and modified at STi's works. Notable features of this early version are foglamps in place of covers, different wheels and an unusually tall rear wing.**

↑ **Easily distinguishable by its crackle-red paint, the STi engine was always blueprinted and tuned to produce more power than the standard WRX engine. STi powerplants varied between 250PS and 300PS. Note the strut brace fitted to all STi Imprezas.**

sodium-filled manifold, free-flow larger-diameter silencers and a three-inch wide chromed tailpipe with an STi logo embossed on it. The result was a boost in power over the WRX, listed at 250PS at 6,500rpm for the 1994 Model Year, with torque standing at 228lb ft (309Nm) at 3,500rpm. The engine revved higher too – up to 8,250rpm, some 750rpm higher than the WRX.

Equally significant was the STi's gearbox. Rebuilt with closer ratios and a quicker shift action, it was allied to a lower (4.444:1) final drive and more durable internals. There were stronger front and rear differentials and heavy duty drive shafts too. All very handy for those gravel stages.

The overall effect of the engine and transmission changes was devastating in-gear performance. The STi was a genuine 150mph (241kph) car (with the electronic limiter removed, at least) and it boasted real supercar-slaying acceleration: how about 0–60mph in 4.6 seconds and a 50–70mph time of under three seconds?

As for the suspension, one highly important change was die-cast aluminium lower front wishbones that significantly reduced weight. These were supplemented by a carbon-fibre strut brace between the front suspension struts, plus stiffened STi springs and dampers, all of which provided superbly focused handling.

Also the brakes were much stronger thanks to four-pot front callipers and uprated brake pads, while it kept the WRX's four-sensor, four-channel ABS system. There was additionally a wide range of accessories and tuning parts available direct from STi to produce yet more performance, even better braking and even more finely tuned handling.

You could spot an STi by many details. The most obvious was the tall rear spoiler (bigger in fact on the first edition than in subsequent years) and the reddish-pink front grille badge. The first series STi produced in 1994 was different to later STi versions in that it kept the WRX spotlamps (on later cars these were replaced by blank panels bearing the STi logos) and had an STi logo on the front spoiler. Later STi versions would also have gold alloy wheels – the first edition had split-rim silver alloys – and clear rear indicator lenses.

To save weight, the STi had a standard aluminium bonnet and boot lid. Yet the STi was no stripped-out special, with standard climate control, remote central locking, electric windows and driver airbag, while the rally-style seats had suede inserts.

From launch in 1994 you could buy an STi in either four-door saloon or five-door estate forms, both with identical mechanical specifications. In both cases, STi took WRXs off the production line and modified them to the STi specification.

1995 – more power please

In October 1994, the C-series WRX was launched. The normal WRX received a significant power boost, rising from 240PS to 260PS at 6,500rpm, with torque slightly up at 228lb ft (309Nm) at 5,000rpm. Another major advance was that all four brake discs on the saloon were now ventilated, in contrast to the European Turbo, which kept solid rear discs for some while after this.

Once again, WRX and lightweight WRX RA versions were available in four-door form. The WRX now had colour-coded door handles, while the RA stuck with black handles. The five-

door WRX meanwhile did not benefit from the boosted power of the rest of the range, remaining at 220PS, whether manual or automatic transmission was specified.

The superiority of the STi was maintained. Launched on 17 November 1994, one month after the revised WRX, its power output was raised for the 1995 Model Year, up to 275PS at 6,500rpm, while torque rose to 319Nm (235lb ft) at 4,000rpm. The 1995 Model Year was unusual for the STi in that it was only available in lightweight Type RA saloon form. The STi RA boasted an additional intercooler waterspray, DCCD electro-magnetic centre differential and rear mechanical limited slip diff – fully described in the section on the Type R – plus a roof ventilator, and no ABS. Like the 'ordinary' WRX RA, it went without many items of equipment to shave kilos off its weight. This year's STi had standard

↑ **Every single year there were special editions in Japan – sometimes as many as four in one season. This is a particularly unsubtle one: the 1996 WRX STi Version II 555, with decals to emulate the contemporary 555-sponsored Impreza rally car.**

↖ **Japanese market decals were loud, cartoon-like adhesive patches that looked all wrong to western eyes. UK market Imprezas had chrome-look badges to instil a feeling of quality.**

← **The 1995 Model Year STi was only available in Type RA guise. The RA was always painted white and had a roof-mounted vent mimicking the rally car. Gold wheels were typical of the STi range, as were pink badges.**

→ 555 branded seats appeared on appropriate special editions. STi seats are sought-after items because they are not only attractive to look at, they are also extremely functional for rapid driving.

↘ Thankfully this oddball Impreza was simply a show car. The Impreza Operetta cut the roof off a two-door coupé and added a roll-over bar, soft-top and rear spoiler. It made one appearance at the 1995 Tokyo Show and was quietly dropped.

spotlamp blanking panels with the STi logo in pink and Subaru Tecnica International wording in black, and gold alloy five-spoke wheels.

All 1995 Model Year WRX models had larger, 16-inch wheels. The new design of double five-spoke alloy wheel was fitted with lower-profile tyres to compensate (205/50 R16 as opposed to 205/55 R15 before). The C-series WRX continued unchanged through 1995 and into 1996.

It was a different story for the STi though, for on 22 August 1995 there were significant moves on the STi front. For the first time this became

an official model, rather than a modified version of an already-manufactured WRX. This revised model was called the STi Version II, although no badging identified the new status, nor indeed any of the future annual evolutions (the chassis code provided the only ID data as to what the version was – see the separate panel on interpreting chassis codes). The STi Version II kept its 275PS engine if you bought it in four-door saloon form and this was offered in both STi and lightweight STi RA types (the latter offered with a quick-ratio steering box as an option). After a year's absence, a Sports Wagon version of the STi returned in Version II guise, with manual transmission only (STis were only ever sold with manual gearboxes).

The first special editions arrived in Japan at this time. Project sub-leader Takeshi Ito explained the rationale behind these limited-production Imprezas: 'The various limited edition models featured either comfort equipment or were designed to evoke an image of the WRC car. These were real sport models that matched widespread customer needs.' The first such special edition was based on the normal STi four-door and was called the '555' after the tobacco-sponsored rally car, identifiable by such fitments as 555-branded seats and mudflaps. The second was based on the STi RA four-door and was called the V-Limited, painted in Rally Blue (but not actually the same as the pukka rally cars) in a run of 1,000 units. The third was based on the STi Sports Wagon with the same '555' treatment as the saloon.

DID YOU KNOW?
Impreza al fresco

At the October 1995 Tokyo Motor Show, Subaru presented one of the most curious Impreza experiments of all – a convertible. The Impreza Cabriolet Operetta was a show model that supposedly demonstrated future possibilities. It was a remarkably unconvincing prototype: the fixed central roll-over bar looked heavy, the electrically operated folding canvas roof did not disappear out of sight but stacked up high behind the cabin and the boot spoiler looked out-of-place. This was not, however, the first two-door Impreza: a mild-mannered coupé was launched in Japan as early as January 1994 and the American market also had a two-door Impreza on its price list in 1994. In both cases this was two years before the Japanese market received the turbocharged Type R coupé. Unlike the Type R, however, neither the US nor Japanese coupés could be described as performance machines in their early incarnations, boasting a mere 110bhp in the USA and only 97–100bhp in Japan.

1997 – Mid-life facelift

On 9 September 1996, the Impreza range was thoroughly overhauled with a new look and more power. The major facelift given to the Impreza worldwide earned the domestic market version the title 'Brand New' and was noted as the D-series in Subaru's chassis sequence. The facelift consisted of a lower, more deeply contoured bonnet line, different bonnet scoop and bonnet grilles, and a new front grille, squarer headlights, while restyled rear bumpers were also new, more rounded and 'cleaner' in profile.

The entry-level WRX saloon now boasted a remarkable 280PS at 6,500rpm as standard, with a highest-yet torque output of 242lb ft (328Nm) at 4,000rpm. The WRX Sports Wagon had a power hike too, up to 240PS at 6,000rpm (torque 304Nm (224lb ft) at 3,000rpm), regardless of whether it was fitted with manual or automatic transmission. Once again the WRX was available in normal and RA lightweight versions. The post-1996 RA and STi-RA versions differed in that they changed from a closed-deck engine block to an open deck block, as this proved to be a satisfactorily rigid set-up.

The STi now progressed to a Version III. Most development engineers will tell you that their favourite car is 'the next one' – and indeed Takeshi Ito says just this. However, candidly he also explained to the author: 'If you allow me to give you the most impressive Impreza, it is the STi Version III. We were able to show a significant improvement for performance with this model.'

Now that the World Rally Championship rules had changed so that manufacturers no longer needed to homologate rally parts on road cars, the spec altered to become a little more road-use friendly.

All STi models now boasted the same power output – the maximum 280PS allowed by Japanese custom. Officially the STi Version III powerplant developed the same output as the 1997 WRX at 280PS at 6,500rpm but many sources quietly whispered that the figure was actually more like 300PS. The main improvement for the Version III STi engine was that it now boasted more torque (and certainly much more than the WRX's), at 235lb ft (319Nm) at 4,000rpm, with a 7,900rpm red line and an 8,400rpm rev limiter. The Version III boasted a competition clutch to cope with that extra torque.

Autocar magazine reported on the STi Type RA Version III in February 1997. It praised the 'amazing acceleration' (0–60mph in 4.9 seconds), adding: 'In first gear you have to strain to keep your hands on the wheel.' But it panned the appalling 8mpg fuel consumption if you kept the turbo spinning for long periods.

The 1996–97 STi Version III was available in four-door saloon, five-door Sports Wagon and RA four-door forms. Once again there was a special edition, the STi Version III V-Limited, offered in four- and five-door guises. Also in 1997 came a '555 Individual' special edition based on the five-door.

Type R time

But the biggest news for the 1997 Model Year was the arrival of the STi Type R on 22 January 1997. This was unusual in that it was the first roadgoing two-door turbocharged Impreza in the world, and was basically marketed as the car that formed the basis for the 1997 World Rally Car. No doubt about it, this was the most extreme Impreza yet conceived.

The Type R was instantly distinguished by its extended front spoiler, colour-coded side skirts and deeper rear valance. The two-door bodyshell had the usual solid rear bulkhead for extra strength but was 10kg (22lb) lighter than the four-door shell. One other small difference between this and the four-door was dark-tinted rear windows.

The Type R also gained a pukka Group N gearbox that gave it even closer gear ratios than the STi, as well as a final drive equating to just 19mph (30.5kph) at 1,000rpm (in place of 22mph/35kph per 1000rpm). At the red line of 8,250rpm, that meant a top speed rather less than other Imprezas, while motorway cruising was adversely affected. But that was not the point of the Type R. This was a car designed for pure acceleration and for anyone who loved shifting gears a lot. Perhaps it was a little too full-on for most drivers, but it certainly gained an enthusiastic following in Japan.

Probably the most significant of the Type R's rally-orientated features was a mechanical centre differential – rather than viscous coupling of other models – that could be altered by the driver. There remained three differentials of course, but the Type R had a front viscous unit, an automatic mechanical limited slip diff at the rear and a manually adjustable centre diff. This was in contrast to the ordinary set-up of centre and rear viscous units and an open diff up front.

The Type R set-up offered tremendous opportunity to adjust the handling of the car at the turn of a dial. In the open position (when the dashboard indicator would be fully green), the centre diff would transmit more power to the axle with the better traction (usually the rear), in a ratio of 36/64 front/rear. In addition to this, the mechanical diff in the rear axle locked both rear driveshafts very quickly once slip was detected. This enabled the driver to indulge in rear-drive antics such as power oversteer. Winding the knob forwards would send power more and more to the front axle. If one of the front wheels began to slip, the viscous unit would ensure drive was directed to the wheel with most grip.

Pushing the dial fully forward (indicated in yellow as 'locked' on the dash bar) would lock the centre diff, keeping torque at 50/50 front/rear. This was not advisable on tarmac because the axles would then be locked and transmission wind-up ensued. This position was really intended for loose gravel or ice surfaces, when high-speed stability was enhanced by locking the differential.

The front limited slip differential on the front axle replaced the normal ABS system – confirming this variant as a car for the experienced enthusiast who demanded driver-adjustability over fail-safe

mechanisms. To compensate for the lack of ABS, the rear brakes gained twin-pot callipers. The Type R also had a standard quick ratio steering rack.

Bringing the McRae experience even closer was a waterspray for the intercooler on the 280PS STi engine. A switch on the dashboard sent a jet of water on to the intercooler on demand to reduced air charge temperature. Although there was also an automated computer setting for the waterspray, because the reservoir was so minute, it would only last a matter a miles in this mode.

At the beginning of Type R production, a special run of Type R coupés was produced under the 'Signature' label, all painted bright yellow with mean-looking dark grey anodised alloy wheels. It was such a car that *Autocar* magazine drove in November 1997, when it commented: 'It's one of the those cars that can't be driven in any other manner than too fast … A wonderfully reassuring chassis offers all the encouragement needed to hurtle into corners at huge speeds… The ratios are super-close.' Pitched against the Mitsubishi Lancer Evo IV in its back-to-back road test, it was the Type R that took the honours. This was indeed a serious, uncompromising performance machine.

1998 – A dozen WRXs

On 1 September 1997, the E-series Impreza WRX heralded the 1998 Model Year Impreza, which gained the all-new dashboard also seen on the European Turbo, with its Forester-type dash-top box. Now the domestic WRX range spiralled up

↓ **Two doors on the Impreza signalled the arrival of the 1997 Type R, the most focused WRX yet. Not only was it lighter but it gained a true Group N rally gearbox with outrageously close ratios, plus quicker steering and a manually-adjustable mechanical centre differential to let you select the handling balance: oversteer or understeer.**

into no less than 12 different versions. The base WRX was offered, as usual, in four-door normal and RA guises (with 280PS) and as a five-door, as ever with rather less power (although at 250PS it was 10PS up on the previous year, unless you went for automatic transmission, in which case it remained at 240PS). If you think things are starting to get complicated, we've only just begun …

At the same time came the STi Version IV, which kept its power output at a nominal 280PS but boosted torque again, to 36kg m (260lb ft) at 4,000rpm. The STi was offered in the same range of four-door STi, four-door STi RA and five-door STi forms. As ever, standard STi equipment included a competition clutch and four-pot front brake callipers. One major change occurred in the exhaust system: up until 1998 the STi models had had two catalysts, but now this changed to a single unit in the downpipe.

Then there was the STi Type R two-door, available this year in a limited edition Type R V-Limited package. For the first time, there was also a quirky special edition, yet another example of WRX nichedom. The WRX Type R V-Limited two-door was the only non-STi coupé ever made

for the Japanese market, and this curious special edition would reappear for the 1999 and 2000 Model Years. Another special edition on offer for the 1998 Model Year was the STi RA V-Limited four-door saloon.

Autocar magazine tested a four-door STi Version IV against the Mitsubishi Evo V in May 1998. The Impreza was faster off the line, its 0–60mph time a phenomenal 4.6 seconds (compared to 4.7 for the Evo): 'Think of a mixture between the Japanese entry in the Cannonball Run and warp drive mode on the Starship Enterprise and you won't be far from the feeling,' it said. While favouring the Mitsubishi as an overall package in this particular back-to-back, *Autocar* described the Impreza as 'a giant-slayer'.

The ultimate Impreza – the 22B

All this activity was totally overshadowed by the spectacular charge of what was undoubtedly the ultimate version of the first generation Impreza series. The spectacular STi 22B was to be as close to Colin McRae's 1997 rally cars as it was possible

↑ If you really wanted a rally car on the road, the remarkable 22B was designed to deliver it. Ultra-wide wheel arches – the body was tweaked by designer Peter Stevens – hid broader-track suspension.

← Crucial to the 22B brew was its expanded 2.2-litre engine. This was perhaps one of the disappointing areas, because although torque was improved, power output was not. Like the Type R, the 22B had a driver-operated intercooler waterspray.

↓ The rear spoiler was not quite an exact replica of the WRC car but it was close enough to fool most people. Its aerofoil was manually adjustable by up to 17° in two stages to alter downforce on the rear end.

↑ Special blue trim adorned the 22B interior, including the specially embroidered seats. The Nardi steering wheel had no airbag.

to get in an off-the-shelf Impreza. The 22B would enter Japanese dealerships on 16 March 1998, to celebrate 40 years of Subaru car manufacture.

The 22B owes its origins to a Prodrive-built 'super Impreza' concept that was constructed for Fuji Heavy Industries and shown to them during 1997. Head office was impressed and rubber-stamped a production version to be built by Subaru Tecnica International. Plenty of rumours were flying around about twin turbos and sequential gearboxes but by February 1998 much of the specification was known and the car had its name – 22B – which is hexadecimal for '555' incidentally.

STi basically hand-built the 22B. Each car started life as a WRX STi Type R Version IV, which was

removed from the production line to have its modifications completed by STi. First the front and rear wheel arches were cut away and new, wider wings welded in place, increasing the 'body width by some 80mm (3in), almost identical to the rally car. The body was then seam-welded and repainted by a specialist (because it was now too wide for the regular production line paint shop).

The 22B's Type R based two-door bodyshell was given a course of steroids courtesy of McLaren F1 designer Peter Stevens. He added an even deeper front spoiler, different WRC-lookalike bonnet vents, big wheel arch blisters and side skirts, and a new rear spoiler. The wider wheel arches covered wider tracks, an extra 20mm at the front and 40mm at the rear.

It all looked very much like the WRC98 car. But contrary to many reports, the rear spoiler was not quite an exact replica of the WRC car but it was pretty close with its adjustable foil (this was manually adjustable by up to 17° in two stages to generate more or less downforce as required). Special WRC lookalike Sonic Blue Mica paint and a titanium STi badge on the front wings hammered home the rally car message. Inside, the

22B received a unique blue-trimmed treatment, matt black finish dashboard, a Nardi rather than Momo steering wheel, specially embroidered seats and a special plaque on the console box. The spec included air conditioning but no airbags.

Underneath the body bristled a unique chassis with wider forged-aluminium suspension arms, and massive 235/40 ZR17 Pirelli P Zero tyres on BBS 17 x 8.5 forged aluminium gold wheels to fill the huge arches. Uprated brakes, joined significantly enhanced suspension to complete a serious driver's chassis. The front, 292mm front discs had the usual four-pot STi callipers, but at the rear, new two-pot callipers with larger ventilated discs made things even sharper. All callipers were painted bright red. The suspension changes included redesigned rear suspension arms, upgraded bushes, rose-jointed lateral links and extremely firm inverted Bilstein dampers and Eibach springs. Incidentally, the dampers bore Prodrive stickers, simply because Prodrive had commissioned them from Bilstein, but the specification was in fact decided in Japan to suit Japanese roads.

Easily the strongest ingredient in the 22B cauldron was its larger capacity flat-four engine, bored out from 1,994cc to 2,212cc – and renamed EJ22 to suit. Magazine articles quoted a rumoured output of 350PS power levels – way over the Japanese 'gentleman's agreement' of 280PS – but in reality the engine did stick to Japan's 280PS upper power limit. Torque was boosted to 265lb ft (360Nm) and it arrived at only 3,200rpm, while the torque curve was almost entirely flat between 2,800rpm and 5,200rpm. The maximum power output was also delivered 500rpm lower down at 6,000rpm.

The turbocharger was a large, IHI VF23 roller bearing unit, the larger, lightweight pistons were forged, the fuel rails were specially made and the larger head gaskets were made of metal. Underlining the rally origins of the 22B, there was a driver-operated water-spray for the intercooler.

A racing-style STi ceramic/metal twin plate lightweight clutch was responsible for transferring the power to the wheels via the same gearbox as the STi Type R, with its driver adjustable viscous centre differential and multi-plate clutch, although the tolerances were even higher. The propshaft and driveshafts were also tougher to suit the extra torque.

Despite the enlarged engine, the 22B was disappointingly no faster than the normal STi Type R, its urge is offset by a 30kg (66lb) increase in weight, while the larger frontal area affected aerodynamics at higher speeds. Without sound proofing, ABS or traction control, the 22B STi was as close to a roadgoing rally car as Subaru had yet achieved.

Demand was unprecedented for the limited supply – amazingly, within three days the entire limited edition run was sold out in Japan – which led to premiums being charged on top of the list price of 5 million yen, already a full 2 million yen more than the STi Type R on which the 22B was based. Although the intention was to make cars for Japan only, in fact many cars were privately exported (the first export being to Hong Kong in April 1998).

A plaque inside the car informed you that only 400 had been made. However, as stated in the previous chapter, the actual number built was 424, as further cars were made for overseas, including 16 specially produced for Subaru UK. Celebrity owners of grey imports in Britain included Manchester United footballer Ryan Giggs and boxer Prince Naseem Hamed. In Australia five examples of the 22B were imported, one being kept by Subaru Australia. However, these cars were never able to pass local road regulations, and therefore none was ever registered for the road.

Three cars are known to have been issued with the number 000, one each belonging to Colin McRae and Nicky Grist, who purchased their cars directly from Subaru for an undisclosed sum, and David Lapworth of Prodrive who also drove a 22B number 000, in this case a development car. Incidentally, contrary to rumour, 'unlucky' number 013 was indeed issued, being used as a demonstrator for Subaru USA.

Magazine testers were agreed that the 22B was an animal to pilot. In all respects it boasted knife-sharp responses: super-sensitive quick-rack steering, biting clutch action, hugely powerful non-ABS brakes, ultra-grippy tyres and a completely lag-free turbo. Frankly frantic to drive, the 22B was the car that really transported you into McRae's boots, as *Evo* magazine pointed out in its November 1998 issue: 'If you want a peek at what it feels like to be Colin McRae,

the 22B will take you there.' But alongside praise
for the 'prodigious' power, 'inspired' steering
and 'the best' brakes, there were a few hints of
disappointment: 'It doesn't like bumps and it's
not keen on rain either. Ironically the standard
Impreza Turbo deals with them superbly.'

Car magazine drove a Japanese-spec 22B in
September 1998 and described the 'psychotic
acceleration,' the 'juddering race-spec clutch'
and stopping power that felt like you had been
'hit in the face.' Comparing it with the Porsche
911 Carrera, it said: 'In its heart the Impreza
is closer to the 911 RS than the new Carrera:
noisy, light and uncompromising … After a hard
thrash in this car, most of us will be suffering from
exhilaration fatigue.'

In America, *Car & Driver* (March 1999)
recorded a top speed of 144mph (232kph)
and a 0–60mph time of 4.7 seconds. They
estimated the 22B's power output at 300bhp
and recorded phenomenal lateral grip of 0.96g
– but fuel consumption was a paltry 15mpg (18.9
litres/100km).

No question that the 22B was the pinnacle
– albeit a very specialised one – of the first
generation Impreza tree. It was the committed
rally fanatic's ultimate roadgoing fantasy. Or as *Car*
magazine put it succinctly: 'This rally replica is *it*
now, the peak, the summit, the ultimate, the fat

lady singing for all she's worth.' So few cars were
produced that it will undoubtedly remain the holy
grail for the Impreza enthusiast.

1999 – Version V

Following a predictable pattern, on 3 September
1998 the F-series and Version V Imprezas arrived,
although many of the changes seen on the Japanese
WRX had actually been previewed on the
Australian-market Impreza, launched in August (the
very first time that a new Subaru model had been
launched outside Japan).

The range available was identical to the previous
year, with the notable absence of the 22B. Even
the range of special editions was identical, with V-
Limited versions of the STi Type R and WRX Type
RA two-doors and the STi RA Version V four-
door, all painted in the same Sonic Blue as the 22B.

All WRX models gained a reprofiled front
spoiler with lower 'ears' and extra vents below the
foglamps (mirroring Mitsubishi's Lancer Evo VI),
with new-style apertures for the indicators. Air
flow to the brakes was much improved as a result.
New colours for the Version V included a darker
silver and Cool Grey (a pewter metallic shade that
was oddly called Blue Steel in Britain when it was
used for the RB5 special edition).

Once again the engines were improved. The non-STi WRX remained at 280PS at 6,500rpm but torque rose another step to 249lb ft (338Nm) at 4,000rpm. The five-door's engine now stood at 240PS at 6,000rpm.

The Version V STi saloon was most notable for its much bigger, reprofiled WRC-style rear spoiler, while all STi models had new vaned STi spotlamp covers. Top speed was claimed to have increased as a result of the front and rear aerodynamic modifications. New inverted dampers were said to provide higher resistance to lateral force, while ride quality was also better.

It is also worth mentioning the arrival of the Impreza SRX at the same time as the Version V. The SRX was a sub-WRX addition that used a non-turbo version of the 2.0-litre twin-cam engine but had a WRX-style body kit and dinner-plate spotlamps. And I cannot round things off without mention of the bizarre Subaru Casa Blanca, launched in December 1998. This was a 1.5-litre Impreza Sports Wagon treated (if that is the right word) to the Japanese fascination with retro style in the form of an upright chrome grille, chrome bumpers and circular headlamps. Merging 1950s Wolseley chromework with a McRae pedigree is about as incongruous as it gets!

2000 – Version VI

On 6 September 1999, the very last of the old-shape Impreza upgrades was announced. The ultimate G-series/Version VI WRX was offered once again in the same range of 11 variants, including V-Limited versions of the Type R and Type RA two-doors and a V-Limited version of the STi RA Version VI four-door.

Very minor changes greeted the Version VI. The colour palette was altered so that black was no longer available and Cashmere Yellow was introduced for the STi and STi RA, while interior colours also changed. On the mechanical side an

↑ It's not a turbocharged Impreza, but the Casa Blanca deserves a mention because it was just such an incongruous addition to the Japanese market: 1950s pastiche meets Carloz Sainz street cred!

↓ The final Version VI evolution of the WRX STi (launched in September 1999) sported many more body addenda than the first types. This Sports Wagon clearly shows its double rear spoiler.

↑ **When the WRX STi Electra One was shown at the 1999 Tokyo Motor Show, few thought it would enter production, with its phantasmagorical aerodynamic package, including a rear wing that was every bit as tall as the roofline.**

uprated clutch was the only major improvement. Bullet-shaped door mirrors were now available as an option to decrease weight and improve aerodynamics.

Once again there were limited edition Version VI Imprezas. These were: WRX STi RA Version VI Limited saloon (2,000 units), WRX RA Limited saloon (1,000 units), WRX Type R STi Version VI Limited coupé (1,000 units) and WRX STi Version VI Limited Sports Wagon (500 units). These all featured RAYS 16-inch alloy wheels, an exclusive instrument panel, aluminium pedals, STi titanium gear knob (except RA Limited), serial number plaque, 'cherry red' emblem (except the WRX RA Limited which was black), and 'exclusive' body colour.

S201 – the wildest Impreza

Easily the wildest-looking roadgoing Impreza ever was the STi S201. Created by Subaru Tecnica International, it was presented on 3 April 2000 as the ultimate four-door evolution of the soon-to-be-replaced first-generation Impreza.

Chief engineer Takeshi Ito described its role as follows: 'We intended to evoke much of

the atmosphere of race cars. We transferred directly the image of the Electra One, which was introduced at the 1999 Tokyo Motor Show as a concept. Its aero parts were developed along state-of-the-art aerodynamics theories.'

The S201 was indeed very closely based on the Electra One shown at the October 1999 Tokyo Motor Show. Its wild bodykit featured a deeply chiselled front spoiler with integrated small-diameter foglamps, matching flared side skirts and oversized rear valance, and a pylon-sized double-tiered rear wing. The bonnet featured a larger than usual air scoop and the air vents were different too. There were six-spoke gold alloy wheels, bullet-shaped door mirrors and a special decal package, and inside there was a titanium gear knob and a special S201 plaque. However, the unusual headlamp treatment of the Electra One show car was not carried over to the S201.

Mechanically, the S201 was essentially the same as the car upon which it was based, the STi RA Version VI. The main difference was engine output, rated at 300PS at 6,500rpm, slightly up on the normal version (and bestowing on the S210 the highest power-to-weight ratio of any standard Impreza at 235PS per tonne), while torque stood at 260lb ft (352Nm) at 4,000rpm. The improvements were down to enhanced charging pressure thanks to an STi sport ECU, a more efficient turbocharger (reduced intake drag was accomplished through a larger intake duct), and a lower back-pressure exhaust with a larger, 120mm diameter tailpipe.

Only 300 numbered examples of the S201 were produced at the equivalent yen price of £23,000 in Japan (3,700,000 yen).

End of the line

The end of the road for the Impreza came in June 2000, when production was suspended in the run-up to the launch of the 'New Age' Impreza in August 2000. Something over 700,000 first-generation Imprezas had been built by the end of the line. Quite what the percentage of turbocharged models was, is sadly not recorded, but it was certainly a very high figure for a performance derivative.

The WRX had been unquestionably a legend in its own lifetime. Rally star, phenomenally able road car, family transport, Number 1 in customer satisfaction surveys, track day express, engineering masterpiece – the Impreza really was the complete machine.

When asked how he felt about the worldwide acclaim the Impreza received, Takeshi Ito replied to the author in typically understated terms: 'We are very proud and honoured. We believe that a lot of people appreciated Impreza's well-balanced driving performance based on the horizontally opposed engine and our basic development philosophy.'

Australia and New Zealand

As already covered in the previous chapter, customers in Australia and New Zealand were offered a model called the Impreza WRX, but it was certainly not the powerful WRX sold in Japan. Instead it was simply a rebadged version of the 208-218PS Turbo/GT sold in almost every other export market.

However, the 'real thing' did eventually filter through to Antipodean markets as demand for

Japanese-market cars reached fever pitch in Australia and New Zealand. Their close proximity to Japan made awareness of the Japanese-market WRX and STi models even more intense than the UK or the USA. Indeed, the flourishing trade in 'grey' imports in New Zealand led to many Japanese-market Imprezas arriving unofficially on Kiwi roads – which are some of the best in the world for exploiting the potential of the Impreza.

Eventually, the official importers relented and leapt at the opportunity to offer limited numbers of genuine STi Imprezas. In Australia, the first official STi models arrived in January 1999, when a modified version of the STi Version V Type R two-door was offered to the public. Differences between the Japanese Type R and this Australian version included clear rather than dark rear windows, a viscous centre coupling instead of an active diff, no intercooler waterspray, STi Version III non-inverted strut suspension, different instruments, no electric folding mirrors, non-ventilated rear discs, and longer gearing as per the standard car.

A choice of blue or white paint was available. The STi was not cheap at 60,000 Australian dollars (some 50 per cent more than the standard car) but demand was extraordinarily strong for the 400 cars that Subaru brought in. Therefore, anyone lucky enough to get one was able sell it immediately for a premium of up to 30 per cent!

The experience had been duly noted at Subaru. In November 1999, the Australian market received a further 400 STi Imprezas, this time

---

DID YOU KNOW?

How to interpret chassis codes

Subaru uses a seven-digit code for each individual model. This can be found on the vehicle identification number (VIN) plate inside the engine bay.

Model code:	G = Impreza (S = Forester, B = Legacy)
Body type:	C = Saloon and Coupé, F =Sports Wagon
Engine type:	8 = 2.0-litre Turbo (6 = 1.8, 4 = 1.6, 1 = 1.5)
Year series code:	A = MY93, B = MY94, C = MY95/96, D = MY97, E = MY98, F = MY99, G = MY00
Number of doors:	2 = two-door coupé, 4 = four-door saloon, 5 = five-door sports wagon
Model Type:	8 = WRX, 7 = RA, E = STi (from Version III), D = STi Type R and RA, S = 22B
Transmission:	D = five-speed manual, P = four-speed automatic

↓ The impreza always made a perfect track day car.

based on the four-door STi Version VI. There were suggestions that this version was detuned as a result of some blown engines with the previous STi, but independent tests showed these rumours were unfounded. The spec closely followed the Japanese spec, including the electronic speed limiter that kept top speed down to 112mph (180kph) and the latest inverted strut suspension.

In New Zealand, the Impreza Turbo was also marketed as the WRX, which was sold in saloon and estate guises. New Zealand literature boasted that 'our ABS system has been specifically tested for Australasian conditions

and the result is improved performance on our unsealed roads.'

The pukka WRX STi also eventually arrived officially in New Zealand. The full range of STi models was available: saloon, estate and coupé. All the usual STi features were present: the 280PS (205kW) engine, big four-pot calliper brakes, intercooler waterspray, short-throw quick-shift gear lever, shorter gear ratios (the coupé having a Group N-type gearbox and adjustable centre differential), firmer suspension, carbon-fibre strut brace, forged aluminium lower wishbones, gold alloy wheels and aluminium bonnet.

Other worldwide markets

While New Zealand and Australia did eventually receive lightly modified versions of the STi, the genuine Japanese specification WRX and STi models were only ever officially sold in four countries outside Japan, namely Brunei, Hong Kong, Singapore and Cyprus. These were all notable as right-hand-drive markets with Type Approval regulations that accepted Japanese standards. The WRX five-door automatic was also sold in these markets.

Deadly rivals: Impreza WRX and Lancer Evo

The Subaru Impreza really had very few genuine rivals throughout its life. Turbocharged four-wheel-drive performance cars are a genuine rarity. The Lancia Integrale was perhaps the only contemporary rival for the Impreza Turbo in Europe, but even this had left production by 1994. Audi's S4 quattro was no match for the Impreza in terms of performance, handling, driver enjoyment or value.

No, there was only one genuine rival for the Impreza, and that also came from Japan. Mitsubishi's Lancer Evolution shadowed the Impreza for its entire production life, and provided the number one opposition to the Impreza both in the showroom and in the World Rally Championship in the late 1990s.

The Lancer Evolution first appeared in October 1992, fractionally before the Impreza. If the spec of tenacious four-wheel-drive transmission and a mighty turbocharged 2.0-litre four-cylinder engine with an IHI turbocharger, twin-cams and four valves per cylinder sounds familiar, it should: it replicated the Impreza's spec exactly. The major difference was the Evo's in-line rather than boxer engine, which boasted an extra 10bhp at 250bhp, and its transverse engine/gearbox layout. The Evo II, which arrived in January 1994 to coincide with the very first Impreza STi, boasted 260bhp and tweaked suspension. The Evo III of February 1995 marked far-reaching changes, with power up to 270bhp, an intercooler waterspray and better brakes, suspension and transmission. It began to look a bit wilder, too, with a deeper, more sculpted front spoiler, side skirts and a larger boot spoiler. Mirroring the Type RA versions of the Impreza, the Evo was always available in an alternative stripped-out lightweight RS version in addition to the normal GSR. Each Lancer Evolution was shadowed by an improved Impreza STi Version.

In the early days, the Impreza definitely had the edge over the Evo. It was innately more balanced thanks to its low-slung left/right symmetrical boxer layout, and it was slightly lighter too to counter the Evo's extra horses. McRae's Impreza was also beating Eriksson's Evo in world rallying – and the Impreza STi was cheaper to buy than

the Mitsubishi. While the Impreza was produced with no upper production limits, each version of the Lancer was available in strictly limited numbers (5,000 each of Evo I, II and III, 9,000 Evo IV, 8,000 Evo V, 7,000 Evo VI and 2,500 Evo VI Tommi Mäkinen).

The Evo III scored its first blood when Mäkinen won the first of his WRC championships in 1996. The magic rubbed off on to the road car programme, but outside Japan Mitsubishi would only sell cars to serious rallying contenders.

The biggest evolutionary change came in August 1996 with the Evo IV, which finally came up with something that took it to a different level than the Impreza – Active Yaw Control. This used sophisticated sensors to track a variety of dynamic information and adjusted traction to the wheels with most grip. Combined with front and rear limited slip differentials, it imbued the Evo IV with a car's equivalent of superhuman strength through corners.

Also the engine was rotated through 180° to improve weight distribution and balance, and was boosted to 280bhp. An all-new bodyshell made it bigger in all

areas, too, but that included its weight. The Impreza and Lancer were now much more evenly matched.

With the Evo V of January 1998, Mitsubishi may just have tipped the balance. Brembo four-pot front callipers were joined by a Torsen front differential, mechanical rear diff and a viscous coupling centre diff with a waterspray. The track grew wider and the look more purposeful, while weight was saved by introducing aluminium front wings and bonnet. The Evo VI of January 1999 took the original Lancer to its ultimate form, especially in tuned Zero Fighter guise.

When Subaru announced the New Age Impreza STi in October 2000, the ball appeared to bounce back in Fuji's favour. Here was a car with greater rigidity, better refinement and extra space. In response, Mitsubishi brought the launch of its all-new Lancer Evo VII forward to January 2001. It was lighter than the Impreza, so slightly quicker, while its Active Yaw Control continued to deliver sublime handling. The match was as close as ever, and the tussle set to last until that inopportune and hopefully far-distant time when fast cars are no longer in demand.

Few cars were ever so closely matched as the Subaru Impreza WRX STi and Mitsubishi Lancer Evolution. Both Impreza and Lancer Evo were launched in 1992 and went on to become rally legends, while vying with each other in the showrooms to take the honours as just about the best tarmac performance cars in the world.

The Impreza WRX bloodline

Type	Chassis code	Max Power	Max Torque
1993 MY A-series (Nov 1992–Sep 1993)			
WRX	GC8A48D	240PS @ 6,000rpm	224.3lb ft (304Nm) @ 5,000rpm
WRX Type RA	GC8A47D	240PS @ 6,000rpm	224.3lb ft (304Nm) @ 5,000rpm
1994 MY B-series (Oct 1993–Sep 1994)			
WRX	GC8B48D	240PS @ 6,000rpm	224.3lb ft (304Nm) @ 5,000rpm
WRX Type RA	GC8B47D	240PS @ 6,000rpm	224.3lb ft (304Nm) @ 5,000rpm
WRX STi Version	GC8B48D	250PS @ 6,500rpm	228lb ft (309Nm) @ 3,500rpm
WRX wagon	GF8B58D	220PS @ 6,000rpm	206.6lb ft (280Nm) @ 3,500rpm
WRX wagon automatic	GF8B58P	220PS @ 6,000rpm	206.6lb ft (280Nm) @ 3,500rpm
WRX wagon SA	GF8B58D	220PS @ 6,000rpm	206.6lb ft (280Nm) @ 3,500rpm
WRX wagon STi Version	GF8B58D	250PS @ 6,500rpm	228lb ft (309Nm) @ 3,500rpm
1995 MY C1-series (Oct 1994–Aug 1995)			
WRX	GC8C48D	260PS @ 6,500rpm	228lb ft (309Nm) @ 5,000rpm
WRX Type RA	GC8C47D	260PS @ 6,500rpm	228lb ft (309Nm) @ 5,000rpm
WRX Type RA STi Version	GC8C47D	275PS @ 6,500rpm	235.4lb ft (319Nm) @ 4,000rpm
WRX wagon	GF8C58D	220PS @ 6,000rpm	206.6lb ft (280Nm) @ 3,500rpm
WRX wagon automatic	GF8C58P	220PS @ 6,000rpm	206.6lb ft (280Nm) @ 3,500rpm
1996 MY C2-series (Aug 1995–Aug 1996)			
WRX	GC8C48D	260PS @ 6,500rpm	228lb ft (309Nm) @ 5,000rpm
WRX Type RA	GC8C47D	260PS @ 6,500rpm	228lb ft (309Nm) @ 5,000rpm
WRX STi Version II	GC8C4ED	275PS @ 6,500rpm	235.4lb ft (319Nm) @ 4,000rpm
WRX STi Version II 555	GC8C4ED	275PS @ 6,500rpm	235.4lb ft (319Nm) @ 4,000rpm
WRX Type RA STi Version II	GC8C4DD	275PS @ 6,500rpm	235.4lb ft (319Nm) @ 4,000rpm
WRX Type RA STi Version II V-Limited	GC8C4DD	275PS @ 6,500rpm	235.4lb ft (319Nm) @ 4,000rpm
WRX wagon	GF8C58D	220PS @ 6,000rpm	206.6lb ft (280Nm) @ 3,500rpm
WRX wagon automatic	GF8C58P	220PS @ 6,000rpm	206.6lb ft (280Nm) @ 3,500rpm
WRX STi Version II wagon	GF8C58D	260PS @ 6,500rpm	228lb ft (309Nm) @ 5,000rpm
WRX STi Version II 555 wagon	GF8C58D	260PS @ 6,500rpm	228lb ft (309Nm) @ 5,000rpm
1997 MY D-series (Sep 1996–Aug 1997)			
WRX Type R STi Version III	GC8D2DD	280PS @ 6,500rpm	259.8lb ft (352Nm) @ 4,000rpm
WRX Type R STi Version III Signature	GC8D2DD	280PS @ 6,500rpm	259.8lb ft (352Nm) @ 4,000rpm
WRX	GC8D48D	280PS @ 6,500rpm	242lb ft (328Nm) @ 4,000rpm
WRX Type RA	GC8D47D	280PS @ 6,500rpm	242lb ft (328Nm) @ 4,000rpm
WRX STi Version III	GC8D4ED	280PS @ 6,500rpm	253.1lb ft (343Nm) @ 4,000rpm
WRX STi Version III V-Limited	GC8D4ED	280PS @ 6,500rpm	253.1lb ft (343Nm) @ 4,000rpm
WRX Type RA STi Version III	GC8D4DD	280PS @ 6,500rpm	253.1lb ft (343Nm) @ 4,000rpm
WRX wagon	GF8D58D	240PS at 6,000rpm	224.3lb ft (304Nm) @ 3,000rpm
WRX wagon automatic	GF8D58P	240PS at 6,000rpm	224.3lb ft (304Nm) @ 3,000rpm
WRX STi Version III wagon	GF8D5ED	280PS @ 6,500rpm	253.1lb ft (343Nm) @ 4,000rpm
WRX STi Version III V-Limited wagon	GF8D5ED	280PS @ 6,500rpm	253.1lb ft (343Nm) @ 4,000rpm

Type	Chassis code	Max Power	Max Torque
1998 MY E-series (Sep 1997–Aug 1998)			
WRX Type R V-Limited	GC8E2DD	280PS @ 6,500rpm	242lb ft (328Nm) @ 4,000rpm
WRX Type R STi Version IV	GC8E2DD	280PS @ 6,500rpm	259.8lb ft (352Nm) @ 4,000rpm
WRX Type R STi Version IV V-Limited	GC8E2DD	280PS @ 6,500rpm	259.8lb ft (352Nm) @ 4,000rpm
WRX	GC8E48D	280PS @ 6,500rpm	242lb ft (328Nm) @ 4,000rpm
WRX Type RA	GC8E47D	280PS @ 6,500rpm	242lb ft (328Nm) @ 4,000rpm
WRX STi Version IV	GC8E4ED	280PS @ 6,500rpm	259.8lb ft (352Nm) @ 4,000rpm
WRX Type RA STi Version IV	GC8E4DD	280PS @ 6,500rpm	259.8lb ft (352Nm) @ 4,000rpm
WRX Type RA STi Version IV V-Limited	GC8E4DD	280PS @ 6,500rpm	259.8lb ft (352Nm) @ 4,000rpm
WRX wagon	GF8E58D	250PS @ 6,000rpm	225.8lb ft (306Nm) @ 4,000rpm
WRX wagon automatic	GF8E58P	240PS @ 6,000rpm	225.8lb ft (306Nm) @ 4,000rpm
WRX STi Version IV wagon	GF8E5ED	280PS @ 6,500rpm	259.8lb ft (352Nm) @ 4,000rpm
1998 MY 22B (Mar 1998–Aug 1998)			
STi Type R 22B	GC8E2SD	280PS @ 6,000rpm	264.2lb ft (360Nm) @ 3,200rpm
1999 MY F-series (Sep 1998–Aug 1999)			
WRX Type R V-Limited	GC8F27D	280PS @ 6,500rpm	249.4lb ft (338Nm) @ 4,000rpm
WRX Type R STi Version V	GC8F2DD	280PS @ 6,500rpm	259.8lb ft (352Nm) @ 4,000rpm
WRX Type R STi Version V V-Limited	GC8F2DD	280PS @ 6,500rpm	259.8lb ft (352Nm) @ 4,000rpm
WRX	GC8F48D	280PS @ 6,500rpm	249.4lb ft (338Nm) @ 4,000rpm
WRX Type RA	GC8F47D	280PS @ 6,500rpm	249.4lb ft (338Nm) @ 4,000rpm
WRX STi Version V	GC8F4ED	280PS @ 6,500rpm	259.8lb ft (352Nm) @ 4,000rpm
WRX Type RA STi Version V	GC8F4DD	280PS @ 6,500rpm	259.8lb ft (352Nm) @ 4,000rpm
WRX Type RA STi Version V V-Limited	GC8F4DD	280PS @ 6,500rpm	259.8lb ft (352Nm) @ 4,000rpm
WRX wagon	GF8F58D	240PS @ 6,000rpm	228lb ft (309Nm) @ 4,000rpm
WRX wagon automatic	GF8F58P	240PS @ 6,000rpm	228lb ft (309Nm) @ 4,000rpm
WRX STi Version V wagon	GF8F5ED	280PS @ 6,500rpm	259.8lb ft (352Nm) @ 4,000rpm
2000 MY G-series (Sep 1999–Aug 2000)			
WRX Type R V-Limited	GC8G27D	280PS @ 6,500rpm	249.4lb ft (338Nm) @ 4,000rpm
WRX Type R STi Version VI	GC8G2FD	280PS @ 6,500rpm	259.8lb ft (352Nm) @ 4,000rpm
WRX Type R STi Version VI V-Limited	GC8G2FD	280PS @ 6,500rpm	259.8lb ft (352Nm) @ 4,000rpm
WRX	GC8G48D	280PS @ 6,500rpm	249.4lb ft (338Nm) @ 4,000rpm
WRX Type RA	GC8G47D	280PS @ 6,500rpm	249.4lb ft (338Nm) @ 4,000rpm
WRX Type RA V-Limited	GC8G47D	280PS @ 6,500rpm	249.4lb ft (338Nm) @ 4,000rpm
WRX STi Version VI	GC8G4ED	280PS @ 6,500rpm	259.8lb ft (352Nm) @ 4,000rpm
WRX Type RA STi Version VI	GC8G4DD	280PS @ 6,500rpm	259.8lb ft (352Nm) @ 4,000rpm
WRX Type RA STi Version VI V-Limited	GC8G4DD	280PS @ 6,500rpm	259.8lb ft (352Nm) @ 4,000rpm
WRX Type RA STi Version VI S201	GC8G4DD	300PS @ 6,500rpm	259.8lb ft (352Nm) @ 4,000rpm
WRX wagon	GF8G58D	240PS @ 6,000rpm	228lb ft (309Nm) @ 4,000rpm
WRX wagon automatic	GF8G58P	240PS @ 6,000rpm	228lb ft (309Nm) @ 4,000rpm
WRX wagon STi Version VI	GF8G5ED	280PS @ 6,500rpm	259.8lb ft (352Nm) @ 4,000rpm
WRX wagon STi Version VI V-Limited	GF8G5ED	280PS @ 6,500rpm	259.8lb ft (352Nm) @ 4,000rpm

CHAPTER 4
AMERICA'S RS

No global car maker can ignore the United States, which is by far the largest single market for cars in the world. North America has become pivotal for the Japanese car makers, with Toyota and Honda – not Ford or Chevrolet – vying for the number one best-seller spot and large manufacturing and assembly plants sprouting up from many overseas car makers on US soil.

America is no less significant for Subaru, which produces around 100,000 cars annually (principally the Legacy) in the USA at a Subaru/Isuzu joint venture plant in Lafayette, Indiana. Models such as the Outback were conceived in the United States, and by far the largest market for Subaru outside Japan is the USA. America even imported Subaru's first-ever car, the tiny 360, in the 1960s.

While the Legacy was easily the most significant Subaru model in North America, the Impreza would be pivotal too. The Impreza first made it to the USA in 1993, sold in four- and five-door guises but with a rather feeble 110bhp 1.8-litre flat-four engine.

For the 1995 Model Year, two new models that had a special resonance in the USA were added to the range. The first was a two-door coupé version. This was to prove highly significant because it was this bodyshell that would be used to homologate Subaru's World Rally Car for the 1997 season. But the roadgoing coupé was no rally special: it merely slotted in as alternative body style in the Impreza line-up and was offered in the same trim level range and with the same engines as all other Imprezas. Which meant a standard 110bhp . . .

The second new model was the Impreza Outback Sport, a station wagon inspired by the smash hit success of the Legacy Outback. The younger Outback was decked out with a special two-tone paint scheme, slightly higher ground clearance, bonnet scoops, four-wheel disc brakes and unique wheel covers. The 1997 version even had a WRX-type bonnet scoop! A similar model was later marketed in Japan as the Impreza EX from October 1995.

In terms of power output the Impreza was going in the right direction at least: the 1995 Model Year saw the arrival of a 135bhp 2.2-litre flat-four that was also unique to America. The 2.2 powerplant was standardised for 1996 (except on the curiously named Brighton coupé), with its power output later rising to 137bhp.

But in the wake of Subaru's all-conquering World Rally successes, there was pent-up demand in America for a car that had some of the WRC kudos, even though as *Car & Driver* magazine put it: 'Most people in the US follow the World Rally Championship with about the same enthusiasm as they follow synchronised swimming.' Perhaps this was why the USA would never receive a turbocharged first-generation Impreza. Or maybe it was a combination of tough emissions regulations and a marketplace that shunned small-capacity turbo engines. Whatever the reason, Subaru USA was forced to try a different tack.

Its solution was the 2.5 RS, launched at the April 1997 New York show as a 1998 Model Year car to go on sale in the autumn. For turbo-unfriendly America, it had a normally aspirated engine. With a capacity of 2,457cc, this was an engine fitted to no other Impreza (although American Legacies also had the powerplant).

The enlarged 2.5-litre engine retained twin overhead camshafts. It produced a more healthy 165 horses at a lazy 5,600rpm and 162lb ft (220Nm) of torque at 4,000rpm, but there was no hiding the disappointment compared to the turbocharged models in other markets. The standard transmission was a five-speed manual gearbox with the same short-throw linkage as the WRX, but the RS's sporting credentials were seemingly decimated by the availability of a four-speed automatic as an option; still, the Japanese also had a 250bhp automatic WRX . . .

Performance was reasonable, if not breathtaking. Top speed was 124mph (200kph)

← The 2.5-litre engine in the 2.5 RS produced only 165bhp at a lazy 5,600rpm. The standard transmission was a five-speed manual but there was also an optional four-speed automatic. North America was the only market to receive a first-generation Impreza fitted with a 2.5-litre flat four-cylinder engine. The performance from the 2.5-litre RS was lively rather than breathtaking.

← The 1999 2.5 RS was notable for its larger dinner-plate foglamps and Japanese-style bumper. Under the bonnet there was a new 'Phase II' engine with extra torque and superior throttle response.

and 0–60mph was achievable in 7.5 seconds, with a standing quarter-mile of 16 seconds. The lacklustre figures were also partly down to the extra weight of the engine: the 2.5 RS weighed 1,280kg (2,822lb) compared with 1,235kg (2,723lb) for the European four-door Turbo.

Testers universally raved about the handling. The improvement compared to other North American Imprezas was mainly down to the stiffer suspension and legendary four-wheel-drive with viscous centre coupling, distinct from other members of the US Impreza family.

Despite its performance disadvantage compared with turbocharged Imprezas, the 2.5 RS certainly looked the part. It was sold in coupé form only to start with. Despite the lack of a turbocharger, the 2.5 RS still sported an intercooler intake and straked vents on the bonnet. The side skirts were there and although the rear under-valance was not, the RS did boast a pretty big rear spoiler. Rally Blue paint was the obvious choice, set off by gold, five-spoke 16-inch alloy wheels shod with 205/55 R16 tyres. The front spoiler was also unique to the RS, featuring tiny projector-beam fog lights either side of the

air scoop and long, thin indicators. The headlamps were unique too.

Slotting in as the top-of-the-line Impreza, the RS came loaded with features. Standard items included air conditioning, variable speed intermittent wipers, electric windows, electrically powered sunroof, 80-watt stereo, 60/40 split rear seat and five seat belts. Safety features included ABS, twin airbags and side impact beams. Priced at $19,195 it was pretty good value.

The RS gained something of a cult following in the USA and Canada. Parts interchangeability allowed many owners to improve their RS by fitting aftermarket wheels, suspension and exhaust systems, as well as cosmetic items. There is now a flourishing performance market in the USA, with both turbo and supercharger conversions available. Surprisingly for a country that largely ignored World Rallying, the names WRX and STi seemed to have a meaning for a select band of owners who had 'discovered' the Impreza.

This was not lost on Subaru America, which was already gearing up for expanding its influence in this area by opening a new driving school near Atlanta, Georgia. This was claimed to be the only driving school in the country that offered AWD vehicles.

For the 1999 Model Year, the 2.5 RS was given a facelift. The front spoiler was now the same as Imprezas in other markets, with the trademark WRX-type dinner-plate foglamps and strakes between the indicators (except in Canada). The alloy wheel colour changed from gold to silver and the interior gained a leather steering wheel, gear knob and gaiter, plus white-faced dials.

More significant perhaps was a revised 'Phase II' engine. Power remained the same at 165bhp but torque rose marginally to 166lb ft (225Nm) at 4,000rpm. The engine was claimed to rev much more freely, with superior throttle response, although the redline dropped by 250rpm to 6,250rpm. Transmissions were also smoother and more efficient, said Subaru.

New for 2000 was a four-door version of the 2.5 RS to join the coupé. Cosmetically the 2000 MY 2.5 RS had the latest front spoiler of the Japanese Impreza WRX but retained a much lower rear spoiler (the four-door version's was even smaller). The colour black was discontinued and replaced with Sedona Red Pearl, while the most popular colour (Rally Blue Pearl) was replaced with a darker Blue Ridge Pearl.

The engine was improved again this year, offering 50 per cent more torque at 3,250rpm, although peak torque remained at 166lb ft (and power remained static too at 165bhp). After problems, the 'hot wire' mass air sensor was replaced with an absolute pressure mass air sensor. Cruise control was a new standard item for 2000.

↓ **The American Impreza interior was well-equipped compared with European cars, with standard air conditioning, electric windows, electric sunroof, 80-watt stereo and twin airbags.**

DID YOU KNOW?

Almost a WRX ... the 2.5 RX

The powerful impact of the WRX on the American psyche – albeit infuriatingly out of reach – was proven by the 2.5 RX show car of 1998. This was created as 'a work in progress, active test bed for a line of performance parts being considered for the US market.'

The RX was a far meaner machine than the RS. The biggest changes occurred in the chassis. At the front end, it had the forged aluminium lower wishbones of the STi, plus stiffer struts and springs, uprated bushings and 'precise ball and socket' anti-roll bar links. The front track (tread) was just under an inch wider.

At the rear end, stiffer springs and struts were supplemented by reinforced trailing links, a reinforced crossmember, tube-type lateral links, stiffer bushings and a thicker anti-roll bar with ball and socket links. The rear suspension was also slightly lower. Big 18-inch alloy wheels were TR Motor Sports Typhoon shod with Pirelli P7000 tyres. Subaru commented: 'The suspension has been tuned to work with the all-wheel-drive system to allow throttle induced oversteer.' Sounds like fun.

Other changes for the 2.5 RX included a tuned exhaust, heavy-duty clutch, new front bumper/spoiler, WRC98 aluminium bonnet, WRC98 rear spoiler and Prodrive Rally Blue paint scheme. Inside there was a bespoke two-tone leather finish with Recaro seats, Momo steering wheel, carbon fibre effect gauge trim and white-faced dials. It also had a very special 200-watt audio system.

New 16-inch six-spoke alloy wheels were new this year too, in addition to a rear limited slip differential (it had previously been a mere open diff). You could also now buy an RS with a front strut cross brace, carbon-fibre interior trim, leather upholstery and a new gauge pod. Overall the 2000 MY RS was 20lb (9kg) lighter.

For the final model year, 2001, all Impreza 2.5 RS models gained a standard single-disc CD player, 2.5 RS embroidered floor mats and carbon-fibre patterned interior trim. Prices rose by only $200.

For all its rally car looks, the 2.5 RS never really lived up to the Impreza Turbo promise of its appearance. As one road tester, Miles Cook, commented: 'With only 165 horsepower, the 2.5 RS had sand kicked in its face by foes such as the VTEC Integra and VR6-powered VW GTI.'

However, the tide would eventually turn for the USA and Canada. With the launch of the New Age WRX, North Americans were finally offered a turbocharged Impreza. More than that, it boasted more power than the European version, which made up some of the lost ground. This particular part of the Impreza story is covered in the chapter on the New Age Impreza.

↑ American road testers cottoned on quickly to the Impreza's amazing grip and handling. A large aftermarket built up in the USA to tune the 2.5 RS up to rival the STi in performance and road behaviour.

← New for the Year 2000 was a four-door version of the 2.5 RS. This is a 2001 example. America would have to wait until the 'New Age' car to get a turbocharged Impreza.

← ← America came close to the WRX with the 1998 2.5 RX – but it was only a show car. Many STi parts, plus 18-inch wheels, tuned exhaust, heavy-duty clutch, Japanese-type front spoiler, WRC98 aluminium bonnet and WRC98 rear spoiler were designed to show how a planned range of tuning parts could emerge for the US market.

CHAPTER 5
PRODRIVE ROAD CARS

The name Prodrive has become synonymous with Impreza rallying and enhanced Impreza road cars. It is rare that any independent company has had such a pivotal role within a major car company, which is a measure of the qualities that the British-based company offers. Prodrive's motorsport pedigree and its background as an engineering company is fully covered in the chapter on rallying, so in this chapter we will concentrate solely on Prodrive's enhancement programmes for roadgoing Imprezas.

As the force behind Subaru's rally team since 1989, and the company responsible for the Impreza rally car, Prodrive was ideally placed to offer enhancement packages for the Impreza road car, and ultimately to create its own visions of the ultimate roadgoing Impreza. The temptation to upgrade the Impreza Turbo proved too strong for many road drivers and Prodrive was there at the outset catering for owners wishing to extend the car's performance, handling, cosmetics or interior fittings.

In fact, Prodrive's Impreza programme predated the launch of the Turbo. Prior to the Turbo it was already offering a limited range of parts – wheels, tyres, Recaro seats and suspension components – for the Impreza 1.8GL. These transferred neatly to the Turbo when it arrived in 1994.

When Prodrive fitted its range of parts to an Impreza Turbo it called it the Prodrive Edition, and only around 25 of these were produced each year to start with. One such car was reviewed in the June 1994 edition of *Performance Car* magazine, fitted with upgraded suspension, wheels and tyres, as well as a Recaro/Prodrive interior at a cost of just under £4,000 on top of the standard Turbo price. A variety of 16-inch and 17-inch wheels was offered as time progressed.

Initially the parts were available through Prodrive dealers but for 1997 Subaru UK took on distribution and parts stocking itself, and many of the parts were now fitted by Subaru dealers.

While tuning or modification would normally invalidate any official manufacturer warranty, because Prodrive's work was backed by Subaru UK, the warranty remained unaffected. This was crucial to the marketing drive.

Prodrive also developed the Series McRae of 1995, which is fully described in the Turbo chapter. By 1996, Prodrive was offering a 'Driver Enhancement' package, which consisted of uprated suspension (stiffer springs and dampers and a thicker anti-roll bar) plus 7 x 17-inch Speedline Supertourismo alloy wheels on Pirelli P Zero tyres.

Going one step further there was a new 'Performance Package' in 1996 that was always fitted by Prodrive at Banbury. This boosted power up to 240bhp at 5,600rpm and torque up to 240lb ft (325Nm) at 4,000rpm. The Prodrive Performance pack was unique in that it did not affect the three-year/60,000 mile warranty. The early (pre-1997) enhancement pack included a new rear silencer, RamAir filter element, enhanced engine management and an uprated Mintex disc brake pad set. The main benefit of the mods was more flexible torque throughout the rev range. Up to 300 Performance Packs would be sold in any one year.

Interior upgrades continued to be offered, and were very popular because the standard pre-1997 interior was rather uninspiring – no less than 250 were sold in the first year out of around 1,200 Impreza Turbos bought in the UK. Recaro sports front seats were the main change, with rear seats and door side panels reupholstered in matching material. Prodrive also offered the console and gear knob in either wood effect and or carbon-fibre effect, plus Prodrive-branded mats. Going the 'Full Monty' and ordering every pack from Prodrive cost a substantial £9,000 on top of the £18,499 price of the base Impreza.

Autocar magazine drove a Prodrive-modified Impreza in October 1996 and commented that it 'feels capable of shaving half a second off the standard car's 5.8sec 0–60mph time.' It also felt the suspension improvements 'tighten the car up noticeably and turn an already capable chassis into a real peach – grippy yet adjustable, neutral with just a hint of power oversteer on the exit of corners.'

In December 1996, *Car* magazine drove a Prodrive Impreza with gushing prose following: 'Terrific grip, fine poise, go-where-you-point-it accuracy, quirk-free chuckability, impeccable stability … In the wet, not even the purebred Elise is a match for Impreza tenacity.'

Prodrive extended their product range in 1997 to include cosmetic bodykits, both for saloon and estate models. The first item on the list was a deeper front air dam with integral PIAA 120w driving lamps. These driving lights replaced the usual fog lights, and operated in tandem with the main high beam (rather than the independently-switched foglamps). Also included were colour-coded skirts and mirrors and a taller rear aerofoil (on the estate, twin aerofoils). The 1998 Model Year would see a front lip spoiler introduced.

Also in 1997 came an upgraded suspension package. Previously the dampers had been merely revalved; now they were replaced by specially selected Bilstein dampers and Eibach springs. As Subaru introduced a thicker anti-roll bar as standard for 1997, new 20mm lower suspension was introduced by Prodrive.

Prodrive's engine upgrade (incorporating the smaller turbo of the standard Impreza) could now be run on standard unleaded (95RON), rather than the previous 98RON super unleaded. The Driver Enhancement package now included high performance brake pads and a quickshift gear linkage. Prodrive's Quickshift was one of its most popular products, replacing the gate mechanism and shortening the throw, although it became of less interest once Subaru reduced the standard gear lever throw for 1998. Finally, the 1997 interior package boasted electrically adjustable Recaro seats.

When all three packages – interior, exterior and driver enhancement – were fitted all at once, that justified special badging for the car, which became known as the Prodrive WR Sport. The performance package was optional on top of this. As well as WR Sport badging, you received an individual, numbered plaque on the dashboard. Prodrive could apply the WR Sport package to either new or used cars, although in practice very few were applied to used vehicles. Arguably this was the best roadgoing Impreza of its day, even though the whole caboodle added £10,000 to the purchase price of an Impreza Turbo. Only around 25 cars each year were produced to WR Sport specification, as Prodrive's Mike Wood recalls: 'These were typically bought by customers who just wanted everything. One customer managed to spend £37,000 on his car – remember that the basic car was £20,000 at the time.'

Performance Car magazine tested a Prodrive car in December 1997, but recorded a disappointing 0–60mph time of only 5.6 seconds. The same magazine reputedly tested (but did not print the story on) a 1998 Prodrive demonstrator, which did the 0–60 blast in just 4.94 seconds – that's more like it! However the emphasis of Prodrive's engine package was always on real-world driving, and therefore mid-range performance was the most impressive characteristic.

Autocar magazine tested a full-blown Prodrive WR in September 1998 but there was some disappointment that performance was actually

↓ Prodrive created its own specially modified Impreza derivatives. This is the WR Sport pictured at the October 1997 London Motor Show. Only very small runs of the genuine article were produced each year.

↑ Road testers acclaimed the Prodrive packages applied to the Impreza. The Performance Package boosted power to 240bhp, with resulting improvements in acceleration.

← Prodrive's Driver Enhancement package boasted uprated suspension and larger alloy wheels to deliver even more leech-like grip and handling feedback.

down on the standard Impreza Turbo (*Autocar* also recorded a 5.6 second 0–60 time), while the 'uprated' brakes were actually inferior. However, Prodrive's Richard Taylor commented to the author: 'When *Autocar* criticised the brakes on the 1998WR they didn't realise that the pads were the same as had been fitted to every press car since 1995. The only difference was that the car had more power and therefore ran out of brakes a little earlier than the previous standard engined cars they had tested!' The suspension was judged better, being adjustable to suit and with a better ride quality. It concluded the WR was 'sensational, but the standard car is better.'

We should not forget Prodrive's input into the 22B Type UK, which is fully covered in the chapter on the Turbo. Meanwhile, Prodrive answered the UK Turbo engine improvements of 1999 with a totally redesigned Performance Pack. This included an upgraded ECU, new centre/rear stainless steel exhaust (replacing the second exhaust catalyst) and improved intercooler pipework. The 1999 engine upgrade boosted peak power to 240bhp at 6,000rpm but more impressive was torque of 258lb ft (350Nm) at only 3,500rpm (no less than 20 per cent up on the standard car and exceeding the standard car's peak torque from 2,900rpm through to 5,500rpm).

↑↑ **Any Prodrive branded item carries extra kudos. This is the tall rear spoiler as fitted to the Prodrive-developed RB5 special edition.**

↑ **The Impreza's lacklustre interior was an area where Prodrive invested a lot of effort. Specially branded Recaro seats and matching trim were standard, while this example of a 1998 WR Sport has a dash-mounted triple gauge set.**

As the standard 1999 Impreza Turbo had much better brakes, uprated pads were no longer offered as part of the Prodrive performance upgrade. However, a Prodrive/Alcon calliper and disc upgrade was made available. The calliper was in aluminium rather than cast iron, providing better heat dissipation and less brake fade and sponginess. This upgrade would only fit 17-inch alloy wheels and became very popular, with up to 300 sets sold in 2000 alone, for example.

As the 1999 Model Year Impreza gained a taller rear spoiler, Prodrive developed an even taller rear wing that year, one that resembled a WRC rear spoiler, although it was not the same as the STi Version 5/22B type, notable by the fact that its integral brake light was mounted higher. As

ever, twin aerofoils were fitted on five-door cars. As the standard Turbo front bumper was more aerodynamic in 1999, the lip spoiler was no longer needed. Thus the 1999/2000 Exterior Package consisted of the rear spoiler, a PIAA high intensity performance driving lamp conversion and body-coloured sill extensions and door mirrors. The Prodrive Interior Package included Prodrive Recaro Sport front seats with electric height adjustment, pneumatic lumbar support and extendable seat base, an aluminium or carbon-fibre gear knob and a tailored carpet mat set.

Also new for 1999 was the ST2 alloy wheel, a six-spoke Speedline that resembled that fitted to the WRC Impreza. With Subaru's switch to four-pot brake callipers for 1999, the old-style Speedline wheels no longer fitted, hence the ST2 style. A seven-spoke design was also offered.

Richard Taylor, Prodrive's director of sales for three years and intimately connected with Prodrive's road car programme since the start, obviously feels a great sense of pride about the enthusiastic customer response to their packages: 'The Prodrive enhancement programme has been incredibly successful. At one point, we estimated that as many as 50 per cent of new Imprezas being sold had some sort of Prodrive accessory being fitted. The most popular items are wheels and tyres, suspension, cosmetics and performance packs. We will certainly be turning our attention to the new Impreza, so there are many more developments in the pipeline.'

The P1 project

Nobody could ignore the huge flood of Impreza grey imports arriving in Britain from Japan. Tempted by extra power and better specifications, UK enthusiasts lapped up the WRX and STi models from Japan, even though they were only available via 'grey' channels, and Subaru (UK) actively discouraged the practice.

However, Subaru UK did fight back. Enlisting Prodrive's help, it aimed to create a fully European type-approved version of the two-door STi Type R. This partnership had to convince Fuji Heavy Industries in Japan that the project should get the green light, and at a meeting between Prodrive's David Richards and Subaru President Tanaka, the go-ahead was duly granted. Subaru UK said that its objective was, 'to work with Prodrive to achieve the same exciting yet reassuring high-quality ambience carefully nurtured by BMW and Mercedes Benz with their M-Technic and AMG-developed performance flagships.'

The project was instigated at the end of 1998 and brought to fruition in less than one year, ready for a public debut at the 1999 Earl's Court and Scottish motor shows. To answer the challenge of the grey imports, the so-called P1 (Prodrive One) would have to have the same 280PS power output. Subaru said of the Impreza P1 that it was intended to be 'the ultimate 'real world' driver's car,' and was 'planned to be the first in a line of ultra high-performance models which comply with all official noise, emission, environmental and safety rules.'

Prodrive took the STi Type R two-door as its basis and set to work. This was to be no 'back door' grey import special. Unlike the 22B-UK, which had to go through Single Vehicle Approval in order to be registered in Britain, the P1 was to get full EU homologation. While the two-door had never been sold in Europe, Prodrive and Subaru

felt confident with the coupé bodyshell, because its crashworthiness, was actually better than the four and five-door cars.

Perhaps the biggest problem to overcome was emissions. The Japanese-spec STi engine would not pass full EU emissions regulations, so Subaru Tecnica International reworked the ECU to Prodrive's specifications and also modified the exhaust so that it had a single catalyst that was more efficient than the contemporary Japanese market STi. There was also the issue of noise, alleviated slightly by the P1 being able to go through EU 'supercar' rules which allowed an extra one decibel during the tests. Thankfully the P1 was quick enough to qualify as a 'supercar' under EU rules!

The whole type approval effort was a tortuous process: Keith Hadley (group homologation manager at Subaru UK importer International Motors) spent nearly six months getting the necessary certification for the engine and the two-door bodywork. The European Whole Vehicle Type Approval for the P1 was held jointly by Subaru (UK) and Fuji Heavy Industries, although the manufacturer's plate on the suspension strut bore Subaru UK wording.

↓ **The P1 project jointly created by Subaru UK and Prodrive produced a car that brought the legendary STi Type R to Britain, suitably modified to conform to local conditions and regulations.**

↑ **McLaren F1 designer Peter Stevens designed the P1's deep front and tall rear spoilers, as well as the specially commissioned OZ 17-inch alloy wheels, designed to emulate the current World Rally Car.**

In addition to the Type Approval modifications, Prodrive wanted to make the P1 less raw than the Type R and more in tune with European tastes. As Hugh Chambers, Prodrive's marketing director, commented: 'We wanted to create the ultimate Impreza Turbo for UK driving conditions. In response to Subaru's brief, we have gone far beyond what was strictly necessary to make this car pass noise and emission regulations.'

Prodrive tried numerous combinations of wheel and tyre size, spring, damper and anti-roll bar rates from the full panorama of Impreza set-ups. 'Our target was to achieve exhilarating yet safe characteristics on the typical sweeping A roads and pitchy B roads of the UK,' said project manager – engineering, David Stevens. 'We researched the wide variation of spring, damper and anti-roll bar combination that are available for the Impreza Turbo family. For example, the 'grey' import WRX STi is too hard at the front and soft at the back for our roads and suffers front-end bounce which holds back the engine's true potential. We experimented with 22 different spring and damper combinations which we whittled down to eight variations, measuring the effect of every single change. Despite the theoretically harsher low-aspect ratio of the 205/45 tyres, the low-speed ride is superior to the normal UK-spec Turbo, while body control is far better at high speed on an undulating road.'

Engineering colleague, Hamish McEwan, added: 'Our benchmark cars were the standard Impreza Turbo, WRX STi, 22B-STi Type UK, BMW M3 and Mitsubishi Lancer Evo VI. We are now convinced we have them all beaten.'

Prodrive's eventual specification coalesced around Peter Stevens-designed titanium-effect 10-spoke OZ Racing 17-inch wheels shod with 205/45 Pirelli P Zero tyres, EU-type front and rear anti-roll bars, stiff STi dampers and special Prodrive/Eibach springs that lowered the ride height by some 20mm (3/4in). A 22B-style quicker steering rack (13:1 instead of 15:1) was announced as being part of the package but rejected as making the car too nervous. A quickshift gear change was also fitted.

Unlike the Type R, the P1 did not get the intercooler spray. Also, Prodrive favoured a four-channel ABS system rather than the Japanese adjustable centre differential. Two other items of equipment that had to be dropped were the climate control (the switchgear protruded too far, so EU-type air conditioning was fitted instead) and the electric folding wing mirrors (not approved on any European Impreza). Also the glass was changed from the dark tinted Type R to EU-spec green tint all round, and UK-spec lighting fitted. The Japanese-spec rear wash/wiper remained, as did the aluminium bonnet and carbon-fibre strut brace.

As for cosmetics, Subaru said: 'The Impreza P1 features striking looks which are aggressive without being vulgar.' It turned to McLaren F1 designer Peter Stevens to create deep front and rear spoilers. The only body colour offered was Sonic Blue (similar to the Impreza World Rally Car), with colour-keyed mirrors, door handles and side skirts and special 90mm diameter Hella front driving lamps (just like the Impreza WRC2000) and Prodrive driving lamp covers. The front lip spoiler was said to be worth 3bhp at 100mph, while the rear wing had a detachable 'Gurney flap' for additional downforce and 'P1' logos.

Inside the car, the P1 had a UK-style dashboard with twin airbags and a centre lidded storage box. Alcantara was used for the door and seat trim, while Prodrive monogrammed mats were standard. Six speakers were installed even though no head unit was standard. To protect the P1, Subaru fitted RAC Trackstar Guardian and a Category 1 alarm/immobiliser.

Subaru naturally claimed that performance was significantly improved, with an estimated 150mph (241kph) top speed and a 0–60mph time of 4.8 seconds. It said that tests recorded a 0–100mph sprint in 12.27 seconds, with a standing quarter mile in 13.49 seconds and the standing kilometre in 24.54 seconds. The 50–70mph time in fifth gear was despatched in 6.9 seconds. These figures were later revised upwards to 155mph (249kph) top speed, 0–60mph in 4.66 seconds and 0–100mph in 12.28 seconds.

The basic P1 was specially built by Fuji Heavy Industries in Japan alongside other Imprezas and then shipped to the UK. However, the car then had to undergo transformation into the P1 once in the UK and specially trained Subaru staff carried out the various suspension, interior and exterior enhancements at International Motors' £3.5 million vehicle distribution centre in Quedgeley, Gloucestershire. Two man days were required to create the finished P1. Among the jobs required were the fitting of the 17-inch wheels, replacement of Subaru's original springs by Eibach units, suspension geometry reset, bodywork modifications (front and rear spoilers, driving lamps), security devices fitted, and new badges and mats installed.

The P1 was only sold in the UK and therefore only made in right-hand-drive, with deliveries starting in March 2000 priced at £31,500. An initial production run of 500 cars was announced but in the event demand was so strong that the total was upped to 1,000. One of the main advantages of the P1 over grey imports was that it carried a full Subaru (UK) three-year warranty with official parts and service back-up.

Of options there were plenty. An exclusively commissioned Leather Interior Package (blue, black and grey Cheshire hide) cost £1,995, Recaro Sports seats in velour and Alcantara were also £1,995, a gas discharge upgrade for the Hella driving lights was £470, a Prodrive/Alcon alloy brake calliper and 330mm disc upgrade was £1,527, massive 18-inch OZ wheels were £495 each (in titanium or gold finish), and a Prodrive stainless steel rear silencer was £350. Various in-car entertainment and satellite navigation packages were also offered.

The P1 was eagerly awaited, of that there is no doubt. But the press was split as to its abilities. *Evo* magazine (May 2000) was extremely positive: 'It feels stiffer than the RB5 but not as firm as the 22B, which makes it more progressive and predictable … The P1 feels very rapid, very wieldy … There's a click-and-go simplicity to this Scooby that almost beggars belief … Prodrive's P1 treatment has made the Impreza a more devastating proposition than ever.'

In January 2000, *Car* magazine produced the ultimate Impreza group test when it pitched the P1 against the RB5, WRX STi Type R, 22B Type UK, Model Year 2000 Turbo and modified Scoobysport Turbo. The winner was the Prodrive P1.

When the author drove the P1 against arch-rival Mitsubishi Evo VI for *Car Import Guide* magazine, I came down in favour of the P1 and

↑ **The Impreza was always known for its excellent performance in all weather conditions, even when the P1 had 276bhp at its disposal. This road tester's excursion into the sea is perhaps taking the point a little far …**

reported: 'The Subaru is simply more involving. It sounds great: where the Evo's engine is a waste-gate-punctuated frenzy, the PI has the sublime guttural growl that is unique to its opposing cylinders … In essence the difference in approach is like the difference between analogue and digital. The Mitsubishi is all-digital: the LCD watch of the '90s, the NICAM-loaded anti-shock Class I Laser Product of the genre. The Subaru applies modern technology in a more rounded and more relevant fashion. It's the revival of warm-sounding vinyl over clean-but-dead CD, the Swiss precision cog system that was never really swept away by quartz crystal.'

But it was not all roses. The UK-tuned suspension set-up certainly attracted some criticism. The front suspension was softer than even the standard WRX, having been chosen to deal with notoriously bumpy British minor roads, and many drivers felt Prodrive had gone too far. Side effects reported by testers included understeer and disappointing steering response.

There was also criticism of the small diameter brakes (substantially smaller than rival Mitsubishi

Evo VI's), combining a lack of outright stopping power with disappointing fade, and the EU Type Approval requirement that cars be able to wear snow chains scuppered any chance of fitting suitably large wheels and tyres. *Autocar* rued: 'There's little point trying to hide our disappointment with the brakes and steering … It is not the mould-breaker we had expected. Perhaps we expected too much.' Perhaps such criticisms were responsible for the fact that there were still some PIs available new into 2001, offered at a significant discount on the original price. However, Prodrive did come up with an answer …

Prodrive PI WR

With the PI, Subaru had achieved a fully type-approved and European-specific equivalent of the STi Type R. Monstrously capable though it was, the PI was a compromise. Prodrive answered many of the PI's shortcomings by offering, from the summer of 2000, a 'dealer fit' aftermarket package that more truly represented what

↓ **Inside, blue Alcantara trim was used for the seats. The dashboard was the UK type rather than the Japanese type, and twin airbags were standard.**

Prodrive's vision of the Impreza was. The P1 WR followed in the footsteps of Prodrive's other WR packages, but this was undoubtedly the ultimate Prodrive Impreza. In some ways it was the embodiment of a secret Peter Stevens project called P1+. Stevens had originally envisaged bigger wheels and tyres (on which count Prodrive obliged with the WR) and an adjustable rear wing (although that remained on the drawing board).

The most immediately obvious change for the P1 WR was massive 18-inch OZ alloy wheels shod with 225/35 Pirelli P Zero rubber, in the same style as the standard P1 but very much more expensive. Clearly visible behind the alloys were Prodrive-branded Alcon-made four-pot callipers holding Prodrive P-F3 pads and acting on 330mm spiral ventilated discs. Outside, the driving lights were upgraded to super-bright gas discharge spec and there was a P1-branded stainless steel exhaust exiting at the rear. Inside there were Prodrive Recaro seats trimmed to resemble P1 items. The full WR package cost £6,322 (taking the total price up to £37,847).

The upshot was a car that felt much stiffer to drive. Although Prodrive claimed the WR had better ride quality, road testers disagreed: *Evo* said, 'bump absorption is less convincing.' It added, 'The P1 WR lacks the impervious feel of its more modestly shod brother. The wheel control gets ragged and ultimately you have to back off for fear of being thrown off line.' But the WR certainly addressed the steering and braking issues, as *Evo* confirmed: 'The steering feels sharper and more direct . . . The P1 WR can be set up into corners with a lift of the throttle and then powered through in a wonderfully predictable, controllable drift.' The brakes were also highly praised as 'fabulously progressive' and 'some of the most powerful you'll ever find on a road car.'

Prodrive and the New Age WRX

Prodrive got to work on the New Age Impreza as soon as it had the opportunity, developing new performance packages and becoming inextricably linked with the new STi, Subaru officially launching a version called Prodrive Style. For full details of Prodrive's involvement with the new-shape Impreza, please turn to Chapter Six.

↑ Controllable to the point of sublimity, the P1 WR could be drifted with precision. However, the cornering speeds required to perform this sort of antic meant that the P1's prodigious grip was rarely tested.

CHAPTER 6
NEW AGE IMPREZA

Such was the head of steam built up by the first-generation Impreza that it is no understatement to say that the second-generation Impreza was in many countries the most eagerly awaited new car launch of the year 2000. Magazines and internet sites ran cycles of 'scoop' stories about the new Impreza, many including highly speculative computer-generated pictures that turned out to be wildly inaccurate, but then that is the nature of 'exclusives' and ultimately it all adds to the fun and anticipation.

In the real-world headquarters of Fuji Heavy Industries, the so-called 'New Age' Impreza project started as early as January 1997. Takeshi Ito, who had been the sub-leader for the first Impreza generation, was now the whole project leader for the new car. He explained the rationale behind the new version thus: 'The first generation Impreza provided higher performance, functionality, and quality with its chassis and powerplant maturing around the basic policy, "faster, more fun, and safer". This was accepted by more and more customers. With this reputation in mind, the project team for the new generation Impreza developed it with an overall concept that we called "high-density sport-minded" to provide customers with a better vehicle that could give "driving pleasure" and "enjoyable driving as a sport".'

So how would the new Impreza be 'better' than the iconic first generation? This new Impreza would be larger in all dimensions, safer, cleaner, stiffer, more responsive and more refined. But it was also heavier and, by implication, slower.

The working concept for the new Impreza was a 'high-quality sporty vehicle' and within this Subaru included the goal of stylish appearance. While the original Impreza could never have been called pretty, Subaru chose what many viewed as a mystifying route with the new car's styling. While the profile of both the four and five-door cars was unmistakably Impreza, all media attention focused

on one aspect of the design. Why on earth had Subaru opted for those headlamps?

The WRX's chief engineer, Takeshi Ito, explained the design ethos behind the bold circular headlamp treatment: 'The current WRX was eight years old and starting to look it. Our Impreza needed a fresh new look, something to take it into the 21st century.' And that meant ovoid headlamps. Contrary to many contemporary reports, there was actually little internal debate about the new look, a wide degree of consensus being reached about the round lights. Market research in Europe and America supported this view, demonstrating that the new look would re-define the car, and differentiate it from rivals such as the Mitsubishi Lancer Evo.

But at the Japanese launch on 23 August 2000, when Subaru presented what it called the 'New Age Impreza', there was reportedly an uncomfortably long period of silence before the assembled journalists, rendered quiet for once by the unexpected sight, remembered themselves and finally applauded the unveiling. Peter Nunn of *Car Graphic* magazine, commenting in *Evo*, summed it up when he said: 'What was Subaru thinking of when it approved those oddball, three-in-one HID lenses? Suddenly the Impreza has something of the look of a '99 Corolla from the front … If nothing else, they've had everyone talking.'

Relying on its market research, Fuji Heavy Industries was unrepentant. Takeshi Ito responded to my question about headlamp design strongly: 'We have mainly designed the vehicle with driving dynamics, functionality, and distinctiveness in mind. There may be some people who do not prefer Impreza's distinctive styling, but we believe that the headlamp design enabled us to have better visibility and dynamism accomplished by sculpted three-dimensional design.' Subaru UK was equally up-front at its launch: 'Unashamedly distinctive,

← In 2000, once again there was an STi-tuned and modified version of the Impreza WRX, boasting a stiffer body, beefed-up suspension and bigger brakes behind 17-inch wheels. This was without doubt the most impressive driver's car Subaru had ever made.

← As a tribute to rally champion Richard Burns, the RB320 had a fittingly superior spec: a 2.5-litre 320PS engine, quickshift, bespoke 18-inch alloy wheels, Prodrive suspension, mesh front grille and bright orange decal treatment.

these lights are deliberately intended to give the new Subaru presence.' They certainly did that.

Perhaps Subaru hoped the new design would grow on the buying public. An analogous situation occurred with the 1989 Toyota Celica, which was widely criticised at launch for its controversial styling but went on to become the most popular Celica yet. Styling is an important issue for customers but it is not the overriding influence, as indeed the first series Impreza proved.

There were now much more marked styling differences between the four and five-door variants. Both Imprezas were said to have 'a machined, engineered appearance', with an 'aggressive' grille and trademark 'dinner plate' fog lamps. Probably the biggest difference between the two body styles was that the four-door had a wider track than the five-door. That meant prominent new blistered wheel arches haunching over the wheels. In contrast, the sports wagon was described as having 'a less-aggressive and more functional look'. Indeed, the saloon's four-door body was a full 40mm (1.6in) wider than the previous model, with front and rear tracks up by 20mm (0.8in); the five-door was the same width as before.

This was indeed a larger car than the old Impreza. Overall length rose by 65mm (2.6in), with the wheelbase marginally up by 5mm (0.2in) and height up by 35mm (1.4in) on the saloon and 60mm (2.4in) on the sports wagon.

By and large the new Impreza did not deviate from the time-honoured formula under the skin. All-wheel-drive, long-travel independent suspension and low centre of gravity 'boxer' engines all remained.

Despite the need to keep weight down to qualify the bodyshell for world rallying, the new floorpan was vastly stiffer than before. In terms of resistance to twisting, the saloon was improved by 185 per cent (122 per cent for the sports wagon) and 250 per cent with respect to bending (239 per cent for the sports wagon). The rear crossmember joints were also tuned to be stiffer. This was all claimed to reduce road noise, improve crash safety and allow the suspension to work better.

New body structure construction techniques also improved strength and safety. The technique used was called hydroforming, or creating metalwork using pipes which are formed in a mould by exerting enormous water pressure from all angles. Additionally the sills and B-posts were made up of steel plates of varying thickness (from 1.2 to 2.6mm) in a process called 'mash-seam' or 'tailored blanket' welding.

Ring-shaped reinforcement frames connected the centre pillars, roof and floor to disperse impact energy. The front doors gained a second reinforcement beam which worked in conjunction with the rear door beams to enhance side-impact protection.

It was absolutely crucial to build on the legendary handling and roadholding of the Impreza. The development of this aspect could not be in better hands. Project leader Takeshi Ito lived and breathed Imprezas right from the birth of the original car, in whose development he had been heavily involved ten years previously. He confirmed the very special place the Impreza occupied: 'I wanted a car which – even in 1.6-litre form – would turn mere motorists into enthusiasts. Every drive should be an occasion.'

In basic layout, things remained much as before. The front suspension continued with MacPherson struts and an anti-roll bar but extensive revisions provided improved feedback and more steering control, especially, so it was claimed, when covering bumpy roads at speed.

Perhaps the most important suspension change was the repositioning of the struts and wheel hub assemblies 10mm outward on each side without altering the kingpin angle. This 20mm track extension minimised changes in the tyres' contact angles with the tarmac, reducing body roll.

Moving to the rear, there had been strong rumours before launch that Subaru might adopt the larger Legacy's multi-link rear suspension. In fact the new Impreza stuck with rear struts and dual links for reasons of compactness, low unsprung weight and durability. No doubt cost was also involved. The rear roll centre was raised by 33mm, virtually matching the WRC rally car. This had the effect of reducing rear suspension compression during cornering, which improved stability and grip during fast cornering, enhanced straight-line stability and contributed to a more neutral feel when cornering. Revised suspension pick-up points and geometry settings, and fine-tuned evolution rather than revolution greeted the steering, springs, dampers and anti-roll bars.

A new front subframe and stronger crossmember connections reduced engine and road noise, vibration and harshness. The lower rear bushes were improved to reduce road noise transmission into the cabin, the rear crossmember was lighter and stronger, and the rear crossmember-to-body bushings were redesigned to provide more lateral support. The crossmember mounting area was strengthened to boost refinement and minimise brake shudder. Anti-roll bars remained front and rear. We have already mentioned the 20mm wider front and rear tracks of the saloon, but strong mention should be made of the lightweight forged aluminium L-shaped lower arms fitted to the WRX saloon. Previously this exotic specification had been reserved for the STi; now it was standard across the board.

The WRX sat 5mm lower than the ordinary versions of the new Impreza and had wider tyres. In Europe, both saloon and sports wagon models were fitted with larger 7 x 17-inch alloy wheels with 215/45 ZR17 tyres – wider and bigger than the Japanese-market version which had 16-inch wheels and 205/50 R16 tyres (although 17-inch wheels and tyres were optional).

The rack and pinion power-assisted steering was

improved, with a smoother, more consistent feel and better feedback, claimed Subaru. As before, the system was engine-speed sensitive, firming up as revs increaseed. An aluminium cooler pipe now improved the durability of the oil seals by controlling fluid temperatures during hard use and a new pump load pressure-sensitive valve enhanced response. All Imprezas now had a rubber coupling on the middle shaft of the steering universal joint and the steering column itself had an extra 20mm of tilt adjustment.

↑ Under the skin the all-new Impreza launched in 2000 was very much an evolution of the previous generation. On top, its look was a mixture of recognisable shapes and striking new directions. All markets now called the turbocharged version WRX.

Following the last of the old-style Impreza Turbos, the European WRX had ventilated front and rear disc brakes, the front pair benefiting from four-pot callipers. The Japanese WRX had solid rear discs. Four-channel, four-sensor ABS was standard.

At the rear was a Suretrac limited slip differential, the propshaft having a double offset joint. The centre differential depended on the transmission choice: viscous coupling LSD with manual and VTD-AWD (variable torque distribution electronically controlled all-wheel-drive) with automatic. The four-speed auto transmission was launched only in Japan to begin with (the USA also received a WRX automatic in due course). The so-called Sports Shift transmission included buttons on the steering wheel to change gears, following the system used in Subaru's Legacy/Liberty B4.

In Japan a curious first awaited the New Age Impreza. For the first time ever, there was a non-turbo WRX on offer! Even more unexpectedly indeed, all the turbo and non-turbo saloons were called WRX at launch, while none of the sports

↑ Testers found that the new Impreza was more composed through corners, and less prone to understeer. However, many rued the dilution of what had been a magical formula in the original machine.

wagon versions were, the turbocharged five-door being referred to merely as the Impreza 20K.

The domestic WRX saloon was therefore available with two engines: the non-turbo twin-cam NA (155PS) and the turbocharged NB (250PS – significantly more than export versions). These were very much a development of the existing Impreza 1,994cc engine, indeed the powerplant kept the same type designation, EJ20. Both engines used AVCS (automatic valve control System), a variable valve timing system.

On the turbo engine fitted to both the WRX NB saloon and 20K estate, a slightly bigger turbocharger yielded more torque in the middle of the rev band, while a 30 per cent larger intercooler improved responsiveness. On the Japanese WRX, 80 per cent of the engine's peak torque was available from just 2,200rpm. The redline remained as before at 7,000rpm. Moreover this was a cleaner engine, clearing the latest exhaust regulations with 25 to 50 per cent lower emissions levels. The WRX vehicle type designations were TA-GDA (for the NB saloon), TA-GD9 (for the NA saloon) and TA-GGA (for the 20K wagon).

There were now no extra air inlet vents in the aluminium bonnet, which kept its scoop, however. The Japanese version had standard body-coloured electric door mirrors, front fog lamps, high-mounted third brake light, rear wash wiper, remote locking, Momo leather steering wheel, leather gear knob and handbrake, climate control, electric windows, front bucket seats and dual airbags. High intensity headlamps were optional from the outset.

The new Impreza sold well in Japan, with 9,000 sales in November 2000, for example (the monthly target had been only 3,000). Once again the turbocharged versions were far more popular than one would expect in a normal car range.

WRX for the world

So much for Japan – now what about the rest of the world? As before, the export version of the WRX had a notably different specification. Also the nomenclature was new: since the WRX name had become well-known in Europe, Subaru decided to adopt it worldwide.

Indeed, it went further than the Japanese market in one respect: the turbocharged five-door version was badged WRX too, whereas in Japan it was known more humbly as the 20K.

The European debut for the new Impreza occurred at the Birmingham NEC Motor Show on 17 October 2000. Britain had always played an important role in the life of the Impreza, which was perhaps why Birmingham was chosen as the international launch rather than September's Paris show, which had missed out on the new Impreza. There, an old-style Impreza was on display, and an obviously piqued French distributor had pasted a sign saying 'Vendu' ('sold') in the windscreen to indicate that the old car was actually no longer available!

On the Subaru stand at Birmingham, smoke billowed from the sides of the stage and silver sheets were pulled off to reveal a car that Subaru UK called 'aggressive but stylish'. It continued: 'The affordable performance car icon of the '90s has grown up, with a smoother ride, lower road noise and quality feel to its fittings and controls. Yet Subaru has avoided the "middle-aged" dull and stodgy feel which can blight evolved sports models.'

The biggest difference between Europe and Japan concerned the engine. While the Japanese WRX had a 250PS power unit, the European one was 218PS (215bhp), exactly the same power output as the previous powerplant. However, there were changes compared to the first generation. Perhaps the most important was a completely reprogrammed turbo offering 'a more progressive power delivery with reduced "lag" or delay in the engine responding to throttle inputs' which was claimed to produce smoother and less jerky acceleration.

Making the engine much cleaner – the new engine met Europe's stringent 'Step 3' emission regulations – was a third, quick-response catalytic converter between the exhaust manifold and turbocharger that warmed up quickly. This was mainly to benefit emissions after start-up but it was also claimed to improve exhaust gas flow into the turbine and so help engine response.

The intercooler was some 11 per cent larger than before but still not nearly as big as the Japanese market item. While power remained the same, torque did rise but only marginally – by 1lb ft to 215.4lb ft (1.4-296Nm) – but it was delivered 400rpm lower down than before, at 3,600rpm. Indeed, torque was most notably improved between 2,500 and 4,000rpm.

In Europe, Subaru claimed a maximum speed of 143mph (230kph) for the WRX saloon and 140mph (225kph) for the sports wagon. Acceleration was allegedly improved, with a claimed 0–60mph time of 5.9 seconds for both body styles. Extra Urban fuel economy was 35.8mpg (7.9 litres/100km) for the WRX, with 19.9mpg (14.2 litres/100km) in town and a combined figure of 27.7mpg (10.2 litres/100km).

In the transmission department, the five-speed gearbox was retained virtually unaltered, with

↑ **At the WRX's European launch at the Birmingham Motor Show in October 2000, Subaru also presented the 2001 season rally car for the first time. Huge public interest awaited the new Impreza.**

↑ For the first time,
the five-door estate was
mechanically very different
to the four-door. Its track
was some 20mm narrower
at the front and 25mm
narrower at the rear,
so that the wide flared
arches on the saloon were
obviated in the apparently
more mild-mannered
estate.

the same ratios as the original Turbo of 1994.
Subaru claimed lighter clutch action, smoother
gearchanges and quieter drivetrains. As before,
the full-time all-wheel-drive transmission had a
50/50 front/rear torque split, varying to changing
conditions. There remained a centre differential
with viscous coupling and a limited slip differential
in the rear axle to apportion grip between each
rear wheel. The WRX additionally benefited from
a flexible flywheel to reduce vibration, the front
and rear differentials had new gear profiles for
lower noise (transfer gear noise was also lowered
thanks to taper roller bearings), and the clutch
master cylinder grew from 15.87mm to 17.46mm.

There was a concerted effort to give the
interior a much higher quality feel, with a massive
upgrade in the quality of seat cloths and facia
and door plastics. The clunk of the doors – a
particularly unimpressive timbre on the old Impreza
– was far more solid thanks to double door seals.
The dashboard design was centred around large
instruments and a silver finish to the centre panel
and rims to the circular ventilation outlets.

Both body styles boasted increased rear seat
space compared with the previous Impreza. The

sports wagon, for example, had an extra 20mm
(0.8in) front legroom and 71mm (2.8in) more
rear legroom. Other interior space improvements
included interior width up by as much as 20.7mm
(0.8in) and headroom by more than 30mm
(1.2in) on both body styles. The saloon gained
a wider-opening boot lid with a ski hatch centre
folding armrest, and a greater luggage volume.
The sports wagon had an improved quality solid
floor and the rear seat now folded completely
flat instead of lying at an angle. Total load capacity
with the seat up dropped to 349 litres (12.3cu ft)
instead of 363 litres (12.8cu ft), but its shape was
described as more practical: you could now stow
a 26in-wheel bicycle plus a shopping basket.

A new ratchet-type driver's seat lifter
yielded 50mm (2in) of vertical range, while the
steering wheel tilted up to 50°. The rear seat
had a centre three-point seat-belt plus three
head restraints on the sports wagon. Driver
and passenger airbags were now standard.
The WRX saloon could be ordered, from
Spring 2001, with rally-style bucket seats as an
alternative to the standard sports seats that
benefited from side airbags.

Standard equipment in the UK included power steering, electric windows, electric door mirrors, radio/cassette/CD, keyless central locking, a Category One remote alarm/immobiliser, air conditioning and aluminium pedals. In the UK, deliveries to dealers started in November 2000, the new WRX being priced at £21,495 for the saloon and £21,995 for the sports wagon. Subaru said that the extra equipment was worth around £2,000, yet prices were only £545 higher than the outgoing Imprezas. Virtually the same 218PS car was launched in Australia, New Zealand and other world markets at the same time.

So how did Subaru's claim that 'handling agility and suspension control are better than ever' match up in the testers' minds? Could we forgive that styling in the wake of an even better drive than the old Impreza?

Auto Express in October 2000 immediately questioned what Subaru had done to its glorious Impreza: 'Why mess with a formula so successful it has transformed the image of Subaru from a purveyor of sheepdog-carrying pick-ups into one of the most respected performance car manufacturers in the world? The bitter pill for enthusiasts did not taste any sweeter when the first pictures of the replacement were seen. The front was a huge surprise, with round headlamps which drew unkind comparisons with the last model Toyota Corolla or even the droopy-faced Ford Scorpio.'

To decide the issue, *Auto Express* pitted the new Impreza against the old Impreza. The interior

was described as 'more bearable' than before, with everything 'perfectly placed'. On the engine, it said: 'Up until 2,000rpm, you could almost be driving a Nissan Micra, but then the turbo wakes up and starts to build speed rapidly. The power delivery is far less peaky than the old car's, with a steady accumulation of boost up to the red line.

'Refinement may be what some buyers want, but the sensation of driving a special car has been filtered out. The shove-in-the-back acceleration of the Turbo, the noise of the rushing air and the exhaust's bark have gone … There is no question that the WRX is at least as fast through bends and on the straight as the Turbo … In addition, the Turbo's tendency to plough on in fast, tight turns has been lessened to give a more neutral feel, and the body remains perfectly composed even after the car encounters a series of bumps mid-bend … At the end of a long day with the prospect

↓ **The thickness of metal varied according to where the load was greatest. A technique called hydroforming was used to shape the structure.**

↓ ↓ **Let there be no mistake: for all its increased civility, the new Impreza was still a remarkably rapid and fun machine, as this cornering shot of a five-door demonstrates.**

↑ The turbo engine was very much a development of the original EJ20 powerplant. The Japanese version developed 250PS, the American version 227PS and the European version 218PS.

of motorway jams ahead, it was the WRX we wanted to go home in. But the Turbo would be our choice for a cross-country blast.'

Auto Express concluded that the WRX was, 'just as fast as the Turbo it replaces, and is easier to drive, with lighter controls, less weighty steering and smoother power delivery. But drivers have to do without the raw thrills which made the old car special. The WRX will be more appealing to buyers wanting refined, fast everyday transport, but enthusiasts will prefer the old model.'

Broadly concurring, *Autocar* magazine said the new car offered 'less performance, less style' but said the New Age car 'can't help but be a more satisfying ownership proposition … the definitive affordable performance saloon for the enthusiast.'

Japanese journalists recognised the new Impreza's abilities by awarding it the 2000/2001 Car of the Year Japan Special Award, beating 20 other cars produced and launched in Japan between 1 November 1999 and 31 October 2000. The Special Award was created for such attributes as outstanding product concepts and mechanical features. The judges said of the new WRX: 'It's a sports sedan with the greatest

attention to driving pleasure we've seen in recent years, and we were impressed by the safety offered by its highly rigid body.'

STi – best-ever Impreza

But there was more in store from the New Age machine. The author awoke on his birthday (24 October) to find news items on Subaru's latest and finest Impreza in his e-mail in-tray. While the second-generation Impreza WRX had been eagerly awaited worldwide, the new STi was the model that all hard-core Impreza enthusiasts had been waiting for.

The theme behind the STi was, in Subaru's words, 'the thrill of sports driving'. One of the blandest ever mission statements could not hide the very special nature of the new STi. Subaru Tecnica International's chief engineer, Takeshi Ito, stressed how individual and unique the new STi Impreza was: 'It goes without saying that the STi is Subaru's top high performance brand. As a car based on an original basic platform, it features highly tuned hardware for enthusiasts interested in competition and sports driving. So in that respect, it's not as specialized as AMG or M vehicles. Yes, we did launch a Forester STi version in 1999, but unlike with the M series, we do not plan to launch a full STi series. If we did do that, it would confuse potential buyers who may think that the standard cars are not up to scratch.'

Naturally there was a more efficient turbocharger. A high performance intercooler with 50 per cent more core area than the outgoing model was lifted and tilted forward to maximise air flow through the newly devised bonnet scoop. 'Just increasing its size doesn't increase its efficiency,' commented Subaru Tecnica International, which also specified an enlarged waterspray tank, forged pistons and conrods and hollow valves so that the engine could rev to 8,100rpm.

The maximum power output permitted by Japanese convention – 280PS – was delivered at 6,400rpm, while torque was also considerably up to 275lb ft (373Nm) at 4,000rpm. Several sources estimated the power at significantly higher than 280PS (as high as 310PS, thought *Autocar* magazine). Also the torque curve was much fuller,

especially between 3,200rpm and 4,800rpm, primed for overtaking.

Undoubtedly the single most impressive feature of the new STi was its all-new six-speed close-ratio manual gearbox, Subaru's first new manual transmission in 20 years. The STi was the first time it had been seen anywhere. There was a special shift light in the rev counter and even a button to adjust the point at which the change-up buzzer

↑ The new cabin was far superior in layout, materials and design than the old generation. All the major controls were grouped together in a silver-faced centre console. Pictured is the STi version.

← With its all-new six-speed gearbox, the STi was a ferocious accelerator. Not only that, it cornered with a precision and involvement that was lacking in lesser versions of the WRX, and which was sorely missed by drivers of the first series Impreza.

↑ The STi-branded engine again had a red finish. Extra torque was now available, notably down to a more efficient turbocharger and a higher performance intercooler (with 50 per cent more core area than the outgoing model).

↗ As before the STi got a driver-operated waterspray system for the intercooler. A quick burst could improve efficiency in hot conditions, while an automatic function was available too (with a larger water tank to extend its usefulness).

bonnet air scoop, pink badges, STi decals, and brake hardware. On the GL version these were blacked-out rear windows (reminiscent of the old Type R) and high-intensity headlamps. There was also a five-door STi as well as the more popular four-door.

Some commentators felt the new STi was a little toned-down compared with the old STi Version VI, but product planner Hiroyuki Harada tantalisingly mapped out that the STi would evolve as far as it had done before. 'We developed the predecessor over seven years, and gave it something special each year. And this time round, we reset the switch. This is Version I all over again.'

Although the car was fully 100kg (220lb) heavier than the old STi because of the six-speed transmission and reinforced bodyshell, Subaru claimed a 0–60mph of 5.3 seconds and 0–100mph in 13.3 seconds, around the same times as the old model.

Subaru Tecnica International famously took the new STi and a team of engineers to the Nürburgring in Germany to test the car. Test driver Kazuo Shimizu (the first man to lap the 21km/13-mile circuit in a production car – a Nissan Skyline GT-R – in less than eight minutes) said the new STi was good for four seconds off the old STi time, thanks to the effects of the revised suspension, track and wider tyres on cornering, although he thought that in a straight line the extra weight may have played against it.

Launched on 24 October 2000 at the New Pia Hall on Tokyo bay, the Japanese press flocked to see the new car, reportedly causing traffic jams outside. The STi was certainly significant: of the 4,000 WRXs built each month, 1,000 were earmarked to wear the STi badge.

Continuing the bewildering complexity of the Impreza clan, there were actually three versions of the regular STi, plus a lightweight STi RA model. The STi could be ordered in top-spec trim as the GL (with a front limited slip differential, blacked-out rear windows and gas discharge headlamps), the EL (front diff but neither of the other two items) or the KL (no front diff).

It was inevitable that Subaru should launch an RA version of the STi. As ever, it was marketed as a road car that could be converted to rally use and therefore only came painted white and only as a four-door saloon with a roof vent. Crucially, it

sounded. In the top-spec STi version probably the biggest difference over the standard WRX was the addition of a front limited slip differential (rather than a free diff).

Body rigidity was improved even further for the STi, offering more than 20 per cent better bend and twist rigidity. As the standard WRX now had forged aluminium lower suspension arms, the STi was no longer unique in having these, but its suspension was improved with beefier arms front and rear, stiffer springs and dampers and revised suspension geometry.

Brakes were considerably upgraded with a Brembo brake package (gold-coloured with bright red lettering), ventilated front and rear. The standard Japanese WRX had 16-inch wheels but the STi gained 17-inch gold alloy wheels with wider tyres. The only other external differences between the WRX and STi were the foglamp covers, bigger was some 30–50kg lighter than the STi, making do without electric windows, air conditioning, central locking, map lights, hi-fi or rear wash/wipe. The RA had harder suspension and a 13:1 quick steering rack (the standard STi had 15:1) and also smaller diameter vented brake discs with two-pot rear callipers and no ABS. The New Age RA shared its gearbox ratios with the standard STi.

Two versions were marketed. The 'real' RA featured a mechanical rear differential and an adjustable centre diff and made do without the HID lights, Brembo brakes and ABS, and also switched to 16-inch wheels in an effort to save maximum weight. The other version had the same axle differentials as the normal STi, 17-inch wheels and a slightly wider track, but was 20kg heavier. The RA would be dropped briefly in September 2001 in advance of an even more extreme STi RA Spec C launched in December 2001 (see 2002 MY opposite).

From February 2001, something of the RA spirit could be ordered in a new STi model called the STi Version S. This did without a hi-fi, HID headlamps, front limited slip differential, keyless entry system or aluminium pedals and was only available in WR Blue, but was pitched in price a little below the STi saloon and a little above the RA. Confusingly, a Version S with some items like HID headlamps and

front LSD added back in was also marketed in a wider variety of colours.

Auto Express drove the new STi and declared: 'It is everything the new WRX isn't; it is as quick as – even marginally faster than – the STi it replaces.' Of the gearbox, it said: 'Positive in feel with deliciously short strokes, the gearchanges are accomplished with a firm, metallic touch and the ratios are ideally spaced. Plus there's a gearchange warning light that can be adjusted to any choice of rpm.'

And the handling was even more praised: 'You can set the STi lunging toward a corner, leave your braking until the last second and jump on the brakes to wipe off unbelievable amounts of speed in a very short time. As the weight goes forward, turn in to the bend and jump back on the gas for a lightning fast exit. And all the while, the STi does nothing but inspire confidence as the reshaped racing seats hold occupants firmly in place.' Its conclusion? 'If you want a car to use regularly – and fling round a circuit at weekends – Subaru has reached perfection.'

Autocar stated: 'Unlike the WRX, the STi goes. Really goes … Subaru's claims that the STi has less lag are true up to a point but there's still a delay … Once the mayhem starts it just keeps on coming … Yet what makes the STi so eye-wateringly capable across country, and so unique

↓ As before there was a lightweight RA version of the STi, nominally intended for owners to put to competition use – hence the 16-inch steel wheels. A more fully equipped 17-inch version was also offered. This is the ultra-light Spec C version.

among its peers, is not its engine or its straight-line performance. It's the chassis.' The conclusion? STi had again waved its magic wand to create an unfeasibly quick car for a bargain price.

UK300 edition

In May 2001, came the first New Age limited-edition model, the UK300. Uniquely available in the UK and limited to 300 units, the UK300 boasted 'World Rally Car styling cues' and the option of a 245PS Prodrive performance upgrade.

The UK300 was a joint project between Subaru UK and Prodrive. The styling modifications were by Peter Stevens, whose first task was to do something about those ovoid headlamps. New units featured black gloss shells with twin high-intensity Hella light units (identical to the Impreza rally car), with small circular indicators above.

The front spoiler had a matching black gloss extension, while the rear spoiler became a Prodrive-badged rally-style device featuring quirkily droopy aerofoil tips at either side. These

body mods were claimed to reduce high-speed lift by 25.6 per cent at 100mph.

Only one colour was offered – WR Blue Mica – with enormous gold-coloured OZ 10-spoke 18 x 7.5 inch alloy wheels shod with wider, 225/40 Pirelli P-Zero Rosso tyres. The only other external changes were clear side indicators, clear front markers and UK300 badging. Inside, the UK300 had blue suede-effect seats (bucket type up front) with matching door inserts, with deep-pile carpet, boot mats and a numbered plaque.

The cost was £24,995 (some £3,500 more than the WRX saloon). Unique to the UK300 (at least initially) was an optional 245PS Prodrive Performance Pack (fully described in the section on Prodrive at the end of this chapter), which added an extra £1,600 to the cost.

Japan's 2002 MY and Spec C

September 2001 saw the arrival of the first round of Impreza improvements, the so-called Type B (sometimes unofficially referred to as the Version VIII). This was a minor evolution indeed: apart from some new paint colours, a deeper front air intake and dark glass for the HID headlamps, and new STi badging were the only exterior changes. Under the skin, the front cross-member and mounting points were strengthened and electronic brake distribution was added to the ABS system. The WRX NA (non-turbo) engine had improved pistons, ignition and intake system, while the turbocharged NB had new low-friction piston rings. If you ordered automatic transmission on your WRX NB, it now had a keener 4.444:1 final drive ratio.

The standard STi dropped in price at this time as, just one month later, Japan received an STi Prodrive Style version sharing many of the modifications seen on the European version of the model (see 'STi comes to Europe' overleaf). It differed from the European one in having a rally style roof vent, rear wash/wipe, engine bay strut brace, blacked out rear passenger windows and high illumination headlights (as well as mechanical differences such as a 280PS engine and a gearbox with lower ratios for fifth and sixth gears).

In September 2001, the RA was dropped for a three-month period, perhaps because it was so roundly beaten by the cheaper Mitsubishi Lancer Evo VII. Subaru's answer, unveiled in December 2001, was the STi RA Spec C. This was no less than 90kg lighter than the standard STi and was achieved by getting rid of even more items than had the old RA. The Spec C did without a front subframe, sound insulation, airbags, seatbelt

pretensioners, ISOFIX anchors, luggage compartment trim, HID lamps, high-mount stoplight, hi-fi and air conditioning.

Other weight-saving measures included modified steering, front bumper, door beams, rear differential mountings, thinner gauge metal for the roof and bootlid, thinner glass, a smaller, 50-litre fuel tank and smaller wash/wipe reservoir.

The Spec C wasn't just about weight saving, though. The engine had a better ECU, the same IHI turbocharger used in the old 22B, and revised cylinders and intake manifold. Response was keener and torque output rose to 283lb ft (385Nm) at 4,400rpm. Other touches included a larger intercooler water spray tank relocated to the boot for better weight distribution, and a transmission cooler.

The Spec C also received better suspension geometry in direct response to the Evo VII's challenge. Notably, the Spec C rode 10mm lower than the STi. There was a version with 17-inch BBS alloy wheels and Brembo brakes, but you could also buy a Spec C version with 16-inch steel wheels, non-Brembo brakes and a driver-controlled centre differential. The familiar RA roof vent and white-only paint scheme remained.

The Japanese market also received a new WRX NB-R for the 2002 model year. This was the first New Age 'Type R' that was based on the ordinary 250PS WRX, rather than the STi. It had some STi items, such as inverted dampers, STi brakes with four-pot front brake callipers, silver-painted 17-inch alloy wheels, a taller rear wing and blanked-

↓ **The WRX NB-R launched in 2001 was a 'Type R' based on the ordinary 250PS WRX, but added some STi items, such as inverted dampers, STi brakes, 17-inch alloy wheels, a taller rear wing and blanked-off fog lamps.**

off foglamps. Not forgotten, the 250PS Sports Wagon was released in a Type Euro version just afterwards, in January 2002. This featured Porsche Design bodywork modifications – new design front and rear bumpers, front grille, roof spoiler and unique 17-inch alloy wheels – and a choice of silver or black paintwork.

STi comes to Europe

For 2002, European markets received the fairly minor WRX Type B changes described above. In the UK, the service schedule was increased from six months or 7,500 miles up to 12 months or 10,000 miles.

The biggest news for 2002, however, was the launch of the STi in Europe – the first time the STi badge had appeared there officially. This happened one year after the STi's Japanese launch, when, at the September 2001 Frankfurt Motor Show, it was officially announced that a fully Type Approved STi would go on sale in Europe, which it duly did in January/February 2002.

This was the real thing. Kazuo Ogawa, leader of the New Impreza Project Team, said that the European version was 95 per cent the same as the Japanese-spec STi. Apart from changes to the emissions equipment to get the car through Euro III Type Approval, very little was altered.

You got the pukka STi engine with that red crackle-finish intake manifold, semi-closed-deck block, reshaped piston heads, forged pistons, screw-in connecting rods, shimless valve lifters, sodium exhaust valves, hollow intake valves and active valve control variable exhaust valve timing. Plus of course the driver-operated intercooler water spray.

Largely because of an extra catalyst and emissions remapping, overall power was 265PS at 6,000rpm rather than the Japanese car's 280PS, with torque rated at 253lb ft (343Nm) at 4,000rpm.

Of course, there was also a six-speed close-ratio gearbox (but with a different fifth and sixth gear ratio to the Japanese version), as well as the joy of a shift light in the rev counter and even a button to adjust the change-up buzzer point. Suretrac front limited slip differential (rather than the WRX's free front diff), a faster steering rack, WRC-style

inverted suspension struts and uprated bushes and rear suspension arms were the suspension differences over the WRX. And who could ignore those gold alloy wheels and bigger, gold-coloured Brembo brakes?

Visually, the European STi had smoked-glass projector-beam headlamps (which went some way to transforming the controversial ovoid lamp look), a bonnet air intake the size of a shoebox, and pink STi badging. In the UK, there was standard air conditioning, a CD player and satellite tracking. In fact, for the UK version (badged 'Type UK'), two models were on offer: a 'normal' STi version (at £25,995) and a Prodrive Style version for £1,500 extra. The latter had a much bigger WRC-style rear wing, restyled front spoiler with very large foglamp covers, special side skirts and deep blue-faced dials with red needles (all courtesy of Peter Stevens's pen). The STi was available in four colours: WR Blue Mica, Blue Black Mica, Premium Silver Metallic and Pure White, the latter two for special order only. It was immediately a hit: in the UK, almost a third of all Impreza sales were the STi model and the initial batch of just 750 Prodrive Style models had to be extended.

Driving the STi

I attended the European STi launch in Biarritz and filed this report for *Japanese Performance* magazine. 'The STi … applies its power with devastating efficiency. And there are fistfuls of it. Unlike certain other turbo installations one could mention, the delivery of power is smooth and progressive, with no sudden turbo impact. Not much happens below 3,000rpm, where the engine feels frankly sluggish, but when the turbo does come in, it has consistent urge. Maximum power comes in high up the range (6,000rpm) but with a red line of 7,500rpm (and a little red warning light to show you when to change up), you are always in the power band as you progress through the gears.

'Punch up through a very slick-acting 'box and you're never more than a split second away from another phenomenal surge of power. Subaru claims 148mph and 0–60mph in 5.2 seconds, which is possibly conservative. But it's the in-gear pace that's most eyebrow-raising: this feels as fast as any supercar. Yet with 24.5mph per 1,000rpm,

↑ The STi arrived in European markets at the beginning of 2002, sharing its specification remarkably closely with the Japanese STi. On the left is the standard version, with its low-level rear spoiler; on the right is the Prodrive Style STi, including a bigger WRC-style rear wing, restyled front spoiler with large fog lamp covers, new side skirts and blue-faced dials with red needles.

← The Peter Stevens-designed modifications for the Prodrive Style enhanced already super-sharp dynamics in the European-specification STi.

cruising is relatively relaxed and certainly a far cry from the 19mph per 1,000rpm of some of the old-generation STi models.

'Have the inverted strut suspension and limited slip front diff returned the old Impreza's raw edge? Broadly the answer is positive. The STi exhibits extremely sharp turn-in, far better than the WRX. Through tightening corners, the STi understeers less, at least as long as you remember to feed the power in progressively. The front limited slip diff certainly works hard here, as does the quicker-rack steering. And when the prodigious grip of the 225-section tyres finally gives, the chassis reveals the true brilliance of its symmetrical balance. Drifting is amazingly neutral, with all four wheels sliding briefly before on-line progress is resumed. It's fabulously adjustable, rewards smoothness and yet is very forgiving of any mistakes.

'The STi eats up the road like some tarmac tyrannosaurus. Criticisms? The STi's wider tyres are more susceptible to tramlining, torque steer can be obtrusive if you apply the power too readily and the steering is over-light at moderate speeds.'

Australian news

Having launched the New Age WRX in October 2000, virtually identical to the European version, Subaru Australia took more of its own course for the 2002 Model Year, when there arrived the $1,950 option of an automatic gearbox in the WRX. At the same time, the manual gearbox had

revised ratios and the final drive went to a more manic 4.444:1 (compared with 3.9:1 previously). This reflected a move towards tailoring the WRX to Australian road conditions, while the range-wide introduction of electronic brake distribution (EBD) was shared with other markets.

Subaru Australia also announced at the 2001 Sydney Motorshow that it would import the STi officially, the car finally coming to market in December. It matched the specification of the 265PS European STi quite closely, although it had Japanese ratios for its six-speed gearbox. Also there was no Prodrive Style bodykit version.

For 2002, Australia also received a US-style Impreza-badged RS using a 2.5-litre non-turbo engine, although it was even less powerful at 153PS at 5,600rpm. There was also a limited-edition WRX Club Spec Evo 5 with striking orange paintwork; only 200 cars were made in all (140 saloons and 60 estates).

USA gets the WRX at last

In the USA, the advent of the WRX's launch in January 2001 at the Detroit Auto Show (as a 2002 Model Year car) was reason for huge celebration. At last America had a genuine turbocharged Impreza to replace the rather lukewarm 2.5 RS that looked but certainly did not perform like an STi Type R. And for once European Impreza enthusiasts had cause to be jealous of their American counterparts, for the US version boasted

12bhp more power than the European one.

The familiar 1,994cc engine – available in the USA for the first time – developed an impressive 227bhp at 6,000rpm, although torque was much closer to European cars at 217lb ft (294Nm) at 4,000rpm. Claimed performance was 0–60mph in 6.1 seconds (with manual transmission), although some testers were able to duck under six seconds.

The optional four-speed electronic automatic transmission was teamed with VTD (variable torque distribution) all-wheel-drive. VTD distributed more power to the rear wheels, providing the vehicle with more of a performance driving feel; the variable torque split was 45 per cent to the front wheels and 55 per cent to the rear. Unlike European Imprezas, both WRX models came with 6.5 x 16-inch alloy wheels and 205/55 R16 Bridgestone Potenza tyres; 7 x 17-inch BBS alloy wheels with 215/45 R17 tyres were optional. Also the rear discs were solid, not ventilated as on Japanese and European cars.

Most of the spec followed the European model, including keyless entry, front foglights, dual and side airbags, twin exhaust pipes and an aluminium bonnet. It was equipped with plenty of goodies, including: air conditioning, a six-speaker radio/ cassette/in-dash six-disc CD changer and cruise control. Aluminium pedals were kept for manual transmission models only.

Two WRX models were on offer in North America: the Sedan and the Sport Wagon. The WRX sedan cost $23,995, with the Sport Wagon slightly less at $23,495; four-speed automatic cost an extra $1,000 for either model. Other non-turbo 2002 Imprezas were the 2.5 TS Sport Wagon, the sporty 2.5 RS Sedan, and the Outback Sport, all powered by the familiar 165bhp 2.5-litre engine. That meant the two-door coupé Impreza dropped out of the US line-up for the first time since 1994.

STi limited editions

In 2002, to celebrate the 30th anniversary of Subaru's association with four-wheel drive, for the Japanese market only there was a limited-edition STi model. With its tuned ECU, the STi Limited boasted more torque than standard – up from

⬇ **The WRX in the USA had slightly more power than European ones. It also had small-diameter projector-beam fog lamps.**

→ The simultaneous launch of the 2003 WRC car and the facelifted Impreza gave Subaru the opportunity to draw parallels between the rally car and the revised STi. Handling was also improved because of better suspension geometry.

↑ Inside, higher-quality cloth was used and the STi pictured had a new, smaller Momo steering wheel and blue carpets.

275lb ft to 283lb ft (385Nm) – while it also had a taller rear spoiler.

Likewise, there was an RA anniversary edition in May 2002. Its name (S202) revived the memory of the crazy S201, but the S202 was a far less extreme exercise. Based on the STi RA Spec C, it was significant in cranking up power to 320PS at 6,400rpm and torque up to 283lb ft at 4,400rpm. This was achieved by adding a specially tuned ECU, silicone intake ducts, special exhaust with some titanium components and a larger rear silencer, as well as an aluminium oil cooler.

Other S202 features included gold RAYS forged alloy wheels and Pirelli P Zero tyres, adjustable carbon fibre rear wing, lightweight grooved brake discs, braided steel brake hoses, upgraded rear suspension, and black interior trim. It weighed just

1,330kg and could be painted yellow, white, blue or blue/black. Only 400 cars were made, and all were sold within weeks of going on sale.

2003: goodbye to those headlamps

Faced with almost universal criticism of the Impreza's headlamp treatment, Subaru finally buckled to the pressures and, only two years into its life, gave the New Age Impreza a facelift that consigned those lights to the scrapheap.

First seen at the September 2002 Paris Motor Show and launched in showrooms across Europe in January/February 2003, the facelifted car had a completely fresh front end, from the windscreen forwards. The design was effected by Peter Stevens and Prodrive and included a new front bumper, spoiler, bonnet and wings. Most significant were new three-dimensional headlamps with circular lamps inlaid to create a striking curved dip.

A character line swept from the lower edge of the headlamps and over a more steeply sloping bonnet. The top edge of the bumper was now more rounded, the front wings were reprofiled and there were larger air-intakes above and below the numberplate. Both the WRX and WRX STi gained larger bonnet air scoops (the former heightened by 20mm and the latter by 30mm).

At the rear, all models had new bumpers and new light clusters with a curved dip to their inner edges which many commentators likened to the

Lexus IS200. Every WRX STi now came with the larger Prodrive Style-type rear spoiler, front corner spoilers and new side sills, claiming to improve high-speed stability. Indeed, the drag coefficient for all saloons dropped to 0.33 Cd, with the WRX five-door scoring 0.37 Cd.

It was not just a cosmetic and aerodynamic job, however. The WRX had more power, rising from 218PS up to 225PS, still at 5,600rpm, while torque grew from 215.4lb ft at 3,600rpm to 221.3lb ft at 4,000rpm. Top speed rose by 3mph to 143mph for the five-door and 144mph for the saloon, while 0–60mph times fell too (5.6 seconds for the saloon and 5.8 seconds for the hatchback).

The WRX engine was retuned to run on 98-octane fuel (although in fact it could still run on 95). Revisions to the exhaust manifold were aimed at smoothing the flow of exhaust gases, and an increased boost pressure and a new engine management system sharpened throttle response. The valve gear and exhaust were also modified to cope with extra heat.

All new-look Imprezas had revised steering, gaining a variable-capacity steering pump to give greater straight-line stability and a lighter, more sensitive feel during low-speed manoeuvring. Helping to sharpen handling were new dampers featuring multiple-layer valves which also enhanced ride comfort.

The STi also received some unique changes. The intercooler water spray nozzle was altered and an air baffle plate installed inside the air scoop. It also received improved front suspension (strengthened mounts for the transverse linkages and new cross-performance rods). Handling and steering response were claimed to improve because of better geometry under hard cornering.

Inside, higher-quality cloth was used, except if you specified a new luxury WRX package called SL. This featured factory-fit black leather seat trim, heated front seats and an electric sunroof, for an extra £1,500. The WRX's rev-counter was resited to the centre of the instrument display, like the STi's. The STi itself gained a new, smaller-diameter Momo steering wheel and blue carpets to match the seats and door trim. On all models, the centre console was now dark metallic instead of silver.

Other 2003 changes included anti-raindrop door mirrors, ISOFIX-compatible child rear seat mountings, dual-stage passenger airbag and high-backed rally front seats with airbags (previously side airbags were only available on the WRX saloon when fitted with standard seats). There was also deadlocking and special shields around the driver's door lock.

As some indication of how much the change was needed, Subaru UK announced discounts of up to £3,000 on old-shape models, bringing the WRX down to just £18,999. But the new WRX had a price cut too, and started at £19,995. The STi cost £24,995 and was now only available in one version (effectively replacing the old Prodrive Style).

Facelift in Japan

In Japan, the facelifted WRX went on sale on 1 November 2002. For 250PS turbocharged models, there was a larger air intake for the intercooler, a smaller diameter turbine for the turbo, hollow

↓ This is a facelifted version of the stripped-out STi Spec C in 16-inch steel wheel form with its driver-controlled centre differential, which was 120kg lighter than the standard STi. The blue paint scheme was a first for the Spec C.

↑ The most powerful STi variant on sale in the world was the 300bhp American version, which was unique in having a 2.5-litre turbocharged engine, rather than a 2.0-litre.

sodium-filled valves and a better exhaust. A new mesh grille was another minor change alongside some interior refinements, while the suspension gained STi-type inverted struts (some two years before the European WRX would do the same).

At last, the old 20K Sports Wagon was rebadged as a WRX and got the same 17-inch wheels, inverted struts and four-pot front/two-pot rear brakes, as on the saloon.

As for the STi, that gained a small lift in torque up to 290lb ft (393Nm) at 4,400rpm, which was due to the Spec C type IHI turbocharger, a better exhaust, wider intake ducts and an improved inlet manifold. Under the skin, a new six-point mounting for the front subframe/cross-member made it tougher and the whole arrangement moved forward 15mm, a support bracket was added to the rear subframe and a jointed link was added to the rear anti-roll bar. These suspension changes were designed to give the STi less understeer. The transmission became lighter, but there were stronger internals and an improved linkage. There were also some extra cosmetic tweaks, namely new front corner skirts, side skirts and a larger rear spoiler, as well as some small interior changes. The five-door STi Wagon was dropped at this point.

The Spec C remained available in two versions, very much as before: a 17-inch wheel model with

a driver-controlled centre diff plus automatic mode, and an even more stripped-out 16-inch wheel version with a driver-controlled centre diff. It remained as much as 120kg lighter than the standard STi and could now also be ordered in blue paint as well as white.

US STi gets 2.5 litres

In January 2003, America finally woke up to the STi. Although it did not go on sale until May, here at last was the icon that Subaru USA had never had before. But it was very different in one major respect from Japanese and European STis: it used a turbocharged engine of 2.5 litres, not 2.0 litres. Developing a massive 300bhp and 300lb ft (407Nm) of torque, Subaru was able to claim it to be the most powerful four-cylinder engine available in the USA.

The US STi did not scrimp on its spec. It came as standard with the driver-controlled centre differential with automatic mode which was optional even in Japan. In other respects it was very similar to the European version of the STi. In 2003, it cost $30,995 in the USA or $46,995 in Canada.

At the same time, the 2004 Model Year US Impreza was launched, sharing its facelift with

Imprezas around the rest of the world. However, there remained detail differences, such as the smaller projector-beam driving lamps in the WRX. The US WRX sedan also received the option of a Premium Package that included a power moonroof, rear spoiler, heated exterior mirrors, heated seats and wiper de-icer. US models remained better specified than European ones, the WRX including standard cruise control and a 6CD changer, for example.

The 2.5-litre STi engine subsequently became very popular among the tuning fraternity in markets outside the USA. In the UK, for example, hundreds of engine blocks were imported to be retro-fitted to Imprezas.

Prodrive and the New Age Impreza

It was reported as early as July 2000 that, perhaps inevitably, Prodrive was to be involved in an uprated version of the New Age Impreza. Some hint of the possibilities was provided in January 2001, when, at the Tokyo Auto Salon, a WRX 'STi Prodrive' show car was displayed. This was the first time that the STi Prodrive label had been used, but it was a natural step: the Prodrive brand had become very well-known in Japan. Prodrive-branded wheels were already being sold officially in Japan and a partnership with Bridgestone saw many more Prodrive parts being offered to Japanese buyers. The Tokyo Auto Salon STi Prodrive featured a special Prodrive grille, deeper front spoiler with extra lights, a WRC-style large rear wing, and Prodrive/OZ 18-inch wheels.

As it happened, the Prodrive name would adorn an official STi version both in the UK and Japan. The Prodrive Style version of the STi, first seen in Autumn 2001, featured many unique features above the standard STi, including a much bigger rear wing, restyled front spoiler with very large foglamp covers, special side skirts, and deep blue-faced dials with red needles.

In fact, the first 'New Age' Prodrive package to market was the Prodrive Performance Pack (PPP), offered from May 2001, initially only for the UK300 and then for any WRX. The £1,600 PPP (also called WR Sport) option got a reprogrammed ECU, uprated intercooler piping and a free-flow exhaust system with a large single tailpipe.

As before, the intention of Prodrive's engine modifications was to boost mid-range power and torque, with stronger throttle reaction from idle to the top of the rev range. There was no discernible tail-off in power from 6,000rpm to 7,000rpm (the standard WRX displayed what Subaru called 'a slight softening of response'). Maximum power was now 245PS at 5,600rpm (instead of the standard WRX's 218PS at the same engine speed). Maximum pulling power was 261lb ft (354Nm) at 4,000rpm. This shaved almost three seconds off the 20–75mph time in third gear.

In this form, the PPP lasted until the arrival of the facelifted Impreza, when the standard WRX engine was upped to 225PS. Prodrive immediately leapt on this new engine and came up with an improved PPP in February 2003. Power was now up to 265PS (the same as the STi) and while torque was actually slightly down on the old PPP (at 257lb ft/349Nm at 3,500rpm), it was still more than the STi's 243lb ft (330Nm).

The PPP-equipped WRX recorded a 0–60mph time of 4.8 seconds and 0–100mph in 14.1 seconds (compared to standard WRX times of 5.6 and 15.9 seconds respectively). Throttle response was also significantly enhanced throughout the rev range. The cost was the same as before at £1,600.

Not wanting to leave the STi in the shade, Prodrive set to work on the STi Type UK and came up with a spectacular £1,995 Prodrive Performance Package to create the quickest

↓ **Prodrive created a 305PS Performance Pack for the STi Type-UK. It was incredibly popular with STi buyers, costing £1,995 and transforming the car's already scorching performance.**

↑ **WRC champion Petter Solberg accepts the tribute of the UK-only WR1 special edition, produced in his honour. Main features were a 320PS engine, driver-controlled centre diff and special paint.**

UK Impreza yet. There was a demonstration to customers as early as May 2002 but the end product did not reach the market until October.

The package consisted of a revised engine control unit, high-flow catalyst and sports silencer. It pushed power up from 265PS to 305PS at the same 6,000rpm and torque up from 253lb ft to 299lb ft (343–405Nm), also at the same 4,000rpm. The torque increase was particularly noticeable between 3,000rpm and 5,800rpm, while at 2,500rpm, the PPP had almost 30 per cent more torque. Overall, said Subaru UK, the Prodrive car had 'startling high-rev performance but also more low and mid-speed flexibility … swifter at any speed and in any gear.' Subaru claimed a 0–60mph time down from 5.2 seconds to 4.6 seconds and a 0–100mph figure of 12.2 seconds instead of 13.7 seconds. The 50–70mph shift in fifth gear was now 4.9 seconds instead of 6.1 seconds.

WR1 special edition

'The fastest and most powerful Impreza ever' was how Subaru described a special UK-only special edition called the WRX STi WR1. Unveiled at the January 2004 Autosport show ahead of a March 2004 production date, and nominally celebrating Petter Solberg's 2003 World Rally title, the WR1 limited edition featured a 320PS power upgrade, courtesy of a revised engine control unit, high-flow

catalyst and sports silencer. Peak power came at 5,800rpm, with maximum torque of 309.8lb ft (420Nm) at 4,000rpm.

This meant the 0–60mph time dropped to just 4.25 seconds with 0–100mph reached in 10.67 seconds. Subaru also claimed 0.7 seconds off the STi's 30–50mph time in 4th gear (at 4.0 seconds) and 0.8 seconds off the 50–70mph time in 5th (4.6 seconds).

The WR1 became the first European Impreza to gain the driver control centre differential (DCCD) offered in Japan and the USA. Also new for the WR1 were Prodrive-developed uprated springs and bump-stops with a 25mm lower ride height. There were also 18-inch P-FF7 (Prodrive Flow Forming seven-spoke) alloy wheels with 225/45 Pirelli PZero tyres.

Externally, Ice Blue Metallic paint looked distinctive, as did driving lamps and a stainless steel mesh grille. Inside, changes included anthracite instead of blue suede-effect seats, a special gear knob, imaged carpet mats and a tax disc holder engraved with the special edition number. Only 500 were built at £29,995 each and they sold out within weeks.

February 2004 also witnessed Australia's tribute to Petter Solberg with a special edition launched at the Melbourne International Motor Show. Unlike the WR1, this was a mere cosmetic job, with WR Blue paintwork, silver gearknob and Petter Solberg WRC console badge and key ring. In total, 200 cars (all four-door) were made available.

The 'Saabaru'

Few motoring pundits foresaw the December 2003 debut of a bizarre motoring chimera: an Impreza without a Subaru badge. The Swedish car maker Saab had been taken over by General Motors and, as part of an expansion into the US market, began to engineer Saab-badged versions of other cars in the GM empire. As GM owned 20 per cent of Subaru, it pressed for the Impreza to be released to Saab for them to develop a badge-engineered version.

So Saab took the Impreza five-door and made the Saab 9-2X out of it. From the A-pillars forward, the 9-2X was all-new: a Saab house-style nose, new lights and a bonnet with a smaller scoop. At the back there was a new tailgate, spoiler and wraparound lights. The alloy wheels were also unique to the 9-2X. However the centre body section (doors, roof and rear quarter-panels) was identical to the Impreza.

Inside, the Impreza had a full Ikea-type makeover: plusher door trim, softer carpeting, drink holders in the metallic-look centre console, and optional leather seats.

The 9-2X was undeniably a softer car than the Impreza. To soften the ride, it had retuned springs, dampers and bushings, while extra sound insulation was installed. Conversely, the steering rack was sharpened up to the STi's 15:1 ratio.

'The Saab 9-2X is the result of a collaboration between two like-minded companies,' said Peter Augustsson, President of Saab Automobile. 'We both have a special aircraft heritage and a successful history in rallying, and our cars are known for being dynamic, safe and fun-to-drive. It makes a lot of sense to combine our strengths in creating a Saab that can be brought to market quickly.' One suspects the final sentence reflects

the real reason why this project went ahead.

Two versions were built for sale only in the USA and Canada: an entry-level Linear model with Subaru's naturally-aspirated 2.5-litre engine and an Aero model with the WRX's familiar 227bhp, 2.0-litre turbo unit. Both had all-wheel-drive, and five-speed manual transmission was standard on both models, with a four-speed automatic option. Because it was 74kg heavier than the US WRX, its 0–60mph time of 6.1 seconds was a little off the pace.

Shown at the December 2003 Los Angeles Auto Show, 9-2X production started in March 2004 in Japan. The 9-2X Aero version cost $27,645, some $2,975 more than the Impreza WRX wagon. The American press seemed to like it, since it added refinement without detracting too much from the Impreza driving experience. The fact that European markets were excluded suggests that it may not have been received so well there. Pundits nicknamed the new car 'Saabaru' but it wasn't a great success. Between 2004 and 2006, only 10,346 examples were made, less than half of them turbocharged.

↓ **When is an Impreza not an Impreza? When it's got a Saab badge. The Saab 9-2X was a mildly reworked Impreza WRX Sports Wagon built in Japan for the North American market.**

↑ **The 2005 Model Year Impreza (sometimes called Version IX) got a huge boost in the chassis department. Revised geometry, active centre diff and yaw control sensor sharpened the handling and ride.**

2005 MY and 'Version IX'

The September 2004 Paris Motor Show was the stage for the Impreza's next step forward. Sometimes dubbed the Version IX, the 2005 Model Year Impreza marked a number of important chassis and cosmetic changes.

We'll start with the STi, whose chassis was the area most improved. The STi's wheelbase and rear track were marginally teased out. The wheelbase grew by 10mm and the rear track by 15mm. But that was only part of the suspension story. The geometry and suspension settings were altered for 2005: the caster angle rose, while spring and damper rates were retuned. The front and rear lateral links were now made from aluminium, the anti-roll bars were bigger, the suspension mounting points were more rigid, and the support arm for the front cross-member and jack-up plate became a single unit. Front wheel bearing capacity was improved, while the rear differential cushion rubber was uprated to make handling more stable. There was also a cannon mount-type attachment for the steering box and a new damper valve to reduce kick-back.

A helical limited-slip front differential replaced the 2004 model's Suretrac diff. A new yaw sensor detected the rate of drift in a corner 50 times per second and automatically adjusted the torque split front to rear.

Understeer was now kept far more firmly under control, as I discovered when I drove the new car at the launch. Turn-in was now tighter and understeer, while still present, was effectively muted. The sense of being suckered on to the tarmac was enhanced by Bridgestone Potenza tyres (new on the European STi) on slightly wider 8 x 17-inch gold alloys (which necessitated small blisters on the rear wheelarches). Ride was notably better too. The only aspect in which the STi took a retrograde step was road noise.

The driver-controlled centre differential (DCCD) was new for the STi in Europe, operated by a thumbwheel to let you change the torque distribution front to rear. The yaw sensor switched off in manual mode, enabling extreme cornering attitudes on loose surfaces.

There was no change to the STi engine or gearbox but new engine and floorpan covers improved underbody aerodynamics. Externally, the only changes were subtle extensions to the rear wheelarches, new design gold alloys and a lack of red paint on the inverted suspension struts.

Inside, things changed more substantially. You now held on to a smaller-diameter three-spoke steering wheel and the door trim and roof lining were in plusher, soft-touch cloth. The gear lever was new and there was grippier black cloth for the seat side supports. The aluminium-effect centre console now swept down in one panel and incorporated new air-conditioning knobs and two new cup holders. In the UK, the STi cost £1,000 more, at £25,995.

The WRX was also changed for 2005. For the first time in Europe, it got the STi's inverted front and rear suspension struts, aluminium front suspension lateral links, more rigid suspension mountings, and the STi's steering revisions.

In Japan, most of the changes were adopted in the home market in September 2004. As concerns special domestic models, Subaru revised the STi's cooling and intake pipework, contributing to a boost in torque from 283lb ft (385Nm) to 304lb ft (412Nm). The STi Spec C Type RA had new, 8 × 17-inch alloy wheels and 235/45 tyres, an ultra-lightweight boot spoiler on stilts, and door decals including a map of the Nürburgring with the words 'Keep attacking the Nürburgring'.

↑ Cabin changes for 2005 included a smaller-diameter steering wheel, plusher door trim, new gear lever, grippier black seat cloth and a new swoopy one-piece aluminium-effect centre console.

← The WRX in Europe also came in for some useful chassis changes for 2005, including adopting STi-type inverted suspension struts.

'Ultimate' S203

In addition to a WRX WR-Limited model (with STi spoilers, STi gold Rays alloy wheels and titanium shift knob), there was one final addition to the Japanese range in 2004. This was the S203 special edition, billed as the "ultimate development" of the STi road car. However, it was a little less hard-edged than the old S202 and more an exercise in going upmarket.

The engine received a new turbo, hand-balanced internals, silicone rubber air intake hoses,

tweaked ECU, titanium exhaust, sports catalyst and oil cooler. The result: an extra 40PS (320PS at 6400rpm) and more torque too (310lb ft at 4400rpm).

More significantly, the S203 chassis was developed with the help of former world rally champion Petter Solberg. It received adjustable damping, lower and stiffer springs, pillowball bushes and aluminium links on the rear suspension, stronger anti-roll bars, power steering oil cooler and larger brakes that were claimed to improve airflow and reduce fading. Solberg was reportedly

2005: UK boosts

May 2005 saw the UK importer offering free Prodrive Performance Packages on the WRX and STi, raising their power outputs to 265PS and 305PS and worth £1600 and £1995 respectively. A matter of days later, Subaru UK announced its latest special edition, the WRX 300. This also had a Prodrive Performance Pack boosting power to

↑↑ Subaru may have billed the S203 the "ultimate" Impreza but it was perhaps less hard-edged than the S202 – despite the input of Petter Solberg in development.

↑ An adjustable rear wing boosted the S203's hardcore credibility.

↗ Only 555 examples of the S203 were made.

↑ Larger brakes were just part if the S203's chassis package, including adjustable damping, uprated springs, pillowball bushes, stronger anti-roll bars and unique soft-compound Pirelli P Zero Corsa tyres.

most impressed with the unique Pirelli P Zero Corsa tyres (on 18-inch BBS forged alloy wheels). Specially developed for the S203, they had a soft compound with two grooves for improved wet weather grip and phenomenal turn-in.

The S203 looked unique with its carbon front underskirt, adjustable rear wing, HID lights, tinted glass, silver mesh grille and special badging. Inside, Recaro supplied what was said to be the world's first fully reclining competition seat, finished in grey, each one reputedly costing £2700.

Other tweaks were a 260kph (165mph) speedometer, pink-stitched leather steering wheel and gearknob, black interior surfaces and a gearknob trim ring with the car's serial number (only 555 S203s were made). Usually finished in Crystal Grey, the S203 was also available in Solid Red, Pure White or WR Blue.

265PS but a few unique features as well. Special 17-inch alloy wheels were fitted with 215/45 tyres, while the WRX 300 received an aluminium gearknob, WRX-branded mats and a 'Subaru World Rally Team' logo on the front seats and front lamp covers, Trackstar anti-theft device and WR Blue paint. The '300' referred to the production run (300 examples), each one priced at £21,495.

Hello to Hawkeye

If the circular headlamps of the original New Age Impreza had been a mistake, Subaru had made amends in 2002 with its more conventional front-end style. Then it appeared to lurch back into controversy again in October 2005 with the debut of an all-new look for 2006, widely known now as 'Hawkeye'. Created by Subaru's Chief Designer, Andreas Zapatinas, it incorporated the new corporate look first seen in Subaru's R1 microcar and the Tribeca SUV.

The most dramatic changes were at the front end, in particular the headlamps, grilles and bumper. The new nose design was described by Subaru as having a 'spread-wings' grille and 'hawkeye' headlamps with cylindrical lamp units, while the ensemble was supposed to resemble the cross-section of an aeroplane fuselage (you had to squint to see that). Also changed were the bonnet (two inches longer) and front bumpers

(with horizontal corner strakes to smooth the airflow down the side of the car). The saloon additionally featured vertical air intakes at the side of the bumper for enhanced brake cooling. Also new were the front wings, side skirts, '3D' cylindrical rear lights with strakes and door handles that did away with keyholes. Every model received updated wheels: the 2.0R 16-inch five-spoke alloys, the WRX 17-inch seven-spoke alloys and the STi a new shade of gold for its 17-inch 10-spoke alloys. Finally, smaller but more powerful projector-type fog lamps were fitted to all models, and all but the entry-level 2.0R five-door had HID headlamps with pop-up washers.

↑ **WRX 300 edition for the UK had a power boost to 265PS, special 17-inch alloy wheels and SWRT logos on the seats and front lamps.**

↓ **Hello to 'Hawkeye', a controversial restyle by Andreas Zapatinas. This WRX shows off its new headlamps, front grille and bumper. The bonnet was two inches longer, too, while the air intakes just ahead of the front wheels improved brake cooling.**

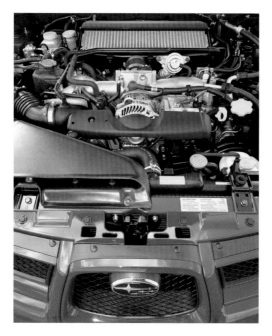

→ Key to the revised 2006 range in Europe was a switch to 2.5-litre turbo power. In WRX form (as pictured) the EJ25 engine had more power and more torque lower down the rev range.

↑ The five-door wagon continued in WRX form with the Hawkeye front, although the long-running STi Wagon was finally dropped in Japan at this point.

→ The STi Type UK got a 15PS power boost in 2.5-litre guise, taking it to 280PS, as well as revised gear ratios for better cruising ability.

The longer and more aerodynamic nose was the main reason why the claimed top speed of the STi rose by 7mph to 158mph. Cooling was also improved so that, for the first time ever, the STi's bonnet scoop actually got smaller (it was now the same as the WRX's).

For the STi, the aero package was not simply a new nose. There was a new under-floorpan panel that smoothed airflow under the car, a ribbed under-bumper rear diffuser and a highly distinctive new aluminium roof vane above the rear window. Shared with the WRC car, it deflected air from the roof down under the boot spoiler, increasing downforce.

Easily the most significant changes, however, lay under the new bonnet. Both the WRX and STi in Europe now got an EJ25 2.5-litre flat-four engine with a larger bore and stroke (as fitted to the US-market Impreza for several years before). The 230PS 2,457 cc engine in the WRX was shared with the contemporary Forester 2.5 XT, but the 280PS STi engine was new for Europe. The move from 2.0 to 2.5 litres was motivated less by the craving for extra power and torque (the 2.5 STi actually had less torque than the Japanese 2.0-litre STi) and much more to do with emissions: it was easier to make the bigger flat-four pass the EuroIV rules that arrived in January 2006. An electronic throttle made for more responsive acceleration and there was a secondary air intake system to reduce emissions. There were also changes to the water jacket in the cylinder head and modifications to the exhaust manifolds to minimise pumping losses and ensure smooth gas flow.

In the WRX, the 2.5-litre engine enjoyed an extra 5PS (230PS) and 15lb ft of torque (235lb ft produced 400rpm lower at 3,600rpm). Response was helped, especially in lower gears, by slightly lower gearing: a new final drive resulted in 23.5mph at 1,000rpm in fifth gear, 1.2mph less than before. Overall, though, the 143mph top speed and 0–60mph time of 5.4 seconds were very similar to the old 2.0-litre WRX. The five-speed manual's shift stroke was also 10mm shorter and the gearchange itself was firmer.

One other minor change for the 2006 WRX was new cloth seat trim with black centres and grey outer panels. Both saloon and five-door WRX versions remained on sale, starting at £20,900, each available with optional 'SL' trim (leather trim, heated front seats and an electric sunroof). The five-door now had hangers on both sides of the load bay for hanging cargo nets.

As for the 2.5-litre STi, the difference in power was much more notable over the old 2.0-litre. For the first time ever, the European STi finally produced the same power as the JDM one – 280PS (some 15PS up on the old EJ20). Overall torque also went up, by 36lb ft to 289lb ft, but it was produced at the same high 4,000rpm, so low-down low-boost engine response remained an issue, even with an Active Valve Control System (AVCS) – a form of variable valve timing – which was claimed to enhance low-speed pulling ability and high-rev power. As for the engine note, this was even more subdued – perhaps even to the point of becoming refined. The bigger engine was not significantly heavier than the 2.0 (the 2006 STi was a mere 20kg heavier than the 2005 one) and the weight distribution remained the same.

The gearchange, always a minor STi bugbear, was smoother thanks to carbon-plated synchronisers on fourth, fifth and sixth gears. Second-to-third gear changes remained notchy and awkward, however, and there was a certain amount of noisiness too. The gear ratios changed for 2006, with longer gaps between the lower ratios and upper gears lengthened to make cruising more comfortable (sixth gear was geared at 26.2mph per 1,000rpm rather than 24.5). Fuel

← The Hawkeye interior changed only a little. The STi was treated to an upgraded Driver Controlled Centre Differential.

→ The hardcore Spec C lapped the Nürburgring in an incredible 7min 59sec. This is a special edition Spec C Type RA.

→ S204 was the predictable badge for the latest STi special edition, boasting 320PS and 318lb ft of torque. Stiffer suspension meant the S204 sat 10mm lower than standard.

consumption was also slightly better, at 25.9mpg for the combined cycle.

The STi now benefited from an upgraded version of the Driver Controlled Centre Differential (DCCD). In auto mode, it split the torque 41/59 front/rear rather than 35/65, or you could dial in your own choice of torque split in manual mode using the console-mounted thumbwheel. Subaru complemented its arsenal of driver aids by adding a sensor for steering wheel angle and a new and faster-acting front helical limited slip diff that was torque-sensitive and reacted earlier to changes in road conditions. Software changes also allowed the power to be funnelled to the rear wheels for longer, which reined in understeer. The DCCD set-up was honed with help from Tommi Mäkinen, no less.

Inside the cabin, very little changed for 2006. The instruments now did an impressive light display when you first switched on, inspired by the Legacy, before the 'STi' logo illuminated. A

gear upchange light was another new addition and side airbags made their first UK appearance in the STi (previously, only the WRX had side airbags). The STi Type UK continued to have a Category 1 alarm, tracking system, window etching, gold alloys, side skirts and blue suede-effect STi seats.

We're only concerned with turbocharged Imprezas in this book, but it's worth mentioning that there remained a naturally aspirated 2.0R model on sale in Europe, which received a new 160PS four-cam 2.0-litre engine, some 35PS more powerful than the old model, and which also came with optional automatic transmission.

Hawkeye in Japan

For Japanese enthusiasts, just as controversial as the Hawkeye's new look was the choice of venue for the debut of the new car: the October 2005 Frankfurt Motor Show, a few weeks ahead of the domestic Tokyo Show. This could be taken as evidence that Subaru was becoming a much more international, globally focused company.

Japanese Imprezas may have looked very similar to European market versions from the outside, but under the skin there was one very big difference: while Europe and the US now had a 2.5-litre WRX and STi, the Japanese equivalents stuck with 2.0 litres.

The WRX was not significantly changed mechanically, continuing to deliver 250PS via a five-speed manual gearbox. The STi received a revised IHI twin-scroll turbo, equal-length manifold and semi-closed deck engine block (all in contrast to the 2.5-litre STi). Torque was up by 8lb ft to 311lbft compared to the old STi, and while the power output officially remained 280PS, independent dyno testing regularly recorded more than 310PS. Other differences from EU-spec cars included a larger intercooler with water spray, slightly wider tyres and a rear windscreen wiper. Incidentally, the Hawkeye finally marked the end of the line for the five-door wagon version of the STi.

The hardcore Spec C became a little more 'mainstream' for 2006, having benefited from extensive testing at the Nürburgring. Its black and dark grey interior differed from the STi (which had black interior trim with blue inserts). The Spec C was, as ever, a little lighter than the STi thanks to thinner glass and roof and an aluminium boot lid. It also featured reinforced strut tower braces, a rear crossbar and other additions to improve chassis rigidity, as well as an intercooler water spray and air-cooled engine oil cooler. To homologate the car as a Group N rally car, Subaru pledged to produce 1,000 units of the Spec C.

November 2005 then saw the launch of the special edition Spec C Type RA, which was limited to 350 units. Before the end of 2005, a standard JDM STi Spec C MY06 had succeeded

in lapping the Nürburgring in just 7min 59sec – an amazing achievement.

Just one month later, in December 2005, Subaru followed up previous limited production specials (the S201, S202 and S203), with the latest version, predictably called S204. Based on the new-look Hawkeye, it featured a new grille, carbon-fibre front apron and boot spoiler, as well as BBS alloy wheels (saving 6kg), 18-inch Pirelli tyres and 17-inch brakes.

Under the S204's bonnet sat a modified version of the 2.0-litre boxer engine producing 320PS and 318lb ft of torque (the biggest torque output yet for a factory car), all courtesy of a reprogrammed ECU, new pistons, crankshaft, exhaust and turbocharger. Stiffer suspension also saw the S204 lower its ride height by 10mm. Inside, there was an exclusive steering wheel, an engraved serial number and Recaro bucket seats.

S204 production began in Japan in January 2006 in three colours: WRC blue, grey and black. Some 600 examples were produced for Japan only, although a further five were sold in New Zealand that were not numbered.

Let's be discreet

The January 2006 Autosport International Show marked the unveiling of what Subaru called a new, "discreet" version of the STi. Dubbed STi Spec D (D for discreet), it was a less in-your-face version

↓ Examples of the 'discreet' Spec D look included a low-level boot spoiler, no rear window roof vane, silver alloy wheels and a lack of badges on the rear end. Inside, you got full leather upholstery.

↑ Discretion was clearly
a virtue to the many
Impreza buyers who
opted for the toned-down
STi Spec D – a model
that originated in the
UK but spread around
the world with various
different badges.

of the latest 2006 Impreza. Subaru (UK) Managing Director, Peter Kinnaird, told the author that this car was a direct response to his wife's refusal to have a car with gold wheels on her drive. In his words, he said: "This car is a steel fist in a velvet glove, offering all the thrills of the regular Impreza STi but not shouting about its abilities."

The Spec D certainly looked more sober with its small boot spoiler, no rear window roof vane, silver 17-inch alloy wheels, front projector foglamps and Prodrive lower front grille. Not only was the rear end debadged, all pink STi badges were removed from the car (apart from one on the steering wheel). Inside it got black leather trim, black instead of blue carpets, extra sound-deadening, an upgraded 200Watt CD/MP3/iPod audio system and Bluetooth hands-free phone kit. The Spec D went on sale in March 2006 priced at £28,495 – in any colour you liked as long it was (very discreet) Crystal Grey metallic.

A road test in Japanese Performance magazine concluded: "The Spec D lives up to its name in one area: its soundtrack. The 2006 2.5-litre engine is surprisingly muted – almost refined in fact. The drive is anything but discreet, though. The Bridgestone tyres offer lots of grip but the ride quality is as bone-shaking as ever."

The Spec D was received so enthusiastically by Subaru head office in Japan that a spate of similar models leaked on to markets around the world with various badges such as 'STi Limited' in Germany, 'Type G' (for 'gentleman'!) in Switzerland and 'STi Club' in France. In Japan, discretion took the form of the 'A-Line', with its silver 17-inch alloys, low boot spoiler, no roof vane, black rather than gold brake callipers, black leather-and-Alcantara interior trim, black dash, aluminium heater controls and better sound-proofing. Unlike the Spec D, the A-Line was offered in a choice of colours (White, Urban Grey and Obsidian Black) and used the JDM 2.0-litre STi engine.

More Prodrive upgrades

In November 2005, hot on the heels of the major facelift, Prodrive accessories became available in the UK, including 8x18 forged alloy wheels with Pirelli tyres (225/40 ZR18 P Zero Nero for the WRX, 235/40 ZR18 P Zero Corsa for the STi), spring kits for WRX or STi, and a Prodrive boot spoiler (echoing the lines of the WRC spoiler). Other accessories launched at the time included reversing sensors, rain sensing wipers and a Bluetooth phone kit.

Then in April 2006 came Prodrive's eagerly awaited Performance Packs (PPP) for the 2.5-litre WRX and STi. Extra power and torque were achieved by reprogramming the engine ECU, removing the rear catalytic converter, and fitting a high-flow catalyst and sports silencer. The STi PPP also got a new high-flow fuel pump. PPP kits were sold through UK Subaru dealers at £1,700 and, as ever, had no effect on the Impreza's warranty.

Perhaps the single most impressive statistic in all this was the WRX PPP, which gained a staggering 74lb ft more torque. The full figures were 270PS at 5,700rpm and 310lb ft of torque at 3,000rpm. That let Prodrive claim a 0–60mph time of 5.3 seconds, 0–100mph in 13.9 seconds and 30–50mph in fourth gear in 4.0 seconds.

The STi PPP was equally impressive. Power leapt to 320PS at 6,000rpm and torque to 332lb ft at 3,700rpm (up 43lb ft). The 0–60mph time dropped to 4.8 seconds, 0–100mph to 12.2 seconds and 30–50mph in fourth gear to 4.3 seconds.

In March 2006, in an effort to boost sales, a special 'Type UK' WRX saloon limited edition was launched. Its only spec differences were a Trackstar theft-tracking system, SmartNav sat nav and touch screen and a Bluetooth hands-free kit. Buyers also got five years' free servicing, a five-year warranty and five years' free roadside recovery in the £20,945 price.

In May 2006, Subaru's 2.5-litre turbo engine got international recognition when it won the 2006 International Engine of the Year Award in the 2.0- to 2.5-litre class. A panel of 61 motoring and technical journalists from 29 countries judged it the best engine in terms of performance, driveability, fuel economy and refinement.

P2: Prodrive's Impreza coupe

The sensation of the January 2006 Autosport International show was without question on the Prodrive stand. For the first time ever, Prodrive had designed its very own roadgoing sports car – the Prodrive P2 based on the Impreza STi – which went from concept to reality in just nine months.

The P2 was the idea of Prodrive chairman, David Richards, who said: "It has been built to showcase Prodrive's innovative technologies and engineering skills and to demonstrate its ability to design and build a unique road car in less than a year."

The Impreza STi donated its engine, transmission and four-wheel drive system but Prodrive added its own rally-inspired spin. The tuned 2.0-litre engine gained ALS, a turbo anti-lag system modified from Subaru's World Rally Cars. ALS kept the turbo on boost at low engine speeds, giving the car more immediate throttle response and improving performance by using more of the engine's 575Nm (423lb ft) of torque throughout the rev range.

↓ **Prodrive created a huge stir with this P2 coupe in 2006. This was effectively an Impreza STi coupe.**

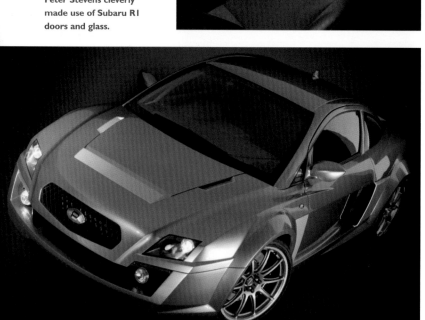

Prodrive also added its own active handling system called ATD, which used active centre and rear differentials to control the torque split between the front and rear of the car and across the rear axle.

The P2 weighed substantially less than the Impreza (1,100kg), giving it a power-to-weight ratio of around 350PS per tonne. Prodrive said it expected the P2 to do 0–62mph in under four seconds and go on to a top speed of 174mph.

The two-seater bodywork and interior were styled by Peter Stevens. Most of the bodywork was in composite material, but it very cleverly used the centre tub of the Subaru R1 (a four-seater microcar sold in Japan), which was completely re-engineered to accommodate the new engine and drivetrain. Despite these humble origins, the sharp styling was well very received by the motoring press. There had been a major focus on weight reduction, but the P2 remained plush enough to boast a six-speaker hi-fi, power-assisted steering and electric windows.

The whole P2 project was realised at Prodrive's facilities at Banbury and Warwick. Despite it being a fully functioning car, which was seen being driven on TV shows, Prodrive declared that it had no plans to put the car into production. However it said that, "should a vehicle manufacturer approach the company" to produce the P2, the price would be around £40,000. After the firecrackers of its 2006 debut, however, the P2 project was quietly forgotten.

Type RA-R roars in

The so-called Revision G for the 2007 Model Year was the last hurrah for the second-generation Impreza. This was only a minor upgrade for the Japanese STi and STi Spec C, featuring a slightly larger VF43 turbo and revised gearing for the six-speed manual gearbox. The 2007 STi also used top-feed injectors instead of side-feed ones, which impacted the design of the intake manifold and tumble valve generators.

Much more extreme was Japan's October 2006 Impreza swansong – a car with one hell of a mouthful of a name: Impreza WRX STi Spec C Type RA-R. Fittingly for the last Impreza of the GD line, the RA-R was a real hard nut of an STi, created for maximum fun at track days but still capable of being used on the road. The final 'R' in the RA-R name either stood for 'Racy' or 'Radical' depending on

← A deep breath was needed to pronounce the name of Subaru's swansong GD Impreza, the STi Spec C Type RA-R. This was a hard track day toy that could still be used happily on the road.

whose true-or-bluff you wanted to believe.

Its specification really was hardcore. As per the Spec C, unnecessary creature comforts such as air con, hi-fi and airbags were dismissed, as were the STi's boot spoiler and rooftop aero vanes. To cut weight further – by some 70kg compared to the regular STi – Subaru used lightweight glass, thinner-gauge roof metal and an aluminium bootlid.

Most attention was paid to the chassis. Changes included reinforced struts, braces, lowering springs, four-way adjustable inverted dampers, pillowball bushes, special STi rear links and thicker anti-roll bars. Specially made white 18x8.5 Enkei alloys were wrapped in Bridgestone Potenza RE070 235/40 rubber. The result was extremely grippy traction and excellent turn-in, if a rather crashy ride.

The RA-R became the first Japanese production car to be fitted with Brembo monoblock six-piston front callipers (although the callipers were actually branded 'STi'); the grooved discs were designed and built specially for the RA-R by Brembo to a pattern inspired by the Super Endurance Impreza racer.

The RA-R shared its 2.0-litre engine with the S204, meaning 320PS and 318lb ft of torque thanks to a remapped ECU, twin-scroll ball bearing turbo, streamlined intake duct and a different exhaust system for better low-rev response. It was even quicker than the S204 because it weighed less (1,390kg).

It looked very distinctive with its white wheels, front lip spoiler and red-outlined front centre grille, and was available in three colours: WR Rally Blue Mica, Pure White or Yellow (the latter limited to 50 units). Sold only in Japan, it retailed at 4.2

million yen with only 300 examples built in all, each one snapped up eagerly by enthusiasts. Options included different BBS alloy wheels, carbon-fibre rear wing and the special Recaro seats could be upgraded to full race seats.

Last gasps: RB320 & GB270

The RA-R had a kind of equivalent in the UK in the form of the RB320, announced in November 2006, although its specification was distinctly different. The 'RB' referred to Richard Burns because this was Subaru's tribute to the former Subaru rally champion who died in November 2005 of brain cancer at the age of 32.

Fittingly, the RB320 had possibly the best all-round specification of any Impreza to date. Its engine was the STi 2.5-litre unit boosted with a PPP to 320PS and 332lb ft. Special features

↑ ↑ The RA-R's 2.0-litre engine offered 320PS and 318lb ft of torque thanks to a remapped ECU, twin-scroll turbo, new intake ducting and an uprated exhaust.

↑ The RA-R has become widely accepted as the most desirable of the Japanese market 'GD' series Imprezas.

included a quickshift gearchange, bespoke 18in alloy wheels and specially developed Prodrive suspension comprising Bilstein dampers, a sports spring kit (lowered by 30mm at the front and 10mm at the rear) and a revised rear anti-roll bar.

It looked utterly unique with its chrome mesh front grille, front lip spoiler, side sill plates and Obsidian Black paint with bright orange decals. Inside were an RB320-branded gearknob, special carpet mats and an individually numbered black alloy tax disc holder.

The cost was £29,995, some £3,500 more than the STi, and there was no shortage of customers. The first RB320 was given away in a raffle in *Autosport* magazine, the proceeds of which went to the Richard Burns Foundation; the following 50 customers being invited to a special celebrity driveaway and track day at Prodrive's Warwickshire circuit.

Many enthusiasts now look on the RB320 as perhaps the ultimate UK-market Impreza but it wasn't the last 'GD' variant. That was announced in July 2007 in the form of the GB270 – a final edition version of the WRX. Named after Rally GB and the 270PS Prodrive-uprated engine, the GB270 looked good and went very well indeed. That was thanks to near-STi levels of power from the Prodrive Performance Pack, which gave the WRX 270PS and 310lb ft. That was good enough for 0–60mph in 5.3 seconds plus great mid-range response. Lowering springs, larger-diameter 18x7.5

GTi alloy wheels and a quickshift gearchange sharpened the driving experience.

Saloon and Sports Wagon versions were offered, both with special mats, Momo Air-Race gearknob, GB270 badging and a numbered plaque. Specific to the GB270 saloon were a WRC-style rear spoiler, stainless-steel mesh front grille, STi front lip spoiler and silver-finished alloy wheels. The Sports Wagon version, meanwhile, received a rear waist spoiler, front and rear aero splash guards, rear privacy glass, black stainless-steel mesh front grille and gloss-black alloy wheels.

Options included a Clarion sat nav/iPod/Bluetooth phone kit system, GB270-branded leather or Alcantara/leather interior and privacy glass for the saloon. The £22,995 price tag was £2,898 more than the standard WRX saloon and £1,898 more than the WRX wagon, but Subaru claimed the GB270 offered around £7,000 worth of extra equipment. Only 300 saloons and 100 Sports Wagons were made, the first deliveries occurring in September 2007, just weeks before the all-new Impreza went on sale in the UK.

Around the world

Australia has long enjoyed a love affair with the Impreza, and has had many of its own unique models. One such was the WRP10 of early 2005. The 'WR' denoted World Rally, 'P' Pirelli and '10' the number of years the Impreza had been sold in Australia (also, perhaps, it sounded a bit like 'Warp 10'). An STi Performance Package boosted the power to 238PS, the suspension was lowered by 15 mm and there were gunmetal STi alloy wheels with Pirelli P Zero Nero tyres. Only 200 numbered cars were built.

Aussie Imprezas switched to the 2.5-litre engine with the Hawkeye facelift and the range included the naturally aspirated RS as well as the turbocharged WRX and STi. One unique Aussie model was the RS-X, a non-turbo 2.5 Impreza with some WRX components, such as the wheels and brakes. Another was the WRX Club Spec Evo 9 of 2006 with its 18in wheels, STi suspension kit, STi front lip spoiler, quickshift gear lever and leather trim. A similar 'WRX Tuned by STi' model of 2007 also had an STi ECU upgrade, lifting the power to 243PS.

In the USA, late 2005 saw the MY06 Hawkeye range launched. A new 2.0R replaced the old RS, switching from a 2.5-litre to a 2.0-litre engine, although it had more power. The WRX, meanwhile, went in the other direction, switching from 2.0 to 2.5 litres. The automatic transmission option was dropped from the WRX at this time but returned in a special 'Limited' package in 2006 which also included heated leather seats, heated mirrors, heated wiper blades and a glass roof. The American STi (still with a 2.5-litre engine) got wider (17x8) wheels.

In early 2006, Subaru in the USA recognised the vast market for tuning by releasing a special WRX specifically for tuning. The WRX TR (Tuner Ready) was priced low at $23,995 and allowed owners to add custom parts themselves. Subaru USA offered a wide selection of performance parts, such as suspension, stiffening bars and gear levers. The TR had a more basic spec than the regular WRX (single-disc CD, non-auto climate control, different side skirts, optional foglights and non-painted door mirrors) but kept its 230PS 2.5-litre engine.

The 2007 US-spec STi ditched the Spec C control arms it had used in favour of standard JDM STi aluminium arms. Other suspension changes included a higher caster angle (and therefore a marginally shorter wheelbase), smaller rear anti-roll bar, longer second, third and fourth gear ratios, redesigned cylinder heads to improve cooling, no sodium-filled exhaust valves, a VF43 turbo, revised ECU and top-feed injectors. Finally, a new STi Limited model mimicked the Japanese A-Line spec, but used 2007MY US-spec STi mechanicals; 800 were produced.

← **Stripped-out look dominates the US WRX TR (Tuner Ready) edition, designed for owners to add their own custom parts.**

← **The very last GD-series Impreza in the UK was the GB270, a special edition offered in saloon and wagon guises. Based on the WRX, it benefited from near-STi power levels (270PS).**

CHAPTER 7
HATCHED: THE NEW IMPREZA

If Impreza enthusiasts had been unsettled by Subaru's sometimes baffling design direction with the second-generation Impreza, they were in for a real shock with the all-new third-generation model.

That shock came in April 2007 when Subaru announced that its all-new Impreza would be a hatchback. In itself this was perhaps no surprise – the Impreza Sports Wagon body style had been an essential part of the Impreza line-up since day one – but the real change came with the announcement that the range-topping STi would be a hatchback and nothing but a hatchback.

The public had been softened up for this revolution as early as the October 2005 Tokyo Motor Show, when Subaru showed the B5-TPH Turbo Parallel Hybrid concept car. This four-wheel drive boxer/electric hybrid used a 256bhp 2.0-litre flat-four engine combined with an electric motor mounted between the engine and transmission, fed by a manganese lithium-ion battery. While the technology wasn't in Subaru's immediate product plans, the hatchback idea was. And although the B5-TPH was a three-door hatch, it could definitely be seen as an indicator of Fuji's future design direction.

The new Impreza GE got its debut at the New York International Auto Show in April 2007 ahead of a summertime on-sale date globally. Subaru's clear intention with the new Impreza was to make it more of a rounded, comfortable, everyday car – in essence, a Volkswagen Golf competitor rather than a roadgoing rally car. As it said, "to compete more directly in the European market with rivals such as the Honda Civic, VW Golf and Mazda 3 while offering the added safety and traction advantage of symmetrical all-wheel drive."

The new Impreza was 50mm shorter than the previous Sport Wagon, despite having a 95mm longer wheelbase, while it was also wider. The body was much stiffer than before thanks to more use of high-tension steel and reinforced

joints. Subaru also said that this was a far stronger bodyshell as far as crashworthiness was concerned.

Also for the first time ever, an Impreza had windows with frames on them, finally abandoning what had become a quaint Japanese tradition for the 'hardtop sedan'. Aerodynamics were improved, too, down from 0.36 to 0.34 in the base 1.5R version, for example. Most models were also lighter than their predecessors.

In design terms, Subaru completely ditched the old family nose for a whole new look, featuring sleek, low-line headlights and a more restrained grille. A tailgate spoiler was standard on all models, while also new were LED tail lamps in clear shells (another styling touch that proved to be controversial).

Most onlookers found it difficult to agree with Subaru's claim that the new Impreza had "a perfectly proportioned body, well calculated panel curves that reflect light and shadow in harmony, and quality details" and that it offered "elegant, restrained design." To many commentators, it was both dumpy and frumpy.

It was clearly more practical, though. Not only was it easier to get into and out of thanks to larger door openings but the cabin also offered significantly more space for passengers, partly because of the

← It would be an understatement to say that not everyone liked the design of the all-new 2007 Impreza, which was designed to have a broader appeal for the 'average' buyer.

↙ The new STi was exclusively offered in five-door hatchback form, but the shell was claimed to be stiffer than the old four-door STi.

↓ An early precursor of the new Impreza was this 2005 Tokyo Motor Show concept, the B5-TPH Turbo Parallel Hybrid. The hatchback format was as an indicator of Subaru's future plans for the Impreza.

and offered enough room for two golf bags.

The Impreza has always been about driving dynamics, but there was a new slant in Subaru's PR spiel for the new-shape GE car: comfort. In a typically bland mission statement, Fuji stated that: "Subaru offers a comfortable, pleasant drive for the driver and passengers; provides peace of mind and reliability; and extends convenience, utility and functionality."

There was one other distinct new direction with the Impreza – extra driver aids. Subaru had always vaunted its all-wheel drive as a great safety boon but the widespread fitment of traction control systems on competitors forced Subaru to follow the electronic stability control route with the new Impreza. Its Vehicle Dynamics Control (VDC) was a first for Subaru. This intervened when excessive wheel slippage was detected, and could be deactivated in two stages via a button on the dashboard.

As for the chassis, the front end now shared many components with the Legacy, while the brakes were taken directly from the Legacy. It was at the back end that things really changed, though. Gone was the old Impreza's MacPherson rear suspension, to be replaced by a newly designed double-wishbone multilink set-up. Subaru gave three reasons for this: it offered improved geometry and hence roadholding; it improved ride comfort; and it reduced intrusion into the boot, boosting luggage space. Subaru also said that by mounting the engine and transmission 10mm lower in the platform, the new car had a lower centre of gravity.

↑ **This is how the new WRX looked inside. The curvy dash design was inspired by the Subaru Tribeca's, and although quality was much improved, road testers criticised it for falling behind class standards.**

↓ **Subaru created this 'Subaglue' marketing gimmick to launch the new Impreza. As well as all-wheel drive, the new model got Vehicle Dynamics Control for the first time in any Subaru.**

longer wheelbase but also because the cabin was some 45mm wider.

Speaking of the cabin, Subaru made special efforts to improve its appeal. The curved dash design echoed that of the Subaru Tribeca, although overall there was perhaps nothing very daring in the design work. Dark fabrics and plastics were the order of the day, only alleviated by metallic silver inserts, with double-stitched seat fabrics raising the feeling of quality.

Due to new double-wishbone rear suspension (more of which below), there was extra room for luggage compared to the old Sports Wagon: up to 538 litres with the rear seat upright. It had 60/40 split/fold rear seats

Japanese launch range

The Japanese domestic market range was launched in June 2007. It started with two non-turbo models: the 15S using the 110PS 1.5-litre EL15 engine, and the 20S using the 140PS EJ20 2.0-litre unit. These were offered in Japan in front-wheel drive versions, as well as all-wheel drive – a surprising move, perhaps, for a company with so much invested in the format of four driven wheels.

The most powerful version at launch was the turbocharged S-GT. This was the replacement for the old WRX and marked the first time that the Japanese market had ever done without a WRX-badged Impreza. Some reports suggested that Subaru dropped the WRX badge because it had a negative stigma for the intended new target audience. In fact, the WRX badge would eventually be restored in Japan, only to be dropped again and the model renamed 2.0GT!

Unlike European and US turbo models, which switched to 2.5-litre engines, the S-GT reprised the familiar turbocharged EJ20 series 1,994cc engine. This was more closely related to the Legacy's engine than the previous Impreza's. Subaru cited better torque low down and a flatter torque curve thanks to the revised intake manifolds and a new twin-scroll turbocharger. Power peaked at pretty much the same level as the old WRX - 250PS at 6,000rpm – while maximum torque was 246lb ft at 2,400rpm. This gave the S-GT effortless performance across its rev range, in contrast to the rather more explosive nature of the previous WRX. It was certainly much livelier than the 230PS WRX that would soon be sold in the UK.

The five-speed gearbox had quite long-ratio gears, which made life on board more comfortable and mature, but perhaps a little watered down and less exciting. Four-speed automatic transmission was also available in the S-GT from launch.

The S-GT carried on the turbo tradition of a bonnet scoop to feed air to the top-mounted intercooler, as well as a more aggressive air dam, side skirts and spoilers. A keyless entry system with an engine start/stop button was optional.

Japanese domestic sales were initially very promising: the 3,829 examples sold in the first week represented a 50 per cent hike over the planned sales target for the whole month. At first, only the hatchback body shape was sold in Japan, but from

↑ The all-new STi was launched at Fuji Speedway in Japan, where the new model banished fears that it would disappoint Impreza enthusiasts. This was a real STi, possibly the best yet.

2008, the four-door saloon body style seen in the USA made a domestic appearance badged as the Impreza Anesis. However, the Anesis was only ever a non-turbo model with 1.5- or 2.0-litre engines.

Impreza hits Europe

Subaru's new Impreza went on sale in Europe in September 2007, initially in a range of entirely non-turbo models. For example, the UK range consisted of three naturally aspirated versions: the 1.5R (priced at a very competitive £12,495), 2.0R and 2.0RX. As ever with Imprezas, every version had all-wheel drive but the 1.5R also included a dual-range manual transmission with a low-ratio transfer box.

The 2.0-litre 2.0R added 16-inch alloy wheels, Vehicle Dynamics Control, xenon headlamps and heated door mirrors. The 2.0RX got a body styling kit (front and rear spoilers, side skirts, chrome exhaust end-cap and rear bumper diffuser), 17in alloy wheels, sat nav, keyless entry, leather steering wheel and gearknob, cruise control and a 10-speaker audio system. 2.0-litre models could also be ordered with automatic transmission for £1,000 extra.

Two months after the non-turbo Impreza launch, in November 2007, the long-awaited turbocharged version arrived in Europe in selected markets such as the UK and Switzerland. In fact, the WRX very nearly did not arrive on European soil at all: Subaru head office had originally not wanted to offer the WRX but European demand was definitely there. The sub-STi turbo model in Europe would continue to be badged WRX, unlike the Japanese S-GT.

Again in contrast to the Japanese-market S-GT, the WRX used not a 2.0-litre engine but virtually the same 2.5-litre EJ25 unit that had made it into European Imprezas in 2005. Indeed, the WRX spec differed very little in the new-shape car: peak power and torque figures were identical but arrived slightly lower down the rev range (power was 230PS at 5,200rpm and torque 236lb ft at 2,800rpm). The EJ25 engine was mated to a five-speed manual gearbox with revised ratios and a lower final drive (which had the effect of making the WRX rather buzzy at motorway speeds).

There was criticism that the new WRX's performance was relatively poor. Its top speed of 130mph and 0–62mph time of 6.1 seconds were decent but not as good, for example, as the original Impreza Turbo of 1994.

More criticism surrounded the handling. In part this was down to a relative lack of stiffness: a five-door shell is inherently less stiff than a saloon's and the WRX didn't enjoy the compensation of the soon-to-be-launched STi's substantial stiffening. The suspension was also set very soft to make the ride appeal to a wider audience and in consequence the body rolled quite a lot. The fast-acting but dead-feeling steering underwhelmed and there was lots of initial understeer. The WRX did offer excellent grip, however, while handling neutrality built up confidently after the initial turn-in. The new mechanical limited-slip rear diff (the old one had been viscous) helped keep it firmly on-line when powering out of bends, while the switchable electronic stability control never felt intrusive.

The author, in his WRX test for *Japanese Performance* magazine, stated: "It's hard to escape the conclusion that the WRX is targeted at the mainstream hot hatch market rather than traditional Impreza fans. Its appeal is clearly wider than the old saloon's: it's more practical, softer-riding and quieter. But is that really what you want from an Impreza?"

Subaru UK announced that "a limited quantity" of the WRX would be available – a suggested maximum of 1,000 – and, once sold, that would be that. Effectively, therefore, it was a special edition – a kind of holding model until the STi arrived. The new WRX was priced competitively at £19,995, less than the previous WRX, but even so it sold relatively poorly in the UK.

STi goes five-door

It didn't take Subaru long to bring the STi to the all-new Impreza party: the range-topping and iconic STi debuted at the Tokyo Auto Show in October 2007.

The biggest single sea-change regarding the new Impreza STi was that it would only be offered as a hatchback, not a saloon. If that raised alarm bells, Subaru was ready to silence them. When the author spoke to the STi project manager, Hiroshi Mori, at the car's launch, he said that the biggest

→ **The UK-only WRX-S was a kind of 'STi light' model with 255PS, 0–60mph in 5.5 seconds and chunky 7.5x18 GT1 anthracite wheels with low-profile 225/40 tyres.**

single advance was the five-door body packaging, which was stiffer than the previous four-door STi body.

In looks, the STi bore a deliberate resemblance to the 2008 WRC rally car (which had already been previewed in concept form). The wheelarches were flared like the rally car's and stylistically linked by bold side skirts and bulging body pressings that were unique to the STi. A deeper front bumper was topped off by a mesh grille and vertical air vents that fed cool air to the intercooler (mounted as ever atop the engine). Hot air exited through slashes in the front wings, passing little 'STi' flashes as it went. At the rear end, a lower diffuser reduced high-speed lift, while downforce was boosted by a rear spoiler mounted on the tailgate. Four exhaust tailpipes added a sense of drama.

The Japanese STi line-up only came with 18in wheels, although other markets (including Europe) would get 17in versions as standard. Japanese buyers could choose from two styles: a chunky five-spoke design or a BBS multispoke (offered in gold, silver or dark grey). Bridgestone 245/40x18 tyres were specified in Japan, whereas EU cars got

235-section Dunlops. Inside, the STi got standard leather-and-Alcantara seat trim (deeply bucketed and very supportive Recaros were optional), while curtain airbags were now standard.

As for the mechanical side, the Japanese STi stuck with the EJ20 2.0-litre engine fitted with a twin-scroll turbocharger. It had a higher torque output than the 2.5-litre version (311lb ft) but it wasn't delivered until a lofty 4,400rpm, some 400rpm higher than the EJ25. It was the same with power: 308PS at 6,400rpm versus the EU STi's 300PS at 6,000rpm.

For the first time, Subaru's 'Si-Drive' made an appearance on an Impreza, taken from the Legacy 3.0R Spec B. This gave you the option to switch between three different engine maps: Intelligent, Sharp and Sports Sharp. These were set by a rotary dial next to the gear lever. Each mode made a noticeable difference to the way the throttle responded, the torque/power curves and the amount of fuel used.

Another driver aid was more familiar to STi drivers: the Driver Controlled Centre Differential (DCCD). As before, this allowed you to dial in the

↓ **Si-Drive was a new arrival on the STi, offering a choice of three engine maps to boost either fuel economy or performance. There was also a choice of manual or automatic functions for the centre differential.**

proportion of torque directed to the front and rear axles, but the old thumbwheel was replaced by an up-down switch. You also now had the option of switching to automatic mode. In fact, there were three different presets: normal Auto mode, Auto+ (emphasising traction in slippery conditions and favouring straight-line stability), and Auto- (enhancing turn-in during cornering). Alternatively you could switch to manual and vary the torque split yourself.

The six-speed gearbox was carried over from the previous STi but with some revisions. The lever had less distance to travel between gears and got better synchromesh for lighter gearchanges.

Although the new STi's wheelbase was 95mm longer than the previous generation, overall length was shorter by 50mm, thanks to smaller front and rear overhangs. This combined with tracks some 45mm wider at the front and 40mm at the rear, plus a lower centre of gravity because the engine sat 22mm lower and the differential 10mm lower. As before, the STi got inverted front suspension struts (in contrast to other members of the Impreza clan) plus aluminium lower wishbones, but in more rigid mounts than before, with less propensity for camber change. The Impreza's new multi-link rear suspension was kept for the STi.

The STi used Brembo four-pot callipers up front and two-pots at the rear, clasping ventilated discs on all four corners. Together with four-channel ABS and Electronic Brakeforce Distribution, they worked sharply. And the STi had its own version of Vehicle Dynamics Control System operated by a little button to the right of the steering wheel. You could turn the system off or to a half-way 'Traction' mode that delayed its onset.

The press was split over the new STi. Some thought its broader appeal was to be welcomed, while others thought it had become less raw and hard-edged. The author said: "It's improved in significant ways: it's easier to live with, has extra safety features, a better gearchange and a classier interior. However, it's certainly not perfect. The sound the car makes is pretty muted, for example, and Subaru has perhaps missed its opportunity to use all those extra driver aids to eliminate the STi's understeer. But there's plenty to celebrate: the excellent grip, uncanny balance and phenomenal performance that have always marked out the STi remain undiminished."

Europe's 2.5-litre STi

The European-spec STi was first seen in December 2007, when it was launched at the Bologna Motor Show. Its first UK appearance was at the January 2008 Autosport Show in Birmingham, with the first deliveries arriving in March 2008.

As with the previous STi, European buyers got a very different version to the Japanese. Principally this centred around the engine: the 2.5-litre EJ25 engine as opposed to Japan's 2.0-litre EJ20. In fact, the powerplant was one of the least changed features on the new STi. It gained a larger and more efficient intercooler and a new four-exit exhaust system that reduced airflow resistance by a claimed 38 per cent. A single-scroll turbo was retained (in contrast to the Japanese version's twin-scroll turbo), while variable valve timing for the intake and exhaust also remained. Power-wise, the UK car developed 300PS at 6,000rpm, compared to the old STi's 276PS and the JDM car's 308PS. Torque was also up, by 11lb ft compared to the old STi, to 300lb ft at 4,000rpm. The top speed was a claimed 155mph and the 0–60mph 4.8 seconds. Fuel consumption was better than the old model at 27.4mpg in the combined cycle.

The new STi was launched at £24,995, some £1,600 less than the old STi and, crucially, £2,500 less than its arch-rival, the new Mitsubishi Evo X. UK standard equipment included cruise control, curtain airbags, 8x17 alloy wheels with 235/45 tyres, HID headlamps, Alcantara-and-leather front seats, climate control and six-disc CD autochanger. Options included 18in wheels with 245/40 tyres.

Prodrive gets involved

It took until the July 2008 British International Motor Show for Prodrive's work on the new Impreza to reach the public. There was a spectacular trio of Prodrive-modified Imprezas: WRX-S, 330S and 380S.

The first of the three, the WRX-S, was a new special edition Impreza for the UK market, offering more power and equipment. Based on the WRX, the 'S' model offered a claimed £4,500 worth of extras for a £2,500 premium (£22,495).

Prodrive was called in to reprogramme the ECU and modify the exhaust system. The direct result of

The July 2008 British Motor Show saw the unveiling of this Prodrive-developed STi 380S concept, with an intended 380PS power output thanks to a complete engine overhaul. The 380S also received uprated suspension and 18x8.5 BBS alloy wheels. Sadly, economic conditions relegated it to the back-burner and it never made production.

this was a jump in power from 230PS at 5,200rpm to 255PS at 5,400rpm, while torque rose from 236lb ft at 2,800rpm to 287.6lb ft at 3,000rpm. The claimed top speed was the same (130mph) but 0–60mph came up in 5.5 seconds (WRX 6.1 seconds), with greater in-gear flexibility as well.

There were no suspension changes for the WRX-S but it gained larger 7.5x18 GT1 anthracite wheels with wider and lower-profile 225/40 tyres (the WRX had 7x17 alloys with 205/50 rubber). The WRX-S looked rather like an 'STi lite' with its STi front grille, STi front lip spoiler and STi rear wing, even though it retained the narrow-arch WRX body. Inside there was a Momo Air-Race gearknob and WRX-S branded seats and mats.

The *Japanese Performance* magazine road test concluded: "There's huge grip here and the 'S' likes to attack bends. Yes, it still understeers but it feels much more confident, and the new wheel/tyre choice hasn't affected the ride quality."

Also at the July 2008 British Show was the new STi 330S. This was the equivalent of the old Prodrive Performance Pack STi, including Prodrive's tweaks to the engine and exhaust. Modifying the ECU and using paired twin 90mm diameter stainless steel exhaust pipes, Subaru claimed that it would "bring back the burble so loved by Scooby fans."

Power rose to 330PS at 5,400rpm compared to the standard STi's 300.5PS at 6,000rpm; torque was boosted from 300.2lb ft at 4,000rpm to 346.6lb ft at 3,400rpm. The 0–60mph sprint time dropped from 4.8 seconds to 4.4 seconds.

Priced at £30,345, the new 330S had lots of luxury touches, including leather-faced Recaro front seats, sat nav and push-button start. Visually, the

330S boasted new five-spoke 18x8.5 alloy wheels wearing 245/40 R18 tyres and one or two unique paint colour options.

It was very well received. Ben Barry in *Car* magazine said: "We'd pretty much given up on extracting any pleasure from the new Impreza. Then we drove the new 330S and – shock, horror – it's very good indeed." The author also ran a 330S for a year for *Japanese Performance* magazine and concluded "Overall, the 330S proves that the Impreza remains one of the great performance cars. In fact, I'm now firmly of the opinion that it's the best all-round Impreza that Subaru has ever made. Not only is it extremely fast, it's also got compliant suspension, a practical layout and easy-to-live-with refinement. The only slight disappointment is that the current STi hasn't significantly moved the game on."

Also at the July 2008 British Motor Show was the spectacular STi 380S concept. As its name hinted, this had a target power output of no less than 380PS, which would have made it the most powerful production Impreza ever. Prodrive's modifications for the 380S included a complete engine rebuild with many uprated components, including a new exhaust system. Also there was uprated suspension and bodywork tweaks. It was planned to offer either gold or silver 18x8.5 BBS alloy wheels with 245/40 tyres.

Subaru said tantalisingly: "The 380S could reach dealers within six months pending positive response. Its final specification will be finalised following customer input and will be hand-built to order." However, despite a fully functional prototype being built and extensively tested by Prodrive, the 380S never made it to market: it simply became a victim of economic conditions. Instead it was put on display in the foyer of Prodrive's Warwickshire test HQ.

In due course, Prodrive also offered upgraded aftermarket parts for the STi, including 19in alloy wheels with 235/35 Pirelli tyres, a quickshift kit, lowering springs and various bodywork dress-up items.

↑ To most people, a turbocharged Impreza means a fire-breathing rally escapee, but the turbodiesel-powered Impreza Boxer Diesel brought flat-four engineering to a whole new type of customer.

← Prodrive leapt on the new STi and helped create the 330S for UK buyers. As its name suggested, power was now 330PS, while its luxury spec included leather Recaro seats and sat nav.

→ Sumptuous leather swathed the A-Line's cabin.

Impreza Boxer Diesel

A new type of turbocharged Impreza arrived at the September 2008 Paris Motor Show: a turbodiesel. Despite some speculation that this version might wear WRX badges, in fact it went on sale with simple 'Boxer Diesel' badging.

It used Subaru's flat-four diesel engine, which had first been seen in the Legacy. This was a 1,998cc unit with 150PS and 350Nm (258lb ft) of torque whose flat-four layout (a world first in a car) endowed it with unusual smoothness. However, its raw power was too weak to make it a real performer, topping out at 127mph and managing 0–62mph in 9.0 seconds. It used a new six-speed gearbox with a wide spread of ratios, so motorway cruising was very relaxed.

The diesel Impreza went on sale in several European countries in early 2009, although the UK did not receive it until September 2009, where it was priced from £20,000.

2009: anniversary year

2009 marked the 20th year of Subaru's rally effort and the company decided to celebrate with a special edition STi in Japan. The sad irony that Subaru pulled out of world rallying in December 2008, just ahead of the 2009 season, was not lost on pundits.

A precursor of the forthcoming 20th Anniversary model had been seen in October 2008 at Tokyo's Motorsport Japan show with the STi Takumi Concept. Small visual differences included a blacked-out rear spoiler, front lip spoiler and 12-spoke wheels. This spec was pretty much carried over to the real thing, the STi 20th Anniversary launched for 2009. Subaru Tecnica International built only 300 examples, all in white, and all for Japan. As well as extrovert 12-spoke 18in wheels, a matt black roof spoiler and a front lip spoiler, the cabin was upgraded with red-stitched Recaro seats, leather gearknob and a red start/stop button. Keeping the STi 2.0-litre turbo engine untouched, the special edition did, however, get a chassis makeover: different springs and dampers and front arms with special bushing were claimed to sharpen up the handling and improve ride quality.

In February 2009 came another Impreza variant: the STi A-Line. This brought automatic transmission to the Impreza STi for the very first time. While this may seem anathema to European enthusiasts, in Japan automatic transmission has always been the default choice of the market. Mitsubishi had successfully marketed a GT-A version of its Lancer Evolution with an automatic gearbox and Subaru decided to follow suit.

The A-Line marked the first time a JDM Impreza STi had ever used the 2.5-litre single-scroll version of the EJ turbo engine, which developed 300PS at 6,200rpm and 258lb ft at 2,800rpm. But the big news was the transmission: a so-called 'Sportshift' five-speed automatic sourced from the Legacy (Sportshift was actually a registered trademark of Prodrive).

You could change gears fully automatically, or select a manual change option with the gear lever, or use paddle-shift controls by the steering wheel. A 'Downshifting Blipping Control' system interacted with the engine management to blip the throttle on downchanges to match revs to the gear. Si-Drive and All-Wheel Drive systems remained

↓ ↓ **The STi A-Line was a new niche for Subaru: a plush automatic-transmission STi with, uniquely for Japan, a 2.5-litre engine.**

↓ **The A-Line's Sportshift five-speed automatic featured 'Downshifting Blipping Control' to blip the throttle on downchanges.**

but the DCCD system did not, so the centre console switching was different.

The A-Line got an extra dose of comfort in the form of eight-way power adjustable front seats (with optional leather and heating) plus leather door trims with silver stitching, while you could order a new body colour called Satin White Pearl.

Return of the Spec C

July 2009 saw the debut of the all-new version of a legendary badge – the Spec C. For fans of the hardest version of the Impreza, this was the moment of truth: would it be as good as previous versions?

On paper, the STi Spec C was just as hardcore as the previous Spec C, boasting engine and chassis

The 'Toyobaru' coupe

In April 2008, Toyota told the world that it would be doubling its financial stake in Fuji Heavy Industries to 16.5 per cent. It took this moment as an opportunity to announce that Toyota and Subaru were already working on a joint project to create a compact rear-wheel drive two-door coupe together. Both brands would share development but produce its own distinct version of the sports coupe.

So what's the Impreza connection? One thing for sure was that the new car was scheduled to use Subaru's flat-four engine, in the form of the next generation unit (dubbed C-45) equipped with Toyota D4-S direct port injection.

Although the details were speculative at the time of writing, it was thought that Toyota would use a 2.0-litre naturally aspirated version of the engine, with

Subaru more likely to use a turbocharger. Speculation also surrounded whether Subaru's coupe would feature all-wheel drive, taking it more up-market than the Toyota.

Toyota's version was previewed at the October 2009 Tokyo Show, when it presented a concept car called the FT-86 (a name that reflected its inspiration, the AE86 Corolla GT). Although some sources said that the car would use an all-new platform, it was widely believed that the joint project would be based on a modified Subaru Impreza platform. The FT-86's dimensions were quoted as 4,160mm long, 1,760mm wide and 1,260mm tall, while its wheelbase of 2,570mm did perhaps suggest a slightly shortened Impreza chassis.

The plan was to introduce the new coupe by the end of 2011, with both Subaru and Toyota versions assembled in a new factory at Subaru's Gunma Manufacturing Division.

No it's not a Subaru – this is Toyota's FT-86 concept as shown at the 2009 Tokyo Motor Show, marking the first public outing for the Subaru/Toyota coupe joint project.

tweaks and lightweight parts. The turbocharger featured special ball bearings and the ECU was uniquely tuned, resulting in quicker throttle response and improved acceleration. Intercooler water spray made a reappearance, too, reducing intake temperatures, and there was a special fuel pump to cope with increased cornering forces. The 2.0-litre engine's maximum output was 308PS at 6,400rpm and 422Nm (311lb ft) at 4,400rpm.

In the chassis department, the Spec C received a reinforced front crossmember, new rates for the dampers and springs, more rigid bushes in the rear sub-frame and anti-roll bar and a switch from Torsen rear limited-slip differential to a mechanical type. Also, Bridgestone Potenza RE070 245/40 R18 were selected and, to firm up steering feel, Subaru increased oil flow volume in the power steering system.

Lightening the Spec C involved fitting an aluminium bonnet, smaller battery, thinner glass in the front and side windows, lightweight 18in alloy wheels (optional 17in) and no spare tyre.

Other small details included gold Brembo brake callipers and bucket front seats with red stitching (on 18in-wheel cars, optionally Alcantara-and-leather Recaros). Five colours were available, including WR Blue, silver and black, plus two that were exclusive to the Spec C: Sunrise Yellow and Pure White. Subaru announced that it would only be making 900 units.

Autocar's test commented: "Gun it in second, third or fourth from about 4,000rpm on and the pick-up is instant, relentless and frankly gob smacking all the way to the 8,000rpm red line… Bottom line: this is the best-sorted new-shape STi to date."

One final curious surprise of 2009 was the STi Carbon. Released at the October 2009 Tokyo Motor Show, the STi Carbon sounded like a lightweight hardcore version but was in fact a curiously mixed-up Japan-only special edition with a carbon-fibre roof, suede seats and five-speed automatic transmission. The carbon roof, Subaru claimed, reduced weight and lowered the centre of gravity.

Then in January 2010 came the latest 'ultimate' special edition, the STi R205, the new-shape equivalent of the legendary S204. The extra 'R' stood, said Subaru, for 'Road Sport', and the R205 made use of many Spec C items, as well as drawing on Subaru's experience fielding an Impreza in the 2009 Nürburgring 24-hour race.

The R205's engine was even more powerful than the Spec C's, boasting 320PS at 6,400rpm and 431Nm (317lb ft) at 4,000rpm. This was thanks to a ball bearing twin-scroll turbocharger, specially tuned ECU and sports exhaust with lower back pressure. The handling side was addressed with uprated dampers, springs, a

↓ The STi's twin-scroll turbocharger received special ball bearings in the Spec C.

↑ Intercooler water spray made a reappearance in the Spec C's engine bay, reducing intake temperatures.

← The spirit of the old S203 and S204 was revived in the hatchback STi with the R205 edition of 2010.

↑ → A four-door Impreza certainly did exist in new-shape form, but only in the US was it was marketed (at least initially) in turbocharged WRX guise. The US Impreza WRX had a 2.5-litre engine with 224PS and 226lb ft – actually slightly down on the previous WRX.

flexible strut tower bar, flexible front lower arm stiffener and Bridgestone RE070 tyres.

Distinguishing the R205 were new front and rear under-spoilers, uniquely profiled black rear spoiler, exclusive 18in alloy wheels, black front grille and black side STi garnishes. Inside were the inevitable R205 serial number plates, indicating that only 400 units were built.

Imprezas around the world

It was not Japanese buyers but the American public who were the first in the world to see the new Impreza, which was launched at the New York Show in April 2007.

Right from the outset, a peculiarity of the US market was the availability of a four-door saloon version as well as the five-door hatchback – the only market to get the saloon initially. The saloon's rear overhang was some 165mm longer than the five-door's, which made its boot quite capacious (it had enough room for three golf bags) and it also boasted 60/40 split/fold rear seats.

While the saloon was never offered in Europe, it did eventually go on sale in Japan and certain

other world markets (it was launched in Japan in 2008 as the Impreza Anesis but never in hot turbocharged form). Subaru also stated clearly that there would never be an STi version of the saloon in this generation, although the US did get a WRX four-door.

All US Imprezas were 2.5-litre models. As well as naturally aspirated EJ253 engines, the US also received an EJ255 2.5-litre turbocharged WRX. The US engine produced 224PS at 5,200rpm and 226lb ft at 2,800rpm (slightly down on the previous WRX but both peak figures arrived lower down the rev range). A five-speed manual gearbox was standard.

One American oddity was the Impreza Outback Sport, basically a cosmetic exercise that aped the Legacy Outback's 'soft-roader' appearance. Mechanically, the Outback Sport was a non-turbo 170PS 2.5i Impreza with a slightly higher ground clearance because of its larger wheels. It had contrasting coloured bumpers, sills, wheelarches and door rubbing strips.

In July 2008, the WRX got an update for the 2009 model year featuring a retuned 2.5-litre engine with 265PS and 244lb ft of torque (41PS and 18lb ft more than the outgoing model). Wider and lower-profile tyres (225/45 R17 versus 205/50 R17) were also announced, while the suspension received stiffer springs, uprated dampers, STi upper strut mounts and larger anti-roll bars. The Aero package now became standard, with the five-door receiving the STi's rear spoiler and underbody diffuser.

Also new in 2008 was the 2.5GT, a model that sat in between the 2.5i and the WRX. It had a turbocharged engine but kept the old output of 224PS, and was only available with automatic transmission. Sold in four- and five-door forms, the 2.5GT was actually $2,000 more expensive than the WRX because of its plusher spec.

It's worth mentioning one final US Impreza: a special one-off built by Subaru of America Inc for factory rally driver Travis Pastrana. Painted in bright yellow '199' livery, the Travis Pastrana WRX STi used Subaru Performance Tuning (SPT) and STi parts in the engine, chassis and interior. The look was boosted by Work alloy wheels with 275/35 ZR18 tyres, PIAA HID driving lights and carbon-fibre bonnet and rear wing. Inside there was custom blue-and-yellow Alcantara upholstery, yellow detail stitching and carbon-fibre style trim highlights.

One of the other major markets for Imprezas – Australia – got the new Impreza GE from September 2007, and it roughly mirrored the European range (initially all hatchbacks). The R, RX and RS used the 2.0-litre engine with 150PS, while Australia's WRX-badged model had the larger 2.5-litre turbo engine with 230PS and manual-only transmission. Australia also got the STi in 2.5-litre form, as well as a so-called STi Spec R variant which added lightweight BBS 18in wheels and leather/Alcantara Recaro seats for an extra $5,000. Then at the Sydney Motor Show in October 2008, the four-door saloon body style was added, including a WRX model.

One Swiss-market oddity was the WRX Swiss S of 2009, a model positioned in between the WRX and STi, rather like the UK WRX-S. However, it had slightly more power, at 265PS, and 343Nm (252lb ft) of torque.

The Impreza's Future

At the time of writing, the Impreza remains very much alive. As of 2009, some 1.7 million Imprezas had been made in a lifespan that stretched over 17 years. That's a remarkable achievement for a 'niche' product like the Impreza. It seems like the steam hasn't gone out of the model yet, for 2007

and 2008 were easily the Impreza's best-ever years for production, totalling 157,202 and 126,690 respectively.

There are signs that enthusiasts are finally coming round to the new Impreza, although its glory days are perhaps overshadowed by Subaru's absence from the World Rally Championship – undoubtedly a blow to the Impreza's standing among fans. However it is still one of the most rallied cars of all time, remaining very active in classes such as Group N.

Some clues to the Impreza's future are perhaps provided by Toyota having recently taken a larger financial stake in Subaru. This could lead to more input from Japan's number one manufacturer, and some cross-fertilisation from joint projects such as the 'Toyobaru' coupe. Whatever the future holds, one thing is for sure: the Impreza's alcove in the motoring history hall of fame has already been well and truly filled.

← American rally driver Travis Pastrana had this special STi built for him by Subaru of America. Lucky him!

↓ The US-only Impreza Outback Sport had a raised ground clearance, larger wheels and duo-tone paint.

CHAPTER 8
THE RALLY STORY

Subaru's achievement in world rallying cannot be underestimated. With the Impreza, it dominated the sport in the mid-1990s and continues to win rallies and challenge strongly for the major titles to this day. Plain and simple, the Subaru World Rally Team is one of the most successful in the history of rallying, and yet Subaru is a relative newcomer to the world rally scene, with all its principal successes packed into just one decade.

The baton of World Rally Championship superiority inexorably passes from one generation to the next. It was Ford in the 1960s, Lancia in the 1970s and late 1980s, and Audi in the early 1980s. As the Lancia Integrale bowed out of the reckoning, a foretaste of the future arrived when, for the first time ever, a Japanese company took up the reins. With Carlos Sainz in the driver's seat, a Toyota scored its first championship win in 1992, although Lancia pulled through to take the manufacturers' title for one last year. But then a new era of Japanese domination was ushered in, as Juha Kankkunen and Dider Auriol helped take Toyota to its first manufacturers' titles in 1993 and 1994.

In 1995 the baton would pass to another Japanese manufacturer: it would finally be the turn of Subaru to conquer what many pundits regard as the toughest racing series in the world. Subaru's Impreza became the car to beat, taking a remarkable three manufacturers' championship titles in succession, and Colin McRae in his Impreza was unbeatable in the double victory year of 1995 – undoubtedly Subaru's highest point to date.

Although competing fully in the World Rally Championship was a 1990s phenomenon for Subaru, Fuji Heavy Industries was not a newcomer to the world of rallying. Indeed its engineering philosophy made it a natural for the gruelling rigours of rally competition: in 1980 Subaru was extremely well placed to take advantage of the coming revolution in rallying, namely four-wheel-

drive. Subaru's 1980 4x4 debut was not on the same scale, however, as the overshadowing and all-conquering presence of that other four-wheel-drive newcomer, the Audi Quattro. But Subaru's first small steps were to pave the way for the Impreza's dominance in the following decade.

In fact, Subaru remains the only manufacturer to have contested the World Championship exclusively with four-wheel-drive cars. Demonstrating its commitment to all-wheel-drive, Subaru even attempted the East African Safari with the tiny, 660cc-engined Vivio 4x4, one of the smallest-engined cars ever to finish the Safari (with, incidentally, a certain Mr McRae at the wheel).

Subaru was ready to compete as soon as all-wheel-drive was permitted in rallying in 1980. Neither did it begin in a half-hearted way, instead diving in at the deep end with the gruelling East African Safari, preparing a 1.6-litre Leone 4WD to contest this high-profile event. Japanese driver Takeshi Hirabayashi finished a respectable 18th overall but victory was there at the outset too, as he scored Subaru's first-ever rally victory by winning Group 1. Despite this being the only event that Subaru entered that year, it was an extremely encouraging start.

Subaru's presence at the East African Safari became a fixture, and its performance improved

← The 1995 RAC Rally gloriously confirmed McRae as the World Champion and Subaru in the manufacturers' title. In second place was Carlos Sainz (right of McRae) and in third Richard Burns (behind). This was the clearest possible clean sweep in Subaru's golden year. (Prodrive)

DAVID LAPWORTH

Prodrive's sublimely gifted rally engineer, David Lapworth, left university and went straight into the world of rally engineering, working as an apprentice at the Peugeot-Talbot team. He collaborated in the development of the famous Talbot Sunbeam Lotus Group B car, which took the 1981 title in the hands of the legendary Henri Toivonen. In 1984, he entered discussions with David Richards, already managing Prodrive at the time, and teamed up with him in March that year, and has worked with Prodrive ever since. His involvement with the Impreza has always been the most intimate. As of the 2000 season, Lapworth took on the role of team principal of SWRT as well as being the technical director of Prodrive.

↑ **Subaru has a long history in rallying worldwide, but it got truly serious with the Prodrive-engineered Legacy. This is Colin McRae in action in his Legacy on the 1992 Scottish Rally, one year before he won the New Zealand Rally in the Impreza's older brother.**

year on year. In 1981, Subaru re-entered the event with the Leone and finished 11th overall. Then in 1982, Subaru returned in force with five cars: two Leone saloons, two Leone Touring Wagons and one Leone Swingback. Three cars managed to finish the gruelling event, and in strong positions too: seventh, ninth and tenth. The swing of results was all going in the right direction, as confirmed by 1983's Safari results: fifth and seventh positions.

For 1985 Subaru fielded its new RX Turbo 4WD model, the first time it had used a turbocharged 4x4 car. Although underpowered with just 180bhp, it performed reasonably well, finishing tenth in the East African Safari (Subaru winning Group A) and eighth, tenth and twelfth in New Zealand. In 1986 Subaru improved its performance with the RX, gaining sixth and seventh places on the Safari (and first and second in Group A), while Possum Bourne's third overall in New Zealand in 1987 was another high point.

The 1987 East Africa Safari saw a fresh homologation machine arrive, the new-generation Coupé 4WD Turbo, in the year that saw Group A become the premier category in place of Group B. In the light of this more high-profile move,

Subaru employed some of the world's leading drivers, including the 1981 World Champion Ari Vatanen. However it was Per Eklund who did best for Subaru, coming fifth (with Vatanen tenth and Bourne 11th). Results slipped to sixth and ninth in 1988 and ninth and 1989, and so a change of tack was called for.

Subaru was getting much more serious about its motorsports involvement. It formed a dedicated motorsports wing called Subaru Tecnica International (STi) in 1988 and the following year founded an extremely long and fruitful alliance with one of Britain's leading motorsport teams, Prodrive, whose David Lapworth recalls: 'Our first meeting was Easter 1989, then Mr Yamada (now president of STi but in technical liaison in the early days) came on the 1000 Lakes rally to assess our credentials. STi president, Mr Kuze signed the deal with us in the summer of 1989.'

Prodrive brought crucial expertise in high-level rallying, in which field it had already proven its credentials (see separate panel). Its presence was immediately felt in 1990, the first season of the partnership. This was also the year that the team celebrated securing one of the world's greatest

Prodrive

Prodrive has formed the backbone of Subaru's World Rally Championship effort since 1989, when Subaru Tecnica International (STi) first joined forces with the renowned British motorsport company to form the Subaru World Rally Team.

David Richards was the man who created Prodrive. Trained as a chartered accountant, he eschewed a number-crunching career to become a professional co-driver. Having won the inaugural world title for co-drivers alongside Ari Vatanen in 1981, he retired to set up his own motorsport operation.

What would become Prodrive was formed in 1984 by David Richards (chairman) and Ian Parry (commercial director) out of this initial motorsport marketing and consultancy business. David Lapworth also joined Richards in 1984. He took a pivotal role as engineering director and became widely acknowledged as probably the top rally engineer in the business. The aim of the new enterprise was to develop marketing and promotional campaigns around motorsports. Immediately showing its expertise and potential, Prodrive formed the Rothmans Porsche World Rally team and won three Middle East Rally Championships in its first year. Then, with Porsche, Rover-MG and BMW, Prodrive won championships across Europe, the highlight being its first World Rally Championship victory in Corsica in 1987.

Prodrive was originally based at the Silverstone circuit, but in 1986 the operation moved from Silverstone to its current Banbury site, and took on the Metro 6R4 rally effort. The following year it entered a successful partnership with BMW, including its M3 BTCC entries (winning the BTCC title three times in a row from 1988 to 1990).

Prodrive began its successful partnership with Subaru in the 1990 season, initiating a close relationship that survives to this day. The Legacy RS then being campaigned was a promising rally tool but certainly no Impreza. In 1991, Prodrive won the British Rally Championship with Colin McRae taking the rallying world by storm, winning four rallies for Prodrive in the Legacy, helping Prodrive reach the outstanding milestone of 50 rally victories. This was also the year when Prodrive opened

Rallying is the lifeblood of Oxfordshire-based Prodrive, which signed a deal to run the Subaru World Rally Team in 1989. Pictured in front of a prototype Prodrive P1 road car is Ed Swatman, Chief Executive Officer of Subaru UK (left) and Prodrive's chairman David Richards.

its engineering division to offer design consultancy to other motorsports teams and the mainstream automotive market.

In 1993, Prodrive and Subaru joined forces with British American Tobacco (BAT) for the new 555-sponsored Impreza to take to the rally scene, while a youthful Richard Burns made his debut driving the Legacy RS to victory in the British Rally Championship. The following year looked even more promising for the Impreza, while Prodrive celebrated victory in the British Touring Car Championship with Gabriele Tarquini in the Alfa Romeo 155. Also in 1994, David Richards was already contemplating taking Prodrive into Formula 1, an intention that would eventually be realised when he became head of the Benetton F1 team for a while.

The year 1995 is etched in Prodrive's history book, for Colin McRae took the drivers' and Subaru the manufacturers' World Rally Championships. Prodrive went on to retain the manufacturers' title in 1996 and 1997. By 1995 – the double championship winning year – Prodrive employed 160 staff including the Alfa BTCC team and the core of the business, the Prodrive Engineering consultancy wing. The number of people actually employed on the rally team then was remarkably only 28. (In stark contrast, some 200 were employed at Toyota's rally team.)

In 1997, Prodrive gained ISO9001 accreditation and in April 1998 was awarded the Investors in People award. Then, in 1999, Burns's win at the Rally of Great Britain in his Impreza saw Prodrive reach the milestone of 100 international rally victories, making it the most successful rally team of all time.

Success was never limited to just the factory teams, either, as customers driving Prodrive-prepared cars won national championships throughout the world.

In 2000, venture capitalists APAX took a 49 per cent share in Prodrive, enabling the company to finance some rapid growth plans, spurred on by a fifth British Touring Car Championship victory with Ford Team Mondeo. The expansion continued as Prodrive moved its Automotive Technology business to a 240-acre site near Warwick, which boasted a bespoke proving ground with a 2.5-mile (4km) test track.

Currently, Prodrive consists of three operating divisions: Motorsport, Sales and Automotive Technology. The Motorsport division has already been described. The company employs a large staff in a wide variety of automotive business sectors at its HQ in Banbury, Oxfordshire. The Sales Division takes up Prodrive's integrated marketing approach: marketing is not a separate function, says Prodrive, rather it is 'the very essence of the business'. Prodrive's Automotive Technology Division applies the technology of the competition world to research and development programmes for leading vehicle manufacturers and component suppliers. Currently the company has 500 employees, 350 housed on the main four-hectare site in Banbury, Oxfordshire and a further 150 at the new Automotive Technology Centre in Warwick.

Prodrive says of itself: 'Prodrive is a company committed to excellence and, having enjoyed success consistently throughout its history, second best is never good enough.'

rally drivers, Markku Alen, the ex-World Champion from Finland.

For the 1990 season, Subaru called in the new Legacy, a much bigger car than any it had used before but also far more powerful thanks to its 2.0-litre flat-four turbo engine. In rally tune the new Legacy's quad cam twin-turbo engine pumped out 300bhp plus, but in the event even this was no match for the outputs of the best competitors. Subaru participated in seven of the 12 World Rallies staged that year, its best results being Markku Alen's

fourth in the 1000 Lakes, while Possum Bourne finished fourth in Australia.

In 1990, Subaru also entered five Group A Legacies and one Group N Legacy in the East African Safari. Of 59 starters, only 10 cars made it over the finishing line in Nairobi. Despite this being the Legacy's first time in a rally, the driver of the highest-placed Legacy, Jim Heather-Hayes (with co-driver Anton Levitan), came in sixth overall. Perhaps even more remarkably, the sole Group N Legacy with David Williamson and Patrick Njiru on board, came eighth overall and won Group N. Subaru went on to win the Safari Rally eight years consecutively in the Group N category.

It was an encouraging start for the 'new era' at Subaru. The following year saw another season of 'nearly' results. Subaru fielded cars in nine of the 14 rallies. Its highest placements were Alen's third in the first event in Sweden, followed by fourths in New Zealand and Australia. The main problem was that, although the Legacy was a solid-handling car, it suffered from being a rather cumbersome machine compared with lighter rivals like the Integrale and RS Cosworth.

COLIN MCRAE

The son of successful Scottish rally driver Jimmy McRae, Colin made his mark as early as 1980 by becoming the Scottish Junior Scrambling Champion, aged 12. His first four-wheeled victory came in 1985 when he became the West Scotland Autotest champion in a Mini. He also had his first taste of rallying driving a Talbot Avenger and a Sunbeam in the 1985 Scottish Championship. He first teamed up with his brilliant co-driver Derek Ringer in 1987, when he was driving a Vauxhall Nova. This car also gave him his first FIA World Rally Championship experience, in the Rally of Sweden. He drove Peugeots and Nissans before settling on Ford, driving Sierras, coming second overall in the British Championship in 1990.

But it was his time with Subaru for which rally fans will really remember McRae. He drove a Prodrive Legacy in 1991 to become British Open Champion, repeated in 1992. Moving up to Subaru's FIA World Championship chase in 1992, he scored the historic first of many World Rally victories at the New Zealand rally towards the end of the 1993 season. He then piloted the Impreza for the first time in 1993 at the RAC Rally, starting a legendary relationship. He won two World Rally events in 1994, coming fourth in the title race.

Colin's year was 1995 as he became the first Briton ever to win the world title. He was also instrumental in securing the manufacturers' title for Subaru in 1995, 1996 and 1997. He left to join Ford after the 1998 season, having spent a spectacularly successful eight years with Prodrive and Subaru.

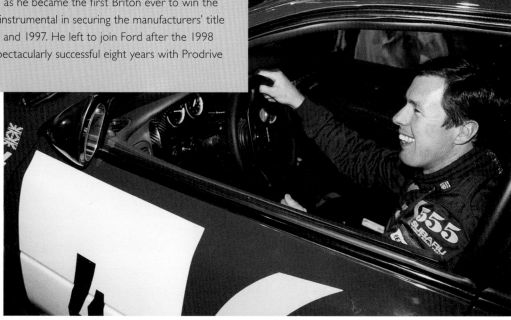

→ The Impreza's World Rally success became synonymous with Scots ace Colin McRae. He won his first title for Subaru in 1991 in a Legacy and went on to become World Champion in the Impreza in 1995.

In the scheme of things, probably the biggest news of 1991 was the arrival on the scene of a very youthful Colin McRae, driving a Rothmans-sponsored Prodrive-prepared Legacy in the British Open Championship. With four victories in individual rallies, McRae was a very impressive championship winner. The lad obviously had potential, but at the time no-one could have guessed to what spectacular extent the relatively unknown Scot would realise it. More promise of things to come was also evident when, in 1991, McRae competed in his first-ever world rally event, the RAC. Amazingly, he actually succeeded in leading the rally when, unfortunately, he crashed out.

Subaru was impressed enough to take McRae officially into the fold to replace Alen in 1992, and he rewarded their faith by scoring the team's best result yet, second place in Sweden, followed by fourth in the Acropolis. McRae was in superb form again for the British Open, winning the title again, with no less than six victories in the rounds. He might have followed this up with a first WRC victory for Subaru as he was leading the RAC Rally on the third day, but a series of events saw him trail back to sixth, with Vatanen's Legacy in second place.

1993 – Impreza impresses

The Legacy remained Subaru's rally tool into the beginning of the 1993 season, with Ari Vatanen and Colin McRae again occupying the drivers' seats. The Legacy was very stable to drive, but rather heavy compared with the Escort RS Cosworth. There was a feeling that the Legacy had to win at least one round in its last year, as David Lapworth recalls: 'We had got very close in Greece and the pressure was on. There was a threat that the Impreza might be delayed if the Legacy didn't win, but Colin came through to reward our faith.'

McRae had managed an encouraging third early on in the season in Sweden but it took until the final event in which a Legacy raced for Subaru to get what it wanted, scoring its first-ever WRC win at the Rally of New Zealand. The winner was a jubilant Colin McRae, who had turned 25 years old on the first day of the rally, qualifying him as the youngest driver to win a top-ranking rally since 1980. It was a great and significant victory but McRae's comment betrayed the pressure behind the win: 'It's a feeling of relief rather than elation,' he revealed.

↑ Testing for the new Impreza rally car (here in Scotland in 1993) showed the tremendous pace of the new car. It was faster than the Legacy straight out of the box.

RICHARD BURNS

Richard Burns started his career aged 11 when he joined a car club for under 17s. He progressed through one-make championships and raced in a self-prepared Talbot Sunbeam, but he really made a name for himself in his first full year of rallying in 1990, when he won the prestigious British Peugeot GTi Cup. At the age of 22, he won the British International Championship driving for Subaru – the youngest driver ever to win this. He went on to the Asia-Pacific for Subaru and raced in World Rally events too. He drove the Subaru Impreza in 1994 and 1995 in a number of World Championship events before joining Team Mitsubishi Ralliart in 1996 to partner Tommi Mäkinen. Two successful years there brought wins on the Safari and British Rally. Burns returned to the Subaru fold for the 1999 season, partnering Juha Kankkunen. He just missed out on the title in 1999 and again in 2000, but looked to be a leading contender for the 2001 title.

↑ **Richard Burns first drove for Subaru in 1993 aged just 23. He went on to replace Colin McRae in 1999 as the team's great British hope in the World Rally Championship.**

Another young Briton also made his debut for the Subaru Team in 1993. Richard Burns, aged just 22, won the British Rally Championship in the Legacy RS, founding a reputation and a relationship with Subaru that would extend into the new millennium. Possum Bourne also took the Asia-Pacific Rally Championship in 1993 – a first for Subaru, and a success that would be repeated the

following year. McRae also impressed in the Asia-Pacific, winning in Malaysia and coming second on the Hong Kong–Beijing rally.

The Subaru/Prodrive team clearly had the expertise and ability to win. All that was required was the right car to take things forward. And waiting in the wings was just the weapon that Subaru needed. In the Impreza was a car that could really build on the potential of the Legacy. Subaru had put together a great team around Prodrive, and had very talented drivers at its disposal. While the Legacy had been a great-handling car, it was getting too bulky by the standards of the day. The Impreza promised lighter weight and the prospect of a far more focused assault on the championship.

Everyone was hoping for great things from the new Impreza. The road car had been launched in November 1992 in Japan but had not been homologated for the start of the season, as the required 2,500 examples had not yet been built. Instead the Impreza arrived (as intended) at the 1000 Lakes in Finland in August, mid-way through the 1993 season.

David Lapworth remembers his first exposure to the Impreza. 'We previewed the new Impreza in 1992 and had the go-ahead to build the rally car towards the end of the year. It was significantly repackaged compared to the Legacy – but all of it was *better* packaged.'

The first wheel turned on 19 May 1993, and the Impreza proved to be significantly improved in just about every area. Prodrive's pre-production input certainly helped. The engine developed much more power than the Legacy's, the bodyshell was stiffer, it was faster-accelerating and better-braking, more responsive and ran cooler. David Lapworth comments: 'We ran it back-to-back with the Legacy with timing beams and it was significantly faster straight in. But looking back, we did very little testing compared to what we would do today.'

The new Impreza looked superb in its blue '555' livery: new sponsors BAT owned the 555 cigarette brand and this was to be the trademark livery of Subaru's rally effort for years to come. Ari Vatanen came desperately close to winning the car's very first outing at the 1000 Lakes. Vatanen was dominating the event when something as trivial as a windscreen demisting problem pushed him back to second place and denied him a historic maiden victory. It would not be long before the Impreza did win its first event, though.

Colin McRae joined Vatanen in the Impreza 555 for the RAC Rally in November. In freezing conditions, McRae was leading the event impressively when a small frozen branch hidden by the snow punctured his radiator, causing an engine melt-down. It was a bitter blow to what could easily have been the new Impreza's first blood. As some small consolation, Vatanen took fifth place in the other Impreza and Burns took seventh in the ageing Legacy.

It was obvious already that the combination of the Impreza and Colin McRae looked set to cause big problems for the other teams. The Impreza had arrived too late to come close to stopping Toyota win the 1993 manufacturers' title

↓ **Ari Vatanen came within a sigh of winning the Impreza's maiden rally, the 1993 1000 Lakes in Finland. A trivial windscreen demisting problem scuppered his chances on an exceptionally brave first outing.**

↑ Carlos Sainz scored
Subaru's first victory of
the 1994 season with
an impressive win at
the Acropolis Rally in
Greece. This was only
the Impreza's sixth-ever
competitive outing.

and become the first-ever Japanese company to
conquer the world of rallying. But Toyota's pre-
eminence would be short-lived …

1994 – Sainz and McRae

For the 1994 season, Subaru had a terrific boost
with the signing of double World Rally Champion
Carlos Sainz (1990 and 1992) from Lancia to
accompany young gun McRae. This was to be the
Impreza's first fully fledged WRC year and one
that would prove pivotal for Subaru. It would
certainly be a challenge though, for the Impreza
was relatively unproven, Sainz was unused to the
car and neither McRae nor the Impreza had yet
competed in the Monte Carlo Rally, which was
the first event of the season.

However, the Sainz/McRae pairing would
prove very strong. David Lapworth said: 'We
really came of age in 1994 with the arrival of
Carlos and Pirelli. Carlos was a very positive
influence on the team, putting in the hard work
to get the car set up right. He taught Colin a lot.
But it was Colin who delivered the speed and the

spectacle, and had the best results, even if at the
end of a rally you couldn't recognise the car – it
always came back with a different wheelbase to
what it started with!'

In the Monte Carlo, at one point McRae was
in second place but by the end of the first day
McRae found himself in 121st position thanks
to some rogue snow dumped on a corner by
spectators. Some measure of his gumption
was evident as he fought back to tenth place
by the end. Subaru gained more solace from
Sainz's impressive third place. McRae had proved
faster over most stages but the Spaniard was
acclimatising to his new steed fast.

McRae retired in Portugal with fire damage,
and in Corsica after an accident. McRae's wayward
rally behaviour earned him the nickname 'Colin
McCrash' but this only betrayed his all-or-nothing
approach. His reputation as the 'wild man of
rallying' – ferociously quick but also not shy of
taking risks – would bolster his popularity with the
fans, if not always with the team.

Sainz was altogether more down-to-earth in
1994, posting a number of good results, including
fourth in Portugal and second in Corsica. But his

most impressive result was a win in the Acropolis Rally in Greece, confirming him as a formidable figure in rallying. This was the first blood the Impreza had taken – and only in its sixth-ever rally. Sainz followed this up with a third place in the 1000 Lakes and second in Argentina.

McRae's first victory in the Impreza arrived in New Zealand, which he won for the second successive year. He led virtually from the start and answered critics who questioned his temperament in a difficult year. He did admit: 'I was beginning to feel I had a jinx. This has set my mind at rest. I just drove as smoothly as I could. To say it was easy would be cheeky but it is true.' Richard Burns also made his debut in the Impreza in New Zealand but was forced to retire, joining Sainz and Possum Bourne in an early bath.

Things were at last going Subaru's way. At San Remo (Italy), Sainz took second place and McRae fifth, gaining valuable extra points for the team. But undoubtedly the high point of the 1994 season for both Subaru and McRae was the Scot's victory in the 'golden jubilee' RAC Rally. This was to be a long-awaited 'home' victory, as the RAC

had last been won by a Brit (Roger Clark) way back in 1976. 'It is a huge weight off my shoulders to win at last,' McRae commented triumphantly. Prodrive endorsed the talent of their Scottish driver: 'Colin is an extraordinarily natural talent, to a level equal to that of the very great rally drivers there have ever been. I think he has the potential to be a World Champion.'

Sadly all the team's efforts came too late to save championship hopes. Sainz finished the season second by a whisker behind Dider Auriol in his Toyota Celica. Likewise, the Subaru team was ranked number two, 11 points behind Toyota. But the Impreza legend was well and truly underway. Thanks to the RAC win, the road car gained sudden cult status, and was voted Rally Car of the Year by the readers of the leading British motorsport magazine, *Autosport*.

Meanwhile, Bourne cleaned up in the Asia-Pacific Championship once more, winning the Rally of Malaysia and one of the world's toughest events, the Hong Kong–Beijing Rally, while McRae found time to win in Australia during the Asia-Pacific.

↓ **McRae did not have long to wait for his first victory in the Impreza, in New Zealand. But far sweeter was the win on home soil, at the 1994 RAC Rally, the first time a Briton had won this event since Roger Clark in 1976.**

1995 – First year of the triple

If ever there was a turning point in the efforts of a company hoping to score from international motorsport, 1995 was the year for Subaru. In a spectacular season, Subaru took its first World Rally titles. As mentioned, it not only did it win the manufacturers' crown but Colin McRae also lifted the drivers' trophy.

It is worth just going through the specification of the championship winning car. The 1995 Impreza developed 300bhp at 5,000rpm and 369lb ft (500Nm) at 4,000rpm on a maximum 2.0 bar boost level. Sequential fuel injection provided variable spark and injection timing, while the engine's computer also controlled throttle response and an electronic anti-lag system to keep the turbo on boost on closed throttle. There was also computerised water injection to reduce inlet temperatures, and a driver-operated waterspray for the intercooler improved low-speed inlet heat.

The gearbox was a six-speed unit with straight-cut Hewland gears in a magnesium casing, operated by a conventional H-gate shifter. Prodrive had

experimented with a semi-automatic sequential transmission but found no advantage because of the unpredictability of gearchanges. The clutch was a triple-plate carbon item. Computers controlled the centre and front differentials and hydraulically powered clutches, and were pre-programmed for each event. Full traction control was under development in 1995 but drivers generally preferred to adjust slide and wheelspin themselves, and there was little benefit in 4x4 cars anyway.

Brakes were 14-inch ventilated discs up front (or 12-inchers on gravel), operated by six-pot front and four-pot rear aluminium callipers. Front-rear brake balance was controlled by a centre differential computer. Up to 18-inch wheels were available for asphalt, with tiny 5.5 x 15s on snow and 7 x 16s on gravel. Pirelli provided a variety of tyres with different tread patterns and compounds. The rally Impreza used titanium hubs and gas-filled Bilstein dampers (with a waterspray for hot events). The suspension was tuned about twice as stiff as the road car on gravel and four times as stiff on asphalt, with around 200mm (8in) of travel in total.

The body was based on the four-door Impreza,

↓ It was McRae's year in 1995. His spectacular driving style and unbeatable pace were overwhelming. On the RAC Rally he overcame a puncture, hydraulic leak and hitting a rock to emerge first in a decisive 1–2–3 for Subaru.

and as required by the regulations, had to look like the road car. The shell itself was seam-welded and reinforced, including a steel alloy roll cage to make the torsional rigidity four times that of the road car.

As for the drivers, the successful McRae/ Sainz pairing continued into 1995. Most experts reckoned the Toyota Celica was favourite to take the title for the third successive year but in its season preview Autocar magazine tellingly described the Impreza as: 'probably the best car in the series'.

Italian tarmac expert Piero Liatti joined the team for Monte Carlo, Corsica and Spain, while Mats Jonsson ran in Sweden, Possum Bourne in Australia and New Zealand and Richard Burns in Portugal, the RAC and, unexpectedly, New Zealand.

Subaru scored the first blood of the season at the Monte Carlo Rally in January. Sainz proved to be the more cool-headed of the drivers, controlling things from the front with only Delecour's Escort Cosworth looking threatening; the Toyotas lacked power. While Sainz looked convincing as the winner, Colin McRae also showed his mettle, setting the fastest time on the first special stage. But he crashed twice, and on the second occasion there was no way back and he scored no points. It had been a very promising start for the team but the next event in Sweden proved to be a disaster, with all three Imprezas retiring with oil leaks.

Fortunes changed in Portugal, as Sainz took his second win of the season and McRae scored his first points (in third place). Moreover, Burns came seventh, his best result yet. The East African Safari was not part of the WRC in 1995 but Subaru fielded a three-car team in the standard production car category, Group N. Amid a series of spectacular crashes, Imprezas came in fourth, fifth and tenth. Corsica was solid if slightly disappointing, the three entered cars coming home in formation in fourth, fifth and sixth.

Colin McRae's comeback began in New Zealand in August with his third successive win there. It was a consistently impressive victory, despite almost being taken out by a low-flying helicopter. The win put him fourth in the title fight. Meanwhile, Richard Burns took over from an injured Sainz but did not finish, while local hero Possum Bourne could only manage seventh. Despite McRae's celebrations, Subaru's challenge for the manufacturers' title was seemingly slipping away.

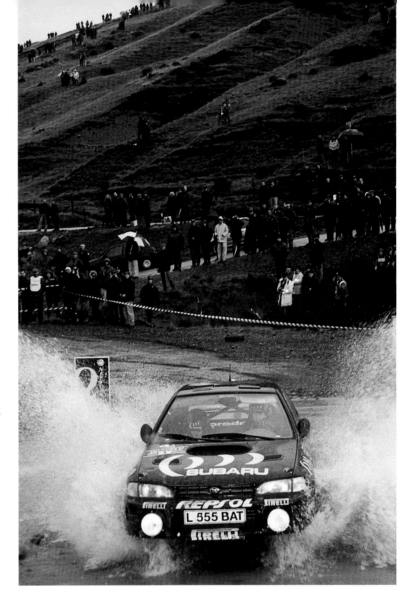

McRae scored an impressive second in Australia to leap up to second place in the drivers' championship behind Kankkunen. Sainz was forced out on the first day and so slipped to fourth in the title chase.

Catalunya was to prove the crux of the season. McRae was clearly, even humiliatingly faster than Sainz on the Spaniard's home soil. But he had to obey team orders and deliberately allowed Sainz to take first place – which meant the two Impreza drivers now tied in the title run. Liatti completed a spectacular 1–2–3 for Subaru. McRae was candid about his feelings and the press stoked an intense rivalry between McRae and Sainz. A further Catalunyan bombshell came after the event, as Toyota was banned, stripped of all its points and its licence suspended for using an illegal turbo restrictor. Also, because Sainz had just signed for Toyota for 1996, it looked like a serious blow for the Spaniard too.

↑ **Crowds watched in awe in very damp conditions as McRae blistered and watersplashed his way to victory in the 1995 RAC Rally – and to victory in that year's World Rally Championship.**

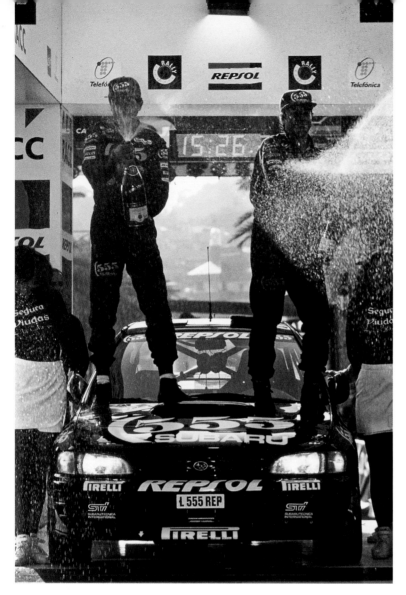

↑ **Rallye Catalunya with Sainz and Moya on the finishing ramp in 1995. (Prodrive)**

David Lapworth summed up the feeling of that time: 'That moment at the 1995 RAC when we cleaned up with a 1–2–3 to take the double in the championship has to be the high point of the team, surpassing even the feeling when Colin had his first win in New Zealand.'

In competition elsewhere Subaru again looked strong, taking second place in the Asia-Pacific manufacturers' championship following a win in Indonesia, while Possum Bourne finished third in the drivers' championship behind Kenneth Eriksson in his Mitsubishi. Subaru would turn the tables in 1996, however, when Eriksson would swap teams and bring victory to the six-star badge in this event.

1996 – Second championship year

Subaru had ended 1995 on the highest possible note, and looked to be one of the strongest teams entering the 1996 season. But with Toyota out of the running, this season was not the classic that everyone had hoped for. Sainz's relationship with David Richards had been the subject of much speculation and, after two years as runner-up with Subaru, the Spaniard transferred over to Ford. That left Colin McRae and Piero Liatti to defend Subaru's title, alongside new signing Kenneth Eriksson of Sweden.

Monte Carlo was a non-championship event this year, so things kicked off in earnest in Sweden. This year's hot ticket Tommi Mäkinen in the Mitsubishi Lancer Evolution proved too strong for a late-charging McRae, who finished third behind Sainz. Things did not improve in the early part of the season. In Indonesia, McRae crashed out in the lead when Derek Ringer's intercom failed, handing Sainz a victory, and his team-mate Liatti a second placing.

At the Safari, Eriksson secured second place, two ahead of McRae. But at the Acropolis Rally in June, it was McRae's turn to return to winning ways. Mäkinen in the Lancer Evo stalked him all the way but McRae emerged victorious, raising him to third in the title chase.

But there was no escaping the lacklustre season that McRae was suffering. Retirements in Argentina and Finland did not help, and

The year 1995 was to end in a fitting climax. In the British RAC Rally, Colin McRae emerged decisively as the new World Champion. That he overcame a two-minute loss due to a puncture, a hydraulic leak and nearly ripping his wheel off on hitting a rock was impressive enough. But McRae's pace was simply blistering. His time on one 17-mile stage was so fast – 28 seconds faster than anyone else – that Sainz refused to believe it was true.

The rally finished with McRae and co-driver Derek Ringer totally dominant. Aged just 27, McRae became the youngest World Rally Champion ever and Britain's first-ever World Champion. Sainz finished second, comfortably enough to wrest the manufacturers' title from Mitsubishi, who had entered the final rally with a slender two-point lead. Richard Burns's third place made the RAC another 1–2–3 for Subaru. The year may not have started well for McRae but it ended on the best imaginable note.

fourth in Italy was two places behind team-mate Eriksson. It took until October and the San Remo rally for McRae to notch up his second World Championship victory of the season, by which stage Mäkinen in his Lancer Evo had already won the drivers' championship. McRae's Italian performance was very impressive, consistently keeping the Fords of Sainz and Thiry at bay.

McRae finished the season in typical style on the last championship event of the year, the Catalunya Rally in Spain in November. He took first place some seven seconds ahead of his strong-running team-mate Liatti, claiming second place in the drivers' championship and securing Subaru's retention of the manufacturers' title. The help of support drivers Kenneth Eriksson and Piero Liatti through the season must also be properly acknowledged, as McRae's title defence had been far from perfect.

The RAC Rally was in a bit of a hiatus in 1996. Not part of the championship calendar, it had hoped to attract interest by allowing the new 1997 WRC cars to take part, but in the event none of the teams had a car ready. Nonetheless Japanese

rally champion Masao Kamioka drove his Impreza impressively in poor conditions to take second place behind Schwarz's Toyota.

Having won the previous year with Mitsubishi, Kenneth Eriksson had also done superbly well in another of Subaru's favoured championships, the Asia-Pacific. He took the 1996 drivers' title and helped Subaru come second in the manufacturers' championship. McRae had also found time to

↑ For the 1996 season, McRae's main team-mate was new signing Kenneth Eriksson of Sweden. Eriksson posted the better results in the early part of the season, McRae taking time to get into his stride.

→ Cars frequently came back bent from the rally, but not usually this bad. This stricken machine is McRae's Number 1 decidedly out of action in the 1000 Lakes in Finland in 1996.

It took until October for
McRae to score his second
championship round of the
1996 season in San Remo,
by which time Mäkinen had
already won the drivers'
championship. However,
Subaru would go on to take
the manufacturer's title for
a second year running.

stack up a first place in Thailand during the Asia-
Pacific. The 1996 Subaru Impreza was again voted
Autosport readers poll winner for Rally Car of the
Year, its third successive such vote.

1997: WRC revolution

A sweeping change hit World Rallying in 1997
with the launch of a new breed of rally cars, the
so-called World Rally Car (WRC). These were far
more purpose-designed machines that, in some
ways, harked back to the halcyon days of Group B.
The regulations changed so that it was no longer
required to build 2500 examples of the specific
rally car for homologation. Instead, manufacturers
were allowed to use any existing model and
develop it for competition, as long as it had sold
more than 25,000 examples. Engines could be
transplanted from another car in the range, the
ultimate restriction on power output of around
300bhp coming from a maximum permitted turbo
inlet size. Speed and cornering abilities were kept
in check by a stipulation on maximum tyre width.
The number of rounds in the rally championship
was increased to 14.

For the Subaru team there was also a change
of approach behind the wheel. The previous year,
1996, had not gone as Colin McRae had wanted,
nor what many had expected at the start of the

season. Reflecting on a disappointing season, in
which an estimated $1 million of crash damage had
been inflicted on the team's cars, McRae sacked his
long-standing (and long-suffering) co-driver Derek
Ringer in November 1996. This was perhaps more to
do with team pressure for not keeping McRae under
control during rallies than his abilities as a co-driver.
His replacement was Welshman Nicky Grist, who
reined in some of Colin's more excessive behaviour
– folklore tales of wild nights in hotels and mad
drives at midnight were widespread – and McRae
commented: 'I think I am now able to balance being
wild and rallying.'

The Subaru World Rally Team was ahead of the
game, being the first to launch its World Rally Car
in Spain in November. This was the biggest single
change for the Impreza since 1993. The team took full
advantage of the broader remit for modifications, and
for the first time based its WRC on the two-door
Impreza bodyshell. Also, for the first time, the WRC
was built entirely at Prodrive (previously Subaru had
supplied cars pre-built ready for preparation). The
1997 car was designed by Peter Stevens, the stylist
behind the McLaren F1. Engineering was, as ever,
by Prodrive's David Lapworth. The cars were built
up from a bare production shell in over 400 man-
hours. Modifications included a much wider shell and
glassfibre bumpers and spoilers. The body was
carefully tuned for aerodynamic performance,
maximising downforce, while weight-saving carbon-
fibre was used inside for the dashboard and
door panels.

The scene was set for a showdown between
the 1996 winner, Tommi Mäkinen in the Mitsubishi
Lancer, and second-placed Colin McRae in the
Impreza. McRae's team-mates remained Piero Liatti
(tarmac specialist) and Kenneth Eriksson
(gravel specialist).

Never was any team's domination of a season so
wholesale as Subaru's, claiming eight wins over the
course of the year's 14 rallies, and a third, successive
manufacturers' crown – although the drivers' title
eluded them.

The season got off to the best possible start for
Subaru, with three successive wins. It was Piero Liatti
who scored first blood in the Monte Carlo Rally. In
his maiden victory, he had a steady drive in difficult
conditions with blistering pace on the final day to
finish ahead of Sainz's Escort. McRae had crashed out
of the event on the second day.

↑ The most gruelling race of the season, the East African Safari, proved that the Subaru and McRae were up to the sternest challenges, as the Scot won the event for his first time ever.

→ The 1997 season saw the arrival of the two-door WRC Impreza. Here, McRae gives the crowds in Australia a demonstration in donuts, after beating Mäkinen's Mitsubishi with startling pace.

At the Swedish Rally in February, McRae again had to cede victory to his team-mate, this time Eriksson. The lead switched often, but ultimately the correct tyre choice saw the Swede take victory on home soil, but McRae had his own tyre problems and finished fourth.

McRae's pre-season promise finally paid off in Kenya for the coveted Safari. With Richard Burns in the Mitsubishi chasing hard, McRae survived

← Colin McRae succeeded in winning his third successive RAC Rally in 1997 – and Subaru's third successive world title for manufacturers – but the drivers' title eluded him once again this year.

147

↑ The Subaru World Rally Team entered 1998 having won three titles in a row but the '98 season would prove to be a tough one for Prodrive and the whole Subaru team. This was McRae's final year in the team.

a gruelling time, including breaking a track rod control arm on a pile of rocks placed in the road by vandals. He had already seen Eriksson go out after breaking his rear wheel and hub on rocks but emerged a full seven minutes ahead of Burns. This was McRae's first-ever Safari victory and his first win of the season, enough to take him into the lead in the championship.

Portugal saw Subaru falter temporarily. Electrical problems relegated McRae to the sidelines and Eriksson was forced out by engine failure while in strong contention with the eventual winner, Mäkinen. The Finn won the Catalunya Rally in April, too, in convincing fashion, although tarmac expert Piero Liatti ran him very close in his Impreza, finishing just seven seconds adrift. Colin McRae could muster no better than fourth, suffering a puncture on day two.

The tables were turned in Corsica in May. Championship leader Mäkinen nose-dived into a ravine after a run in with some stray cows, handing McRae a great opportunity. Surprises of the championship, the two-wheel drive Peugeot team, led in the early stages and Sainz's Escort was leading on the last day. But McRae

performed superbly in wet conditions to leap-frog the Spaniard and win by eight seconds, putting him a mere two points behind Mäkinen in the championship race.

It was a close tussle in Argentina, too, but Mäkinen led McRae from day one, forcing him into second place. Greece would prove to be Ford's rally as Sainz and Kankkunen took first and second. McRae suffered a bent steering column when he crashed into a bank early on, forcing him to retire. Eriksson followed the next day with broken suspension. The Swede did better in New Zealand, inheriting a win once Mäkinen had crashed out and McRae's cam belt pulley had broken. The win put Subaru decisively in the lead in the manufacturers' title chase, although Mäkinen retained his 12-point lead over McRae. Another cam belt failure in Finland forced McRae to admit: 'I think my championship is over' – especially as Mäkinen won his home rally.

It really did seem all over for McRae in Indonesia, when he lost control and hit a tree. Sainz won the rally, with Kankkunen second and Eriksson in the Subaru third. But McRae fought back with characteristic bravery. At the San Remo rally, McRae put in a blistering performance to win unexpectedly, ahead of Liatti in second place.

Then in Australia, Mäkinen made a heavy landing and broke his starter motor, the subsequent delay earning him a 40-second penalty. The Finn clawed back McRae's advantage but could not take victory. He admitted: 'I thought I could do it, but Colin must have driven like a madman.' That put McRae 10 points behind Mäkinen but with just the RAC Rally to go, the odds were slim.

In the event, McRae did what he had to do – win the RAC for the third time in a row – but it was all to no avail. The Scot's drive had been heroic, pulling back from eighth place with two days to go. Mäkinen's team-mate Richard Burns proved very tough competition and for a while looked like winning, but a burst tyre scuppered those chances. Even with McRae in first, all that a flu-ridden Mäkinen had to do was finish in the points. And he did so – in sixth place. That handed him the title by just one point. Eriksson finished in fifth place in the championship.

The drivers' title had proven elusive in 1997 but the manufacturers' crown was decisively Subaru's, with 114 points against Ford's 91 and Mitsubishi's 86. This was a third successive manufacturers' title and a fitting climax to Subaru's domination of the sport.

Meanwhile in the Asia-Pacific, yet another championship victory awaited: Subaru notched up its third manufacturers' title and, with Eriksson on great form, its fourth drivers' title. McRae again scored in the Asia-Pacific on the China Rally. And to round off the year, Polish driver Krzysztof Holowczyc also won the 1997 European Rally Championship.

Finally, Group A waned in importance with the rule changes and Subaru ducked out of any official involvement in the class after the 1996 season. However privateers continued to enter national and international events with the Impreza in this class, scoring numerous successes.

1998 – McRae's final year

The assumption after 1997 was that McRae and Mäkinen would battle things out in their respective Subaru and Mitsubishi. In fact there would be stiff competition from Toyota, which signalled its

seriousness with a win from newly signed Carlos Sainz at the first rally of the year, the Monte Carlo. McRae looked like he might overhaul Kankkunen's Escort to take second but a puncture kept him in third, while team-mate Liatti came fourth.

In Sweden, McRae was on the pace but retired with battery problems. Eriksson came fourth but already Mäkinen and Sainz were opening up a gap in the championship. McRae accepted that to stay in the chase he needed to win in Kenya (as he had done in 1997) but it was not to be: overheating caused irreparable damage. So no points for Subaru on the Safari.

The first of McRae's victories arrived in Portugal. Overcoming the disadvantage of driving first on rough roads, McRae held off the challenge from Sainz in the Toyota Corolla to win by just 2.1 seconds. It was certainly not incident free, as on one of the stages McRae hit a photographer, breaking his legs. But Portugal was a sweet victory: 'I am back in the hunt', declared a relieved McRae.

Two retirements left Subaru with no points in Spain but McRae was back on top in Corsica in May, winning the event for the second year running.

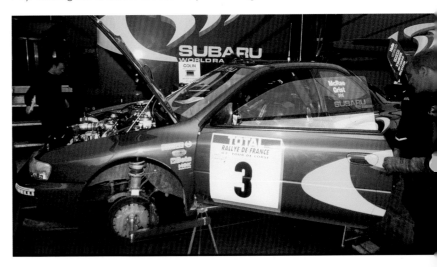

It was not an easy ride, though. A puncture had left the front tyres bald, but the team was exonerated from any suggestion that rules had been broken. The damp weather seemed to suit the Subarus, leaving too much of a gap for the other teams to pull back when the surface dried out. McRae's victory was backed up by a third place from team-mate Piero Liatti. McRae was now leading the drivers' championship, and Subaru the manufacturers'.

↑ **Hard team work kept McRae in the running. Solid support at the 1998 Rallye de France in Corsica helped the Scotsman to one of several victories that year, and to third place in the drivers' championship.**

A great battle in Argentina saw McRae and Mäkinen trade places. But the Scot seemed to lose concentration on the roughest stage and stoved in the rear suspension on a wall. It was enough to drop him to fifth, even though he valiantly set the fastest time on the following stage.

'Nothing cuts through Greece like Subaru,' ran an advertising campaign following another jubilant victory at the Acropolis Rally. It was a hard-fought win, and one that Colin was not expecting; Mäkinen had been forced to retire with electrical problems. With Liatti finishing sixth, McRae and Subaru were once again on top of their championship tables. Sadly this lead was short-lived, for in New Zealand, Toyota took full advantage of McRae's handling problems and finally a puncture, to score a 1–2, with the Scot back in fifth and Liatti in sixth. In Finland, McRae again looked very quick but aquaplaning at 100mph caused him to crash out.

The title fight was now very close, and it became closer after San Remo in October. Subaru's tarmac man and local hero, Piero Liatti, chased Mäkinen hard and ended up in second place behind the Finn, only 15.8 seconds adrift. An even greater battle between McRae and Sainz for third saw the Scot recover from ninth place to pip the Spaniard.

What could have been a great three-way showdown to the wire phuttered out when McRae suffered the most incredible misfortune in Australia. Almost within sight of the finish and in first place, an engine blow-up handed victory to Mäkinen. McRae ended in fourth place, scoring too few points to keep his challenge for the championship alive. So it was that in the Network Q Rally in Britain, Mäkinen and Mitsubishi won both titles as mechanical problems once again forced a sad McRae out when he was in contention for a win. Gregoire de Mevius's fourth in the other Subaru left the Japanese team third in the manufacturers' title, while McRae finished third overall in the drivers' championship. It would be the last time McRae would race for Subaru.

David Lapworth was philosophical: 'Of course it was a significant loss after eight years together. But it was probably the right time for Colin to leave, from his point of view and ours. We had a fresh

↓ **Richard Burns asserted his authority as a potential future World Champion with a win at the 1999 Acropolis Rally in Greece – his first ever WRC victory in an Impreza.**

↑ The Impreza's competition career was not confined to world rallying. It was also a winning machine in Group N. Here, Jane Gunningham poses with her steed in the British Rally Championship.

injection of talent and recent experience of other cars. Richard Burns revealed where development was required, especially regarding tyres.'

1999 – Richard Burns arrives

On the technical front, the 1999 season saw the arrival of ATM (automated manual transmission). This was a new electro-hydraulically controlled semi-automatic gearbox that was very different to most other teams' sequential gearboxes. Prodrive elected to automate the traditional, and tough, H-pattern gearbox using electro-hydraulics via a paddle shift to the right of the steering wheel. The driver could switch to the manual H shift in case of difficulty, unlike the sequential systems where a glitch normally meant a retirement. Another advantage was a dashboard switch to select neutral, then first – vital after a spin, for example. The 1999 WRC Impreza also introduced an electronically actuated 'fly-by-wire' accelerator. The rules now allowed for extensive engine modifications, including larger turbochargers and water injection.

For 1999 it was all change at the Subaru driver roster. Colin McRae left to join Malcolm Wilson's Ford rally team, Eriksson departed to Hyundai and Liatti teamed up with Seat. To fill the void, Subaru shopped around for the best available talent. Richard Burns rejoined the Subaru World Rally Team from the championship-winning Mitsubishi team – which felt like coming home to him – and ex-champion Juha Kankkunen joined from Ford.

A dominant-looking Mäkinen had the season off to the start he intended with a win in Monte Carlo. In a hopeful move, Kankkunen secured second place ahead of Dider Auriol. But this initial success was to elude the Subaru team for the rest of the first half of the season.

In Sweden, the team's tyres suffered because of the unexpected heat and Burns and Kankkunen came fifth and sixth respectively. In Kenya, Burns looked set for a second successive Safari victory until a collapsed bolt smashed his commanding lead. In Portugal a lack of grip kept Burns in fourth and Bruno Thiry in sixth, and the same problem in Catalunya relegated Burns to fifth and Kankkunen to sixth.

→ Appalling weather
conditions at the first ever
Chinese Rally saw all teams
struggling. Burns thought
the rally should be stopped,
and you can see why.

↑ An ecstatic crowd
watched Burns win his first
RAC Rally of Great Britain
in 1999. This was enough to
put him in second place in
the drivers' championship.

With no points in Corsica and the form book
totally upset by Citroën's front-drive Xsara winning
its second successive rally, it took until the seventh
round in Argentina for Subaru to realise its full
potential. It was an emphatic one–two for Subaru,
but what should have been triumphant glee was
overshadowed by Kankkunen taking first, when
team orders should have posted Burns first, instead
of second by a margin of 2.4 seconds. But for the
Finn, this was an emotional victory, his first in
a long time. Also it was Subaru's first win since
Greece the previous year and lifted the team to
third in the manufacturers' title chase.

At the next event in Greece, Burns turned the
tables, emphatically winning the Acropolis rally, his
first-ever victory in the Impreza WRC. He never
looked vulnerable in a stormer of a race that he
described as 'my best win yet'. He led virtually
all the way from start to finish and succeeded in
drawing level with McRae to fourth in the title race.

But Burns's run faltered in New Zealand as he
failed to finish, even though Kankkunen scored
an encouraging second. Then on home territory,
Kankkunen notched up another win in Finland – his
23rd, making him the most successful rally driver in

the world. The victory also put the Finn up to third
in the 1999 title fight. But he had tough opposition
from Burns, who was a rare non-Finnish leader of
the rally on the opening day, and finished second
overall at the end.

At the first-ever China Rally, the wake of a
typhoon caused terrible driving conditions. It was
so bad that Burns wanted the rally stopped but he
came through huge difficulties to run Didier Auriol
a close second by the end. In San Remo, Subaru's
best place was Kankkunen in sixth.

The 1999 season certainly ended on a high for
Subaru, with Burns taking wins in Australia and
Great Britain, but it wasn't enough to stop Mäkinen
take a record fourth successive title in the Lancer.
Burns's fifth WRC victory, on the RAC, confirmed
him as Britain's number one driver ahead of Colin
McRae. It was a convincing performance and justly
saw the Englishman take second place in the drivers'
championship ahead of Auriol. Kankkunen's second
place brought Subaru to within four points of the
manufacturers' title winner, Toyota, and handed him
fourth place in the drivers' championship.

Now that Subaru had won in Finland and
Argentina in 1999, there was not a single World

← Richard Burns led from start to finish in the last event in which the WRC99 competed, the Safari. Kankkunen followed to leave Subaru with a superb 1–2.

Championship event anywhere in the world that the Subaru team had not won at one time or another.

2000 – A close race

Subaru started the 2000 season with the WRC99 car, the reason being that the New Age Impreza was due to arrive mid-way through the year. That meant Subaru could begin mid-season installing the mechanical package from the new car. As much as 80 per cent of the car was new, much improved in terms of aerodynamics, cooling, suspension, electrics, roll cage and weight distribution. Yet another advance was made on active differentials, with all three now computer-controlled via hydraulic pumps. The centre and rear differentials were now almost fully locked all the time, giving better on-the-limit handling on both gravel and tarmac.

Backtracking now, the WRC99 was obviously still competitive, as Kankkunen took third at Monte Carlo. Sweden was not as impressive (fifth and sixth places) but, in the last event in which the WRC99 took part, the Safari, Subaru scored a tremendous 1–2, Burns being followed by Kankkunen. Burns led the rally virtually from start to finish: 'Spending the whole rally in the lead is quite stressful', he commented.

The new WRC2000 Impreza appeared for the first time in Portugal and won it decisively with Burns at the wheel. Overcoming power steering failure and dust clouds, he stormed to victory and the bookies now favoured him to take the title. 'This is the start of a new era,' Burns said confidently, as he became the first Englishman ever

to lead the World Championship. After a near-miss in Catalunya, Burns became the first Briton ever to win in Argentina, coming back from sixth place and overcoming on-board computer problems to take a runaway victory.

But then Burns's fortunes suddenly changed. Retirements followed in Greece, New Zealand and Finland, loosening his grip on the championship and allowing Marcus Gronholm into the lead. Two fourth places in Cyprus and Corsica kept the pressure on but another retirement in Italy, despite being on the pace, put Burns five points adrift of Gronholm's Peugeot 206. Burns tried hard but could not beat the Finn in Australia, leaving Gronholm needing just one point from the British Rally to win the championship.

↑ Argentina has a reputation as a very tough event and Richard Burns became the first ever Briton to score victory there in 2000. It was a decisive victory in a car that already incorporated much of the underpinnings of the New Age Impreza.

DID YOU KNOW?

Allstars team

Prodrive's Allstars team is a factory-backed team service, tailoring rallying packages to individual requirements. The team enjoyed considerable success in 2000, helping to secure the FIA Teams' Cup for Toshihiro Arai (who joined the Subaru World Rally Team for 2001), and supporting other drivers around the world to achieve no fewer than nine major national titles.

For 2001 there were six specified events run at World Rally events: Sweden, Portugal, Cyprus, Greece, Italy and Australia. The team ran full Teams' Cup programmes for Hamed Al Wahaibi (Oman Arab World Rally Team), and Frenchman Frederic Dor.

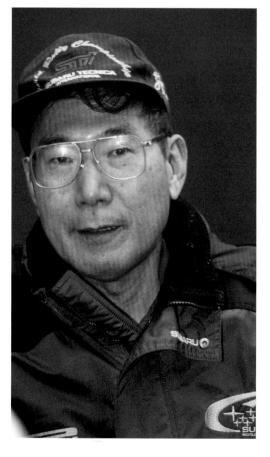

Burns did what he had to back in Britain, winning his third successive Rally of Britain in spectacular style. But Gronholm was cautious yet fast and came second – easily enough to secure his title head of Burns. As some consolation, Burns had set more fastest stages than any other driver and looked to be a firm championship prospect for the future.

Elsewhere, Tom McGeer took the 2000 Canadian Rally Series, and Prodrive appointed former British champion Mark Lovell and Karl Schieble to drive in the 2001 SCCA Pro-Rally Series in the USA. Once again Possum Bourne took the 2000 FIA Asia-Pacific Rally drivers' and manufacturer's championships.

2001 – Dawn of a new age

Subaru consciously hired young drivers for the 2001 season – indeed its oldest driver (Burns, aged 30) was younger than the youngest driver of any other team that year. Three new signings – Petter Solberg (26) of Norway, Markko Märtin (25) of Estonia and Toshihiro Arai (30) of Japan – were all ready to be developed by Subaru.

To join them, the 'New Age' Impreza was ready for the fight, the new platform and underpinnings having already proven themselves during 2000. It was therefore a relatively simple matter to sort the all-new bodyshell and things like the electrics.

The same layout of triple active differentials was kept. Brakes were Alcon-Prodrive 305mm ventilated discs all round with four-pot callipers for the rough stuff. For tarmac stages, ferocious water-cooled six-pot front callipers operated on massive 366mm discs. Wheels changed for tarmac too, going from 6 × 15-inch front and 7 × 15-inch rear on 205/65 R15 tyres on gravel to 225/50 slicks or wets on 8 × 18-inch wheels. The suspension pick-up points were very similar to before and the general layout of MacPherson struts front and rear was carried over.

The 2001 rally car pumped out 300bhp at 5,500rpm and 347lb ft (470Nm) of torque at 4,000rpm. The rally engine had its own dedicated microprocessor, as did the transmission and data-logging system. This produced a 0–100kph time of 3.9 seconds and a top speed of 135mph (217kph).

Of course, the biggest difference was the bodyshell, which reverted to four doors rather than the previous two-door. But the new shell was far stiffer than before – no less than 250 per cent more resistant to flexing than its predecessor, said Prodrive. Despite the extra doors, weight did not increase.

Peter Stevens, styling director at Prodrive, was responsible for creating the rally car's shape. He started work as early as Spring 1999. Air intakes were specially designed to cope with the extreme angles of yaw that rally cars undergo – as much as 15 from straight-ahead on gravel stages. Therefore the front was designed to split air into two streams for the intercooler and radiator.

Reworked inner rear wheel arches allowed longer suspension travel (to the same degree as the old two-door rally car). Designer Peter Stevens also commented: 'You want some downforce but not too much because the springs are relatively soft. And what we really don't want to happen is for the car to land nose first. If we treated the nose like an F1 car that's what we would get.'

Fascinatingly, Peter Stevens produced a sculpted dashboard shape for apparently psychological

↓ The Subaru World Rally team was easily the most youthful in 2001. At 30, Richard Burns was the oldest driver in the team, while Norwegian Petter Solberg, Estonian Markko Märtin and Toshihiro Arai of Japan were all younger.

reasons. 'I've never liked the cardboard box approach to rally car interiors. We've taken care to give the shapes of the console and dash an element of style. If the driver gets the message that some effort has been put into the car, he's more likely to feel confident. It works for the opposition too: they might look at the interior and wonder how we found the time to pay that much attention to detail.' The driver even had a full-colour binnacle giving digital 'pages' of information. The co-driver also had a much improved single digital display providing time and distance measurements, fuel consumption and computer functions. Each car reputedly cost around £350,000 to build.

The 2001 season kicked off in January with Team Principal David Lapworth sounding confident. 'We are in a good position; both quick and reliable. We're not as big as Ford so we have to be clever with our budget, and our reputation is for innovation and we are poised to take advantage of two years of hard work. It's been painful developing the new car but now we have a superb car and very talented drivers.'

The season started badly at the Monte Carlo Rally however. On an event of attrition, all three Subarus ducked out with what David Lapworth described as: 'the most bizarre combination of misfortunes I have ever seen.' Burns was clearly on the pace though, as he proved in Sweden in February. His blistering pace made him the fastest driver there but he beached his car on a snow bank early on and was always playing catch-up.

It got worse in Portugal, where Burns had steering and transmission problems and the other Subaru drivers failed to finish. It was a similar story in Spain, with both Märtin and Arai failing to reach the end and Burns suffering from gearbox problems and a puncture.

Finally some points were notched up in Argentina, where Burns almost succeeded in passing McRae, but the Scot eventually beat him into second place. There was a near-repeat in Cyprus, when McRae again took first with Burns in second, Arai battling home to take fourth.

If things had started to go well, they took a downturn again in Greece, where Burns left the road, Märtin's wheel broke and a fire put Arai out, although Solberg secured a podium finish. In a gruelling African Safari, the Subarus were again afflicted with problems and none finished. Burns

← Richard Burns took his one and only round victory in 2001 at the New Zealand Rally. But he was a consistent scorer, which proved enough for him to take the drivers' title for the first time.

↑ Achieving a championship victory had rarely been so tough, but Richard Burns was overjoyed. Here he celebrates his 2001 title victory by driving through the streets of London with the Union Flag.

admitted that the Championship was now only a remote possibility.

But this was the point at which fortunes turned and Burns put in a string of solid performances. He secured second place in the 1000 Lakes, missing out on first by dint of a puncture, with Märtin in fifth and Solberg seventh. Burns took his one and only victory of the season in New Zealand where his consistency was unassailable. San Remo was Burns's only blip in the second half of the season. In Corsica, Burns damaged his suspension but still led a Subaru 4-5-6 ahead of Solberg and Märtin. His main rivals in the Championship, Mäkinen and Sainz, crucially did not finish. A second place in Australia left it all to play for in the last rally – the RAC GB, where Burns needed to finish fourth to take the title.

In fog and rain, Richard Burns persevered as title contenders Colin McRae, Tommi Mäkinen and Carlos Sainz retired, and he eventually finished third. This was enough for him to take the drivers' title, two points ahead of McRae, and to become the first Englishman ever to win the FIA World Rally Championship for drivers. And this with Burns only winning one round in 2001! Arai finished tenth

in Britain, which ironically left Subaru in fourth, its worst placing in the title for manufacturers since the Impreza arrived.

Burns commented: 'There was massive pressure before this event, and to come through it like this is brilliant. It's a bit of a shame not to win my home event, but I'm overwhelmed by this experience; it's been a great team performance.' Team Principal David Lapworth added: 'People were writing us off in the middle of the season, but we've proved them wrong. Richard has proved himself now to be one of the best drivers in the world.'

2002 – Mäkinen joins Subaru

For 2002, there was a new version of the New Age rally car, with a revised exhaust, better turbo and throttle body, tougher transmission, new anti-roll bar mountings and a new rubber front spoiler splitter. For the new season, 555 sponsorship returned to the SWRT, while Burns left for Peugeot. His replacement was another absolute master of the sport, veteran Tommi Mäkinen supported by Petter Solberg.

It was Solberg who set the early pace, being fastest on stage three of the Monte Carlo. But Mäkinen's consistency handed him the first victory of the season, Solberg having to settle for sixth. A series of three mediocre results in Sweden (no finishes), Corsica (Solberg fifth, Mäkinen out) and Spain (same result), left Subaru suddenly looking adrift against Gronholm's Peugeot.

Things changed in Cyprus, with Mäkinen back on the podium in third place and Solberg in fifth. Mäkinen was looking strong in Argentina but crashed out just as victory seemed to be his while his Norwegian team-mate was eventually placed second. This was followed by Solberg's fifth in Greece and third in Finland (Subaru would probably rather forget an unlucky no-finish in Africa sandwiched between these two).

In Tommi's home rally, the 1000 Lakes, he was surprisingly off the pace, ending in sixth and letting Solberg take third. At the inaugural Rallye Deutschland, a series of problems led to every Impreza retiring except Mäkinen's, but he was out of the points in seventh. Solberg got his first ever tarmac podium at San Remo, where he came third,

a position that Mäkinen repeated in New Zealand and Solberg repeated in turn in Australia.

Going into the final round of the season, the RAC, Gronholm had already won the drivers' title and secured the manufacturers' title for Peugeot, but Solberg lying in seventh place could take second overall if he scored well. And he did – claiming his first ever victory in a WRC event, aged 27. Ford's Markko Märtin and Solberg slugged it out for the spoils, the Subaru driver emerging victorious. This meant he secured a creditable second place in the 2002 Drivers' Championship behind Gronholm. Tommi Mäkinen finished the rally in fourth place, leaving him in eighth place overall in the Drivers' Championship. In the Manufacturers' Championship, the 555 Subaru World Rally Team finished third.

2003 – Solberg's year

There was another new car for the 2003 season, featuring revisions to the engine, roll-cage, body panels and aerodynamics that mirrored the new

→ Tommi Mäkinen joined the Subaru team for 2002 and was rewarded with a victory in the opening round, the Monte Carlo. Mäkinen would remain with Subaru for 2002 and 2003, his last season in World Rallying.

2003 road car. Team-mates Tommi Mäkinen and Petter Solberg seemed very happy about the new car. As winner of the last four Monte Carlo rallies, Mäkinen's hopes were high for 2003, but in an icy first round at the Monte, many drivers came unstuck and both Subarus succumbed to damage sustained during off-piste manoeuvres.

The first points of the season came in Sweden, with Mäkinen performing strongly to take second, and Solberg sixth. The next event was the inaugural Turkish Rally, which proved to be a well-run but tough round. For Subaru, it was especially tough with only Mäkinen managing to score any points. In New Zealand, Solberg maintained his overnight third position on the final day to collect six WRC driver's points, with team-mate Mäkinen seventh.

In Argentina, Tommi was 13 minutes adrift at the end of day one after an incident, but a quick Solberg finished fifth overall, maintaining his solid scoring record. Next came Greece where Solberg was fastest on four of the six last-day's stages, but was delayed overtaking and had to settle for third, with team-mate Mäkinen fifth. A faultless performance in Cyprus saw Solberg

claim the second victory of his WRC career by a huge 4 minute 14 second margin.

In the second-ever German Rally, Solberg battled with flu to finish a creditable eighth overall, with Mäkinen again retiring (with alternator problems). At the 1000 Lakes, Solberg's consistently fast times overturned Richard Burns's overnight advantage so that the Norwegian snatched second overall on the very last stage. Mäkinen's home event was less kind to him, but he still came sixth overall. Solberg's third WRC victory of his career came in Australia, where he traded stage wins with his closest competitor, Citroën's Sebastien Loeb, but he eventually won by a decisive margin. After ten rounds, Subaru had moved up to third in the manufacturers' series, while Solberg was joint second in the drivers' title, seven points behind Richard Burns in his Peugeot.

Dramatically changing weather in Italy upset the order as tyre choice determined the outcome, with only Mäkinen making the top ten for Subaru. At the Tour de Corse, Solberg won by a margin of 36.6 seconds, leaving him just three points off the lead. It became even closer

↑ Norwegian Petter Solberg was Mäkinen's team-mate in 2002. Here he lands spectacularly back to earth on the Australian Rally, in which he finished third.

↑ Petter Solberg takes the crowd's adulation after winning the title at the end of the RAC Rally of Great Britain – an outstanding achievement for the young Norwegian.

↑ ↑ A revised rally Impreza appeared in 2003. It was to be Solberg's year, here proving it in mid-season by winning the Cyprus Rally, the second WRC victory of his career.

after the penultimate round in Catalunya, when Solberg pulled a fifth place out of the bag and ended just one point behind joint leaders Carlos Sainz and Sebastian Loeb, while Richard Burns (only four points behind Solberg) also had a chance of taking the title.

It started out very well at the last event of the season in Wales, with Solberg and Mäkinen ending the first day in first and third respectively. It got better on day two, as Solberg set the fastest time on every single stage, but Loeb was still in touch with him. On a spectacular last day, Loeb beat Solberg on the first stage and took a further

3.5 seconds out of his lead on the second stage. But Solberg was emphatic and pushed hard to win the third stage and ensure his win, by a margin of 43.6 seconds, collecting the fifth WRC win of his career.

Of course, this also meant he secured the 2003 WRC Drivers' title as the first Norwegian ever to win the FIA World Rally Championship for drivers. He commented: 'It's such a great way to finish the year, it's been hard at times and now it's just the greatest feeling.'

The GB Rally was significant for another reason. Poignantly contesting his last event as a full-time WRC driver, Tommi Mäkinen's last race was run at typically blistering pace and the four-times World Champion finished third.

In another celebration, Martin Rowe, driving an Impreza WRX STi, clinched victory in the 2003 FIA Production Car Championship, run alongside the main WRC. Indeed, Subaru achieved a clean sweep of the PCWRC podium, with Toshi Arai finishing second and Stig Blomqvist third.

The year ended with yet more drama. The Subaru team had signed Richard Burns for 2004, but the Englishman had collapsed on his way to the Rally in Wales and was diagnosed with a brain tumour. The team announced that he would not compete in the 2004 season alongside Solberg as planned. David Lapworth said: 'We are very concerned at this news

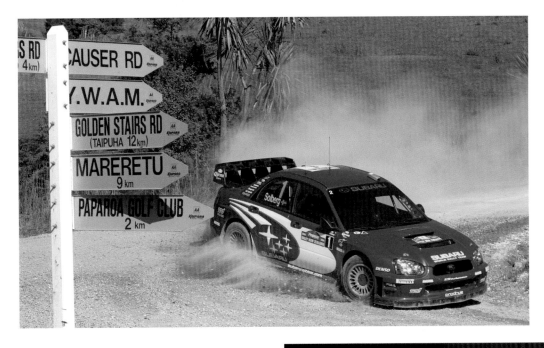

← The new WRC2004 Impreza was improved in terms of aerodynamics, suspension, engine, electronics and bodyshell stiffness. Here in New Zealand, Petter Solberg scores the 2004 car's first victory.

about Richard. There will always be future rallies and future championships, but for now Richard needs to put his own health first.'

2004 – Second place

With Subaru on a high, hopes were strong for another title in 2004. Subaru's driver roster consisted of Petter Solberg with navigator Phil Mills, and Mikko Hirvonen from Finland with Jarmo Lehtinen. But 2004 was to be decisively Sebastian Loeb's and Citroën's year.

The season started with a victory for Loeb in Monte Carlo, while Solberg could only manage seventh after he hit a patch of snow. Solberg got closer in Sweden, with a third place, but Loeb was unmatchable once again.

The new WRC2004 Impreza did not make its debut until the third rally of the season (Mexico), when both cars scored points. Although there were revisions to the aerodynamics and suspension, the main focus was on the engine, electronics and bodyshell stiffness. That the new car was quick right out of the box was proven in the next round, New Zealand, where Solberg took a thrilling victory over Marcus Gronholm.

Victory recurred two rounds later in Greece when Solberg claimed his first ever victory on the Acropolis Rally, making him the only driver to score points in all six rallies thus far. It also marked the

Impreza's 40th rally win and put Solberg just five points behind Loeb.

There was a third place for Solberg in Turkey but three successive rounds with no points on the scoreboard seemed to spell the end of the Norwegian's title hopes. Then, Solberg dramatically reversed his fortunes with three successive victories: in Japan he became the only driver to lead a WRC event from start to finish that season; in Wales he won his third successive Rally GB title, and he also dominated in Sardinia.

There was still a mathematical possibility to beat Loeb but it was all over in Corsica, where Loeb's

↑ Solberg is cheered as he sweeps to a dramatic victory on Subaru's home soil, leading the event from start to finish. It kept alive hopes of a second WRC title, but in the end he had to settle for second in the title battle, behind Sebastian Loeb.

→ The restyled WRC2005 Impreza made its debut at the Rally Mexico, featuring a stiffer, wider shell and minor engine changes.

↑ Petter Solberg won in Mexico in 2005 and had a solid enough season, finishing level on points with second-placed Marcus Gronholm.

shell and minor engine changes. Things initially looked very good for the team, with Solberg winning in Mexico and immediately following that with a second victory in Sweden. Atkinson made his debut at the Swedish Rally, but his first major success would not come until his podium placing at Rally Japan.

However, the 2005 season was pretty much dominated by Sébastien Loeb. Solberg and Marcus Gronholm battled it out for second spot and ended the season level on points. Subaru finished the season in a disappointing fourth place out of six.

second placing overall and Solberg's four points meant that the title was Loeb's. Subaru finished the season in third place in the manufacturers' title, with Solberg second in the drivers' race behind Loeb.

2005

Having finished the 2004 season in seventh place, Hirvonen was not deemed impressive enough to be hired for the 2005 season; instead the second position was occupied by Chris Atkinson, an Australian driver who had competed in one 2004 WRC event in a Subaru (the 2004 Rally New Zealand). Petter Solberg remained Subaru's number one driver.

The restyled WRC2005 STi made its debut at the Rally Mexico in March, featuring a stiffer, wider

2006

For 2006, a new regime banned active differentials and water injection, but the rules were otherwise little changed. Subaru's new 'Hawkeye' WRC2006 car was therefore ready for the very first event of the year. Once again, it was Petter Solberg who blazed Subaru's trail this season, supported by Chris Atkinson at gravel events, and ex-Formula 1 driver Stéphane Sarrazin on tarmac events.

A poor start to the season, with mechanical failures, was perhaps the reason behind team boss David Lapworth's departure from the Subaru World Rally Team in February 2006; he was replaced by Paul Howarth. It wasn't until the third rally of 2006, Rally Mexico, that Solberg scored his first points (he came second). He followed this with two more second places in Argentina and Australia,

162 SUBARU IMPREZA TURBO

but the season was very much a head-to-head between Sebastien Loeb's Citroen and Marcus Gronholm's Ford.

For Subaru, 2006 was to be a very lacklustre season. Without a single win all year, and with podiums in only four rallies, one commentator was moved to describe Subaru's year as "The Season from Hell". In fact, the team finished higher up the championship table in 2006 than in 2005, ending up in third place in the manufacturers' standings, although Solberg could only muster sixth in the drivers' championship.

2007

2007's WRC car featured only minor changes, including new dampers, cooling system, suspension geometry and differentials. Despite the evolutionary approach, the 2007 Impreza proved to be a curiously difficult car to drive. A telling scenario came at Rally Finland, where handling problems forced Subaru to withdraw on the second day of the event. And Solberg's conclusion after coming fifth in Rally Ireland? It was "the most difficult rally I've ever done."

Sarrazin departed the team for 2007, leaving Solberg and Atkinson to fight Subaru's corner (although a third Impreza was campaigned from mid-season by Xavier Pons but was not nominated for manufacturer points). Again there was early promise, with Atkinson coming fourth at the opening rally in Monte Carlo. Solberg had to wait

until the fifth event of the season, in Portugal, for his first podium – a second placing. Another notable success was Solberg's podium in the Acropolis Rally.

But overall, 2007 was another very difficult year for Subaru. Only two podium finishes and no overall wins was a far cry from the glory days. Solberg ended the season in fifth place, with Subaru only able to muster third in the manufacturers' competition.

2008

2008 was momentous for several reasons. Firstly, it was the first time for many years that Mitsubishi did not compete in the championship. Secondly, it saw the debut of the all-new Impreza GE WRC

↓ **Australian Chris Atkinson showed early promise in 2007 but failed to score a single podium finish for Subaru that year.**

← **The WRC2006 prototype featured the new 'Hawkeye' front end, but the 2006 would prove very disappointing for Subaru, with not a single win to its name.**

car based on the hatchback shell. And third, it marked the end of an era: Subaru would pull out of WRC at the end of the year.

The season started with the previous year's car; the new WRC2008 car would not debut until well into the season, at the Acropolis Rally in Greece. When it did, it continued to use the 2.0-litre engine, rather than the 2.5, and it stuck with the old MacPherson rear suspension rather than the new model's multilink/double wishbone set-up. It was certainly a dramatic-looking machine, dominated by a large biplane rear wing.

Solberg and Atkinson continued as the drivers for 2008. As ever with Subaru, there was early promise. On the first rally of the season, the Monte Carlo Rally, Atkinson scored a podium finish (his first ever on tarmac). He followed this up with two second placings in Mexico and Argentina, his best ever results. There was also a good early showing for the new WRC2008 car, which scored second place in its first race at the Acropolis Rally, with Petter Solberg at the helm. Atkinson finished the season just ahead of Solberg, in fifth and sixth places respectively, in a year dominated once again by Loeb in the Citroen.

End of an era: Subaru leaves WRC

After 20 seasons in world rallying, on 16 December 2008 Subaru made a shock announcement: it was withdrawing from the World Rally Championship. That was just one day after Suzuki had made a similar announcement.

The drastic decision came against a backdrop of global economic turmoil in the autumn of 2008. Fuji Heavy Industries said: "Our business environment has been dramatically changed due to the quick deterioration of the global economy." President Mori commented that reaching this decision had been an extremely difficult task, and he acknowledged the countless Subaru fans who had supported the blue-liveried Imprezas over the years.

The announcement marked the end of a 20-year Subaru/Prodrive collaboration in WRC. Prodrive chairman, David Richards, said: "Subaru's departure from the World Rally Championship is a great loss, as it is one of the sport's icons. The Subaru World Rally Team has created true champions such as Colin McRae and Richard Burns and its absence will be felt by many the world over."

Prodrive punctuated its announcement by selling off a number of legendary Impreza rally cars, including the 1997 WRC car driven by Colin McRae, Pierro Liatti and Kenneth Erikkson. A further seven former works WRC Imprezas and 17 Group N cars also went on sale, priced from £50,000 up to nearly £350,000 for a 2008 WRC car.

However, this was not the end of WRC rallying for the Impreza. The 2009 season saw what was essentially the WRC2008 car competing once again but under Prodrive's name, not Subaru's. Prodrive had inherited a handful of Impreza World Rally Cars in the split with Subaru, and made a return to WRC competition in Portugal with a single car. Behind the wheel was none other than double world champion Marcus Gronholm, his first drive in WRC for 18 months. He had a good start, holding second place during day one, but he then clipped a tree, rolled and was forced to retire. And that marked the end of his – and the Impreza's – WRC comeback.

Would Subaru ever return to WRC? Nobody in Subaru had been prepared to rule it out when it withdrew from the series in 2008, but as of 2010 it had still not re-entered WRC. For the time being, at the time of writing, Subaru continues to throw its weight behind its Group N Impreza competition business – for example, by joining the Intercontinental Rally Challenge in 2010. It is thought that as many as 1,000 Subarus were rallying around the world in 2010.

↑ ↑ In December 2008, Subaru announced that it was withdrawing from the World Rally Championship. This WRC2009 prototype wears Prodrive branding.

↑ Prodrive made a fleeting return to WRC competition in Portugal with a single car, piloted by double world champion Marcus Gronholm. His crash in that event marked the end of the Impreza's WRC career, at least for the time being.

← The Impreza continues to be one of the most-rallied cars of all time. Here 13-year-old Sean Galael takes victory in the Junior Rally Sprint in Indonesia.

Subaru Impreza – major factory-backed Rally Championship victories

Year	Championship	Position
2008	World Rally Championship (Manufacturers)	3rd
	World Rally Championship (Drivers)	5th
2007	World Rally Championship (Manufacturers)	3rd
	World Rally Championship (Drivers) 5th	
2006	World Rally Championship (Manufacturers)	3rd
	World Rally Championship (Drivers)	6th
2005	World Rally Championship (Manufacturers)	4th
	World Rally Championship (Drivers)	2nd
2004	World Rally Championship (Manufacturers)	3rd
	World Rally Championship (Drivers)	2nd
2003	World Rally Championship (Manufacturers)	3rd
	World Rally Championship (Drivers)	1st
	Asia-Pacific Rally Championship (Drivers)	4th
	Asia-Pacific Rally Championship (Manufacturers)	12th
2002	World Rally Championship (Manufacturers)	3rd
	World Rally Championship (Drivers)	2nd
	Asia-Pacific Rally Championship (Drivers)	5th
	Asia-Pacific Rally Championship (Manufacturers)	3rd
2001	World Rally Championship (Manufacturers)	4th
	World Rally Championship (Drivers)	1st
	Asia-Pacific Rally Championship (Drivers)	2nd
	Asia-Pacific Rally Championship (Manufacturers)	2nd
2000	World Rally Championship (Manufacturers)	3rd
	World Rally Championship (Drivers)	2nd
	Asia-Pacific Rally Championship (Drivers)	1st
	Asia-Pacific Rally Championship (Manufacturers)	1st
1999	World Rally Championship (Manufacturers)	2nd
	World Rally Championship (Drivers)	2nd
	Asia-Pacific Rally Championship (Drivers)	1st
	Asia-Pacific Rally Championship (Manufacturers)	2nd
1998	World Rally Championship (Manufacturers)	3rd
	World Rally Championship (Drivers)	3rd
	Asia-Pacific Rally Championship (Drivers)	1st
	Asia-Pacific Rally Championship (Manufacturers)	1st
1997	World Rally Championship (Manufacturers)	1st
	World Rally Championship (Drivers)	2nd
	Asia-Pacific Rally Championship (Drivers)	1st
	Asia-Pacific Rally Championship (Manufacturers)	1st
1996	World Rally Championship (Manufacturers)	1st
	World Rally Championship (Drivers)	2nd
	Asia-Pacific Rally Championship (Drivers)	1st
	Asia-Pacific Rally Championship (Manufacturers)	2nd
1995	World Rally Championship (Manufacturers)	1st
	World Rally Championship (Drivers)	1st
	Asia-Pacific Rally Championship (Drivers)	3rd
	Asia-Pacific Rally Championship (Manufacturers)	2nd
1994	World Rally Championship (Manufacturers)	2nd
	World Rally Championship (Drivers)	2nd
	Asia-Pacific Rally Championship (Drivers)	1st
	Asia-Pacific Rally Championship (Manufacturers)	1st

At Prodrive HQ, David Lapworth is justifiably proud of the Impreza WRC's impressive silverware collection.

CHAPTER 9
OWNERSHIP AND MAINTENANCE

For sheer owner satisfaction the Impreza makes one of the most convincing car buys around. Speak to a typical owner and they will rave about its reliability and durability – not for nothing did the Impreza score first place in the JD Power customer satisfaction survey twice. Demand has traditionally been strong so that depreciation has been less crushing than most other cars, and the Impreza continues to enjoy a very strong image.

You gain tremendous satisfaction of ownership from the outset, even with a totally standard car. The performance, grip level and ride quality are way above what you would normally expect at this price level, and the Impreza rewards you loyally, remaining dependable as the miles stack up.

No-one is pretending that the Impreza is some motoring panacea, or that little old ladies should abandon their Metros to discover the joys of Scoobydom. Of course, there are drawbacks to Impreza ownership. The first is the potential expense. You'll want to enjoy the performance to the full and that can work out very costly on fuel bills – mid-teen mpg figures and worse-can result if you're constantly pedal to the metal. Insurance groupings are high because the Impreza has been one of the more popular conveyances of the criminal classes. The situation is tougher with grey import cars, which have the additional worry of potentially expensive parts sourcing for insurance companies, and therefore higher insurance groupings. Also, the turbocharged engine does need meticulous attention to avoid big bills in the future.

Naturally, you need to make sure you buy the right car in the first place. Just because the Impreza has a reputation for being dependable does not mean there are no problem cars out there, or no known areas of weakness. Despite what you may have been told, the Impreza can't defy laws of physics and crash damage is not uncommon. Cars have often been thrashed, so you always need to be careful in your checks.

Engine

The turbocharged boxer engine is what really makes the Impreza special. Gruff-sounding, very powerful, compact, lightweight and highly charismatic, it also has the major benefit of being very robust and reliable.

With proper maintenance (see later), the engine should last a very healthy number of miles. However, because some of the maintenance is expensive, proper servicing sometimes occurs late or is skipped altogether by penny-pinching owners. Always check the service record to confirm that vital items such as spark plugs, lubricants and, in particular, the cambelt have been replaced at the correct time.

Flat-four engines have a sound all of their own. A slightly rough note is how the engine should sing. However if you hear a distinct knocking sound below 2,000rpm, this can indicate piston slap. The problem is known particularly on 1998 cars, occurring typically between 10,000 and 20,000 miles on the number three piston. The

DID YOU KNOW?
'Scooby' do
Just about every car gets a nickname at some point or another. The one that has stuck for Subaru – and by association the Impreza – is 'Scooby'. One suggestion of the origin of this word is that 'Scooby Doo' is Cockney rhyming slang for Subaru, so Scooby is the contraction. This seems more likely than trying to draw similarities between the Impreza and the floppy biscuit-munching canine in Hannah Barbera's cartoon series. In New Zealand, Subaru is sometimes known as 'Subby'. The Impreza name is often contracted to just 'Imp' although owners of the Coventry Climax-powered Hillman may well have something to say about that.

→ **Engines are very robust but do check that the turbocharger is quiet as it spins. Failed dump valves and clogged wastegate solenoids are known turbo weaknesses, especially on early cars.**

only solution is a new block, although by now any problem should already have come to light and the block replaced under warranty.

The turbocharger should also be quiet in operation and there should be no smoke from the exhaust at idle, which is a sign of a worn turbo. Known problems on turbos include the dump valve failing to close properly on 1997 MY and 1998 MY cars (listen for a noise that, on boost, resembles a mooing cow) and clogged wastegate solenoids due to over filling with oil, especially on pre-1998 cars. Aftermarket air filters that are too heavy can break the air-flow monitor.

Replacing a turbocharger is costly, so learn to look after it. After a long journey or hard use, you should always let the engine idle to let the heat in the turbo dissipate before switching off. Failure to do this ultimately results in coked internals.

Exhaust

Luckily, exhaust systems can be long-lived. However, this is an area where many owners have modified their cars, usually with a more free-flowing rear box. Check that the exhaust is not leaking and that the tail pipe is not too wide (which can restrict the back pressure available to spin the turbo). Be aware that big tail pipes can be very loud too – which may or may not be your thing.

Pre-1997 cars are known to suffer from heatshield cracking problems. If they are suddenly cooled when hot (such as being doused with water – flood-strewn Britons and Aussies beware), they can easily fracture. This condition will identify itself by a buzzing sound, particularly around the 3,000rpm level. Packing out the shield so that

temperatures do not get quite so high will solve the problem in the future.

Transmission

The 4x4 system is extremely tough, reflecting its robust, long-lived, tried and tested design and its use in gruelling rally events with little modification. However, gearbox failures are not unknown. These have usually been down to bearings or synchromesh giving way, so always check for smoothness of operation and excessive whine on over-run. Check for a notchy gearchange; first-to-second gearchange quality is a problem on pre-1997 MY cars, so expect some notchiness on early cars. On 1998 MY cars, the bottom of the gear lever sits inside a plastic boot that is held in place by a circlip that is too small and can pop out, especially with a quickshift fitted.

Clutches do tend to have a short life if they are subjected to abuse: in ordinary use they can last up to 45,000 miles but an abused one can give way after only a few thousand miles. It is vital that you get the car rolling before planting the accelerator, as slipping the clutch at high revs for a quick getaway can destroy the clutch in one operation. Clutch slip will usually mean expensive bills, as clutches are very costly to replace: the clutch kit itself is £350 at the time of writing, but fitting is time-consuming (up to five hours) as it involves dropping the gearbox out. Juddering clutches when the engine is cold may simply be down to the sheer torque being applied to the wheels, but if the juddering occurs only when the engine is hot, changing to Dot 5 fluid may cure this. A sticking clutch pedal may be down to pressure loss in the clutch master cylinder or lack of spring pressure in the clutch cover plate.

Brakes

Brakes do take a pounding at the feet of Impreza drivers. Discs can last as little as 20,000 miles before needing replacement at over £100 each. Check for warped or cracked discs and signs of juddering under braking. Pedal feel can become rather spongy on older cars, and brake fade is notorious if you're using the car hard (for example, on a track day). This is easily alleviated by uprating the braking system (see the chapter on Tuning and modification).

Suspension

As the Impreza is expected to cope with high g-forces, the suspension is extremely robust and long-lasting. Nevertheless you need to check things carefully. Listen out for clonking noises, which can indicate worn anti-roll bar bushes. Replacement is an easy job to do, but if left unattended the mounts may need replacing as well. Fitting harder bushes should make them last longer, but they have to be changed all at once and the ride quality may suffer a little.

Look under the car to check for bent or new rear suspension links and distorted inner front wishbone mounts, which indicate accident damage or serious kerbing. Uneven tyre wear may also give this away.

Bodywork

While the Impreza is a tough car, look carefully for stone chipping, a scraped undertray and car park dents. The front spoiler is not as low as some performance cars, but do check for signs of grounding on sleeping policemen and the like. Check that the large front spotlamps are not cracked.

Rust really is not a problem on cars sold in Europe, which came with a six-year anti-corrosion warranty (ensure that the relevant checks have been made at a Subaru dealership at the correct

times). If rust does occur, it will be minor outbreaks in areas like the bumper attachment points. Rust is more of a concern on Japanese grey imports that may not have been undersealed (see the section on buying a grey import). Always run a history check on the car to ascertain previous accident records, whether it has been previously stolen or is subject to any outstanding finance.

Wheels and tyres

This is possibly the most common area of modification on Imprezas. The early (pre-1998) 15-inch alloy wheel type is not very appealing aesthetically. Moreover some of these early wheels are known to be porous, which can lead to air escaping from the tyres, although this problem should have been sorted under warranty. Always check for signs of kerbing, especially as serious kerbing can indicate possible bent suspension. Gold wheels are desirable and carry a premium, while a good new set of Prodrive-sourced alloys always

↖ Brakes tend to be used more in an Impreza than most other cars, so expect a short life. Warped discs and signs of juddering under braking will mean replacement. The brakes are a popular area of modification.

↑ The suspension is very tough but check for worn anti-roll bar bushes. Bent or recently replaced links and distorted front wishbone mounts may indicate accident damage.

← Serious kerbing can result in bent suspension. Be suspicious of uneven tyre wear, which can also give accident damage away. Gold wheels carry a premium if you're buying used.

looks good in the 'for sale' columns; 16-inch wheels are most popular, 17-inch wheels are more suitable for serious driving (especially tuned cars), and even 18-inch wheels are possible.

As for tyres, these can last 20,000 miles but life drops away quickly if the car is being used hard. Front tyres wear more quickly than rear ones. Always ensure that the correct profile tyre is used for the wheel size, and that the width is suitable for the rim. Uneven tyre wear is a sign of possible suspension or steering damage.

↑ Standard interiors are hard-wearing but rather uninspired. The plastic in early cars tended to scratch easily and can tear if subjected to an impact.

↗ The wiring loom is barely enough to cope with standard headlamps. If upgraded lighting has been fitted, check that the loom matches it, otherwise it can melt.

→ Security is an important issue with the frequently stolen Impreza. In Britain, you are unlikely to obtain insurance unless a Thatcham Category 1 alarm/immobiliser is fitted. Only post-1999 cars came with a Category 1 alarm as standard.

Interior

The lacklustre cabin is perhaps the Impreza's weakest area. Early (pre-October 1996) cars were particularly uninspiring. While 1997 MY cars had new cloth trim and high-backed winged sports front seats, a large percentage of pre-1997 cars will have been upgraded at least as far as the seating is concerned. Check that the seats are correctly installed and suitable for you.

Most of the interior trim is pretty hard-wearing but the plastic used in early cars has a tendency to get scratched. The rear-view mirror is prone to vibration. Air conditioning is a very desirable item to have but it was always optional on UK cars (except for some special editions), but was standard in Australia. Climate control is standard on almost all Japanese imports (only the RA versions were supplied as standard without climate control).

Electrics

Most Japanese cars are hugely reliable on the electrical front, and the Impreza is no exception. The Scooby was never the most gadget-laden machine – luxury items were never really its bag – but what is there is usually extremely reliable.

As noted in the chapter on modifications, fitting more powerful headlamps can melt the rather inadequate wiring loom, so check this out when you are looking at the car. The air conditioning wiring terminates near the radiator, and may hang loose on cars where no air con is fitted, so always terminate the wire properly. In the UK, the audio system was changed for the 1997 MY

from a Subaru-badged Panasonic radio/cassette to a Philips unit with a removable front, but many owners replace the system with something with more power and quality.

Security

It's one of the unfortunate facts of life that desirable cars are targeted by thieves, and the Impreza is a five-star favourite among joy riders. Some form of security is really essential. Indeed, in the UK most insurance companies insist on a Thatcham Category 1 alarm/immobiliser in order to insure you, so make sure one is fitted.

In the UK, prior to July 1996, cars were fitted at the docks with a Thatcham Category 2 Cobra 0802T immobiliser (where an upgrade to a Category 1 alarm was possible). Post-July 1996 Imprezas gained factory-fitted transponder immobilisers using the normal ignition key to unlock the engine management system. However this system does not meet Thatcham Category 2

Track days

There is nothing quite like the feeling of edging out of a pit lane on a well-known racing circuit, in the full knowledge that you can explore both your and your car's limits in relative safety. We're talking about track days, an increasingly popular phenomenon among performance car drivers, and especially Impreza pilots.

The variety of track day events is becoming ever wider (for a full listing of UK track day contacts, see the Appendix at the rear of this book). Even a standard Impreza can provide thrills and huge enjoyment, while modifying your car can transform its on-track abilities (see the chapter on Tuning and Modification for full details).

When you attend a track day, the emphasis will always be on safety: track etiquette, wearing of helmets and suitable clothing, proper briefing for drivers and so on. Your car will need to be scrutineered, which usually consists of a brief inspection that the car is safe to take to the track, particularly in the lighting department.

There may be noise limits at certain tracks.

You may be lucky enough to be taken on familiarisation laps by experienced tutors. Depending on the event, you may be assessed as to your experience with performance cars and circuit driving and sometimes put in classes so that you are on track with drivers and cars of a similar standard. Crashing is a rare occurrence, for if you crash on a track day it usually means you are driving well beyond your limits.

Specialised insurance schemes are widely available. You'll certainly go through tyres, brakes and fuel at a rate of knots, and you'll need to keep an eye on fluid temperatures and levels, and the condition of brake pads and tyres during the day.

Track days are great fun and need not be expensive. They provide an excellent way to get to know the limits of your car in an environment that is safe and organised – and, crucially, well away from Gatso cameras.

Track days provide the perfect opportunity to explore the Impreza's abilities and your limits in safe surroundings. Pictured is Nino Morelli's Prodrive WR Sport in action.

standards as the engine is allowed to run briefly before being immobilised. In this case, an after-market system should be fitted along with a remote locking alarm to gain Category 1 status. A good system costs a few hundred pounds. Note that the Terzo special edition has a Thatcham Category 1 remote locking alarm/immobiliser (a Cobra 6422). All UK cars from the 1999 Model Year also gained a Sigma Category 1 system, but check the mounting brackets which are known to be weak. For the most complete protection, you could also consider installing a 'Tracker' type device, standard on the STi Type UK.

Buying Japanese market grey imports

So-called grey imports from Japan have become extremely popular in right-hand-drive markets such as the UK, Australia, New Zealand and Cyprus – and have even been sold officially in the latter three markets. Imports offer extra power, extra

equipment and often a lower purchase price.

The price factor is down to the fact that Japanese cars are far cheaper on the domestic market than in export markets. Combined with high incomes in Japan, this means that vehicles are treated more like white goods, to be disposed of regularly. The Japanese usually sell their cars after three years as the *Sha-ken* – the Japanese MoT – becomes due. It is usually expensive to pass and

↓ A full dealer service history adds to the value and saleability of any Impreza. In the UK, dealers are reluctant to service imports, so a burgeoning specialist industry has sprung up to cater for this market.

→ **Any WRX imported from Japan needs modifications for UK roads. One example is changing the speedometer face to read in miles per hour rather than kilometres per hour. You can replace the whole unit or recalibrate the existing speedo to compensate.**

provides a good incentive to sell. It also has the effect of further battering down prices, as does the punitive tax regime on older cars.

Reputable importers will only buy good quality cars, and should be able to supply finance and warranty and carry out all modifications required for the local market. Always ask for names and addresses of previous satisfied customers.

Do not under any circumstances think of flying out to Japan and visiting dealers to buy a car yourself. To buy a car from a dealer, you need to supply a Japanese postal address and proof of a parking space, and the only way you can buy a car at auction in Japan is if you are a registered dealer.

Instead, you have to use some sort of agent. Usually agents source cars from the massive auctions in Japan, with thousands of cars sold at each one, often including dozens of Imprezas. You can fly out to Japan and choose your car in person at an auction (the import agent will have a local Japanese contact who will do the buying at the auction on your behalf). But it's more common to request that the agent does all the sourcing and purchasing for you. Internet technology now allows you to view pictures and details of specific models in stock or awaiting auction in Japan via many companies. You can specify the exact model you require and any budget you are working to. If you do not feel the need to kick tyres, this is often a good option.

Against the low purchase price in Japan, you must offset expenses such as deregistration in Japan, shipping costs, insurance in transit and any agency fees. You also need to investigate the cost of customs clearance. In the UK, import duty is 10 per cent and VAT of 17.5 per cent must be

paid on all import costs. Then you will need to take care of registration and licensing. In the UK this means taking in certificates for MoT or Single Vehicle Approval test, insurance and Japanese deregistration to the Vehicle Registration Office. In practice, any agent should sort all this for you, but check that all costs have been included in the quote they provide.

Probably the easiest and safest option is to walk on to the forecourt of an established grey importer, find the car you want and buy it. This has the advantages that the car has already been registered and tested and will be ready to drive away. You also have the advantage of actually seeing the car right in front of you.

What do you need to check for when buying a grey import rather than a local Impreza? You do need to exercise extra caution buying such a car. Usually, cars will have been well looked after if they are fresh from Japan but never assume that to be the case. Accident damage and abuse is just as possible with a Japanese import as any other car.

You are unlikely to get a service history with the car; or if you do it will be in Japanese. Also, you will have to use your judgement to decide whether the mileage on the clock is correct. Cars from Japan are usually not undersealed, so this is something that you should always insist on; good undersealing costs less than £100 and you don't want your Scooby to disappear in a pool of orange sludge! Check also that all modifications necessary to make the car legal have been passed. In the UK, a Single Vehicle Approval (SVA) certificate is required to register the car, showing that is has passed safety and emissions standards. On an Impreza, the fuel filler neck needs to be restricted to suit unleaded fuel pumps, the speedometer needs to be calibrated in mph, a rear foglamp needs to be fitted and the control knobs on the dashboard need to be filed down slightly to pass minimum distance from driver conditions. The SVA test was made tougher as of 1 August 2001, with serious implications regarding emissions, such that 1997-99 cars may be uneconomic to import.

Maintenance is also an issue, as dealers in the UK for example will not service grey imports (you have to seek out a specialist), and sometimes specialised parts (such as aluminium body panels or STi items) have to be flown in specially from Japan.

Maintenance

GENERAL MAINTENANCE

Speak to Impreza owners and you will quickly lose count of the number of them who will tell you their steed is the most reliable car they've ever owned. It is most rare for an Impreza to let you down, but equally you would not want to abuse a machine that provides such good service. After all, the Impreza Turbo is a high performance machine and as such regular checks should be made on the most important systems, ideally once a week.

ENGINE

Check the oil level when the engine is cold; the gap between the 'Add' and 'Full' marks is one litre. Stick to one type of oil grade. You can consider using a synthetic oil, which gives superior performance at a certain expense, but you must make sure the engine is bedded in before using synthetic oil (after around 3,000–6,000 miles). Avoid over-filling as this can clog the wastegate solenoids: ideally fill so that the 'Full' mark is not quite approached.

Check radiator hoses for leaks or damage and, when the engine is cold, squeeze them for pliancy; if they are hard, they may need replacing. There should be no cracking on any of the belts in the engine, and they should not move by more than 15mm when pressed.

There are several vital tips to bear in mind on running your engine. When starting, do not press the throttle down, as this can shut down the ECU and result in a non-starting car. As with any engine, especially an all-aluminium one such as the Impreza's, avoid hard use or high revs from cold. Stay below 3,000rpm until the unit has warmed up. When stopping after hard use, always let the turbocharger cool down for at least a minute by leaving the engine running to lubricate the system. 'Turbo timers' are available to keep the engine idling automatically for a pre-programmed time after you have switched off, but security is an issue here if you walk away with your engine still running. Some local laws prohibit leaving a vehicle unattended with the engine still running.

BRAKES

To get the best life out of your brakes, follow a few simple rules. Never apply hard braking when the discs are cold, as they can warp, and never sit with your foot on the brake pedal once the discs are hot, as the same thing can result. Discs are more vulnerable when they are older and thinner. As for pads, these can last anything from 5,000 miles to 60,000 miles, depending on use. If you're going through pads at a rate of knots, consider fitting harder pads which offer better performance and wear, although discs will wear more quickly. Most pads need bedding in (a period of milder use) when new, but some harder compound pads can be used straight out of the box.

TRANSMISSION

Clutch judder when cold has already been mentioned, and may simply be down to the design parameters of the clutch as it tries to cope with putting down so much power through the 4x4 system. Keep revs down when the engine is cold. Likewise, when things get very hot there can be clutch slip – again keep the revs down to prevent frying your clutch.

FLUIDS

Coolant levels need to be checked regularly, ideally on a weekly basis. When topping up the radiator, remember to add anti-freeze in winter. The power steering fluid should be translucent when checked (ideally when the engine is hot). If the fluid is dirty, the system should be drained and flushed. The same comment applies to the transmission fluid. A low brake fluid level could mean worn pads (more fluid fills the calliper pots to compensate), or it could mean a leak, in which case urgent remedy is required. Also, the battery works quite hard in the Impreza and it is relatively small for the duties it has to perform, so regular checks on electrolyte levels are needed.

TYRES

The recommended tyre pressures for 205/55 VR15 tyres are 33psi front, 32psi rear, and some dealers recommend the same pressures for 16 and 17-inch wheels. But Prodrive suggests a lower, 30psi pressure for the rear tyres (or 32psi on longer high speed runs) for all wheel sizes. In Australia, tuning specialist MRT suggests 35psi on both front and rear. Ultimately it is a matter of trial and error and arriving at pressures around these levels that suit your particular use. There is no need to reduce pressures in cold weather.

Combating tyre wear is something you'll want to consider. Over-inflate rather than under-inflate to achieve more longevity and better fuel efficiency. Tyre

→ Restricting the fuel filler neck is a modification that needs to be done to make any imported Impreza suitable for European fuel pumps. It is vital that you use at least 97RON super unleaded fuel for imports.

life varies very much according to use. Front tyres can last as little as 7,000 miles if used very hard, but more commonly they last between 15,000 and 20,000 miles. Rear tyres can remain in service for up to 40,000 miles. Practise tyre rotation to extend tyre life (to around 25,000 miles for each set of four) and always match tyres by buying new tyres in pairs. Never rotate badly worn or damaged front tyres to the rear. If you need to replace a whole set of 15-inch tyres in one go, this may be the ideal time to upgrade to a set of 16 or 17-inch alloys.

SERVICING

In the UK, servicing intervals for the Turbo were every six months or every 7,500 miles, whichever is the sooner (later extended to 12 months or 10,000 miles). The first six monthly service counts as a minor service (checks and adjustments, oil and filter change), which should cost no more than £100. An annual inspection or intermediate service should cost about £130 at a UK official dealer.

As the Impreza ages, naturally its servicing costs increase. The major service at 30,000 miles will cost in the region of £380. Timing belts are relatively costly to replace and need doing every 45,000-miles or three years, and as part of the 45,000 mile service, should cost around £325.

Spark plugs are quite difficult to get to. Early manuals recommended that they be changed every year or every 15,000 miles, but the Turbo model with its special platinum tipped plugs (quite expensive to buy, incidentally) can go two years and 30,000 miles between plug changes.

Servicing for grey import Japanese cars follows a broadly similar pattern. However, in the UK, the official Subaru concessionaire refuses to allow its dealers to service greys, forcing you to find a good independent specialist, of which there are many around now. Import specialist Charlesworth recommends a minor service costing around £100 every 6,000 miles, with a major service costing more like £450 every 12,000 miles.

Fuel issues

Owning a car with such performance potential, it is almost unavoidable to make full and spirited use of the available power, with consequent heavy effects on fuel consumption. A typical average is

↑ Always check the service record thoroughly to confirm that vital components have been replaced, especially the cambelt, lubricants and spark plugs.

20–23mpg (14–12 litres/100km), but enthusiastic use of the loud pedal can see that plunge as low as 15mpg (19 litres/100km). At the extremes, gentle 'touring' use can see the figure rise as high as 30mpg (9.4 litres/100km), while at the opposite end, track day blasts can result in prolonged blasts of just 8mpg (35 litres/100km)! The 60-litre fuel tank gives a typical range of 200–300 miles (320–480km) – not great but better than the Mitsubishi Lancer Evo, for example.

What about the type of fuel to use? In the Impreza's home market, fuel quality is much higher than in most export markets. The octane rating of Japanese fuel is as high as 100RON, far higher than other countries. This is one of the reasons why the engine had to be re-engineered and detuned for export.

'Super Unleaded' in the UK rates at 97RON, but 'Super' in other countries such as the USA and Australia is only 95RON, the same as regular unleaded in the UK. The Turbo can be run on 95RON fuel, although many owners in the UK prefer to run on 97RON super unleaded, reporting extra smoothness and a modest improvement in fuel economy.

Using octane boosters is perhaps controversial, but they should be safe to use, neither generating any more boost nor more power. They modify the flame front and reduce the risk of pre-detonation (pinking), but you should ensure you find one that is suitable for catalysts.

Low octane fuel should never be used in WRX and STi imports from Japan, where adverse effects have been widely reported. In the UK 97RON super unleaded must be used, and even then it is likely to reduce power output: many owners report that engines supposed to develop 280bhp actually develop more like 260bhp. If you are using lower octane fuel than this, there may actually be engine damage. There were certainly reports of this with the STi versions sold officially in Australia, and the problem has also affected some grey import cars in the UK. It's a serious issue, as the reported fault is nothing less than engine meltdown, involving failed pistons, valves and worn bores when 95RON only is used. This is because detonation occurs at lower temperatures, causing knocking. The ECU detects this and tries to compensate but it can reach its limits so that it can do no more to stop the pre-detonation. Such pre-detonation can melt pistons or break down the oil film in the big end bearings.

If you have used lower quality fuel you may need an 'ECU reset'. The engine's electronics react to lower quality fuel, retarding the timing and reducing maximum boost from the turbo. As the ECU 'learns' to cope with poorer quality fuel, it needs to 'unlearn' this too. Eventually it should re-adapt once higher quality fuel is put back in the tank but resetting the ECU will speed things up. This is something that your Subaru dealer should be able to do.

UK SERVICING SCHEDULES (classic-shape Impreza Turbo)

Item	Interval – *months/thousand miles*									See note
	1	6/7.5	12/15	18/22.5	24/30	30/37.5	36/45	42/52.5	48/60	
Drive belts (except camshaft)	I	I	I	I	I	I	I	I	I	
Camshaft belts							R			
Engine oil	R	R	R	R	R	R	R	R	R	1
Engine oil filter	R	R	R	R	R	R	R	R	R	1
Engine coolant				R					R	
Cooling system, hoses & connections	I		I		I		I		I	
Fuel filter					R				R	
Fuel system, line & connections			I		I		I		I	2
Air filter			I		R		I		R	1
Spark plugs			R		R		R		R	
4-Gas Analysis Check			I		I				I	
Transmission & diff. gear oil			I		R				R	1
Brake fluid	I	I	I	I	R	I	I	I	R	3
Brake pads & discs		I	I	I	I	I	I	I	I	
Axle shafts, joints & boots			I		I		I		I	2
Brake lines		I	I	I	I	I	I	I	I	
Park & service brake operation		I	I	I	I	I	I	I	I	2
Clutch system	A		I		I		I		I	
Full geometry check	Perform as required at additional cost									
Steering & suspension system			I		I		I		I	2
Operation of lights, wipers, washers	I	I	I	I	I	I	I	I	I	
Tyre condition and inflation pressures	I	I	I	I	I	I	I	I	I	
Wheel bearing lubricant									(I)	

A: Adjust   R: Replace or change   I: Inspect, correct or replace if necessary   *Details taken from Service and Warranties Booklet*

Notes:
1. *If the vehicle is used under severe driving conditions, replace more often than the usual recommended intervals.*
2. *If the vehicle is used under severe driving conditions, inspect every 7,500 miles or six months, whichever occurs first.*
3. *If the vehicle is used under high humidity conditions or mountainous areas, replace fluid every 15,000 miles or 12 months, whichever occurs first.*

Severe driving conditions are:
   Driving in extremely cold weather
   Towing a trailer
   Driving regular short distances
   Driving on dusty roads
   Driving on rough or muddy roads
   Driving in areas using road salt or other corrosive materials
   Driving in coastal areas

CHAPTER 10
TUNING AND MODIFICATION

Few cars are as impressive as the turbocharged Impreza straight out of the box. Supercar-slaying performance and superhuman grip are standard features to be enjoyed by every owner. The Impreza flatters even the most ham-fisted driver, and few drivers ever get into an Impreza for the first time and fail to be enthralled by the unique feel of the car's package.

Yet there is always the desire to go one better, and there are indeed almost innumerable ways to improve the overall driveability and desirability of the Impreza. Moreover the Impreza is one of the most suitable cars for performance upgrades and modification; indeed the habit can become both infectious and obsessive!

Of course, what you modify very much depends on the type of use you put your car to, and what sort of priorities you have as an owner and driver. If the Impreza is your only means of transport and you just want to make it better to own, you might consider interior and cosmetic upgrades. If you want to take your Impreza out on track days on a regular basis, there is a host of mechanical packages available to create a faster, sharper-handling, better-braking machine. And if you want more straight-line speed, the engine can be happily tuned.

There are myriad opinions about what should and should not be modified, many of which are contradictory. This chapter is intended as a review of common modifications for consideration rather than a definitive guide as to what or what not to do. Common sense should play a large part in any modification programme. Inevitably, cost is also a significant factor, for one of the great things about the Impreza is that it is not an expensive machine, and there is no need to spend a fortune on it to make it even better. Also you must consider legal implications in the country where your car is registered.

Identifying the weak areas of the Impreza does come with time and experience. Many owners of early cars want to do something about the lacklustre interior, poor lighting and dowdy alloy wheel choice. Most owners at some point will rue brake fade after repeated pedal applications during spirited driving. Wheel and tyre choices can bring big improvements, as can suspension upgrades. The steering is over-light for many drivers, the gear lever travel too long, and of course many owners want to extend the power output of their engines.

A whole industry has grown up around modifying and improving Imprezas. Many companies that specialised in Escort Cosworths have now switched to Imprezas, for example, and there is an increasing variety of parts now available for the owner to choose from.

If your Impreza is still under warranty (it lasts three years or 60,000 miles in the UK), you need to be very careful that any modification does not affect this warranty. Subaru's Passenger Vehicles Service and Warranty Book states that the following are not covered under warranty: 'Defects, malfunctions or failures resulting from misuse (e.g. overloading, rallying or racing), negligence, modification, alteration, tampering, disconnection, improper adjustment or repairs, accidents, installation of parts not equivalent in quality and design to parts supplied by Subaru (UK) Ltd, add-on parts, improper maintenance or use of fuels, oils and/or lubricants other than those recommended.' However, for the warranty not to apply, the fitment of the non-standard part must have *caused* the damage. For example, if you fitted a non-standard exhaust and the gearbox developed a fault, the warranty should still apply to this. We should note that modifications available officially (for example, the Prodrive Performance Pack) are warranty-safe.

When modifying your car, you must accept that higher performance parts often have an impact on reliability. In all cases, you must ensure that upgrades in one area are matched by suitable

← As countless enthusiasts have discovered, the Impreza makes a superb basis for tuning, often to stratospheric levels.

improvements in others, especially where safety is concerned. For example, it is most inadvisable to go for a monster tune engine and leave the original braking system untouched, and the suspension and tyres as they came out of the factory. It is always best to seek the advice of other Impreza enthusiasts and specialist tuning and modification companies.

Engine

Owners of European/Australian market Turbo cars have a wide choice of tuning parts and packages for the standard engine. What has always been a healthy power output (211PS in the first incarnation, rising to 218PS for the 1999 Model Year) is sometimes felt as a little 'short-changed' when compared with Japanese-market WRX cars, which have always had more power – a minimum of 220PS and a maximum of 300PS out of the factory. Interestingly, though, some rolling roads have shown that up to 235PS can be produced by standard UK-specification Turbo engines, so the gap may not always be as wide as is supposed …

In the UK, the best-known and most trusted engine packages come from Prodrive. Depending on the model year, this so-called Performance Package would normally comprise a Ramair air filter, stainless steel free-flow exhaust and revised engine management (plus revised brake pads to match the extra power). Available from 1996, the package boosted power up to 240bhp at 5,600rpm and torque up to 325Nm (240lb ft) at 2,400rpm,

with much more flexible torque throughout the rev range and a more urgent response.

For 1999 Model Year cars and later, a revised Performance Pack had an upgraded ECU, new centre/rear stainless steel exhaust (replacing the second exhaust catalyst) and improved intercooler pipework. This boosted peak power to the same 240bhp as before (although at 6,000rpm), but more significant was torque of 350Nm (258lb ft) at only 3,500rpm, comfortably exceeding the standard car's peak torque from 2,900rpm through to 5,500rpm.

In later years, the PPP became even more powerful. The EJ20-engined 'New Age' WRX boasted 265PS and the STi 305PS, rising to 270PS and 310lb ft for the post-2005 2.5-litre WRX and 320PS and 332lb ft for the 2.5-litre STi. This changed again slightly from 2008 in the new-shape Impreza GE: the WRX PPP went down a little to 255PS and 287lb ft while the STi PPP rose to its highest ever level: 330PS and 346lb ft.

The PPP has the advantage of not affecting Subaru's warranty. However, some magazine road tests affirmed that PPP-equipped classic-shape Imprezas were not significantly quicker than standard cars. The PPP is also relatively expensive for what is basically an ECU and exhaust upgrade, and it must be fitted 'officially'. Note that Performance Package engines for pre-1997 Model Year cars must be fed with super unleaded fuel (later cars can use normal unleaded). Many owners choose the Prodrive Performance Package as their number one choice but there are naturally plenty of other options.

Many owners choose to increase turbo boost. There are many ways of achieving this. The most basic form is with a bleed valve, which is crude and potentially dangerous. Imprezas have a built-in fuel cut-off to prevent engine damage in the event of overboost. For pre-1997 UK cars, this limit is set at approximately 1 bar; on later UK models, the limit is approximately 1.25 bar. By running just below this level, one can achieve excellent results on the standard ECU without activating the fuel cut-off. A properly set-up Electronic Boost Controller can work very effectively on a UK car with typical results on later models yielding up to 286bhp with a boost controller, induction kit and de-catalysed exhaust system. There are kits available to remove the safety fuel cut-off but be cautious, as anything substantially over 1.2 bar sustained on a UK-spec car

↓ **The Impreza has a particularly short crankshaft, which is also very durable. If you do want to strengthen it, you can get it Nitrided.**

will introduce too much heat into the engine and possibly cause engine damage.

For Japanese imports, a remapped ECU is a much better option as the original unit is mapped for 100 octane fuel instead of 95 octane. Increasing boost on a Japanese spec car without making suitable adjustments to fuelling and ignition timing can be very risky, particularly for later models. A remap is not just a performance enhancement for a Japanese spec car but also essential for engine longevity.

The standard ECU 'learns' according to data it receives and adjusts itself to suit things like fuel quality and wear and tear. It is possible to reset the ECU fairly easily. Going for chip upgrades has the advantage of keeping the original ECU. The STi chip is probably not the best choice for Turbo engines as it is designed for 100RON fuel. Earlier cars are cheaper to 'chip' than later cars but beware of improperly developed chips.

Replacing the ECU becomes necessary if your intended power output is especially high. A halfway house to getting a full replacement ECU is a 'piggyback' module, of which there are several available, possibly the best known being the GReddy e-Manage. This uses the same connectors as the standard ECU but allows mapping to be altered to get the best from the car. This is a less expensive option than the full ECU route and there are many add-on modules on the market. Many tuners offer standardised base maps for particular applications. Later Imprezas can benefit from tuning via software packages, such as the popular EcuTek system which uses the car's diagnostic port. In general, engine mapping work is highly specialised and should ideally be conducted by experts.

There has been something of an explosion in ECU mapping in recent years. A large number of full replacement ECUs has emerged on to the market from brands such as MoTeC, AEM, GEMS, Hydra, Autronic, A'PEXi and many others.

This route is more costly. The ideal is to go the whole hog and get your engine specifically mapped, either on the dyno or via 'live' mapping using a laptop while the car is in motion. Top mapping experts are few and far between, but the results speak for themselves. It's also possible to make available several switchable maps so that, for example, you can flick between economy and full-power modes.

Going the full replacement route opens up huge possibilities for tuning in all sorts of areas. Many ECUs allow you to alter boost control, for instance, obviating the need to buy a separate boost controller. It's relatively straightforward to alter the mapping for particular fuels (such as 102 RON race fuel) and nitrous oxide injection can be configured as well. Other ECU-controlled areas such as antilag, launch control and traction control can also form part of the ECU mapping process.

Impreza tuning has developed massively over the last few years. Simply by adding bolt-on items – uprated turbocharger, ECU, intake, exhaust and so on – tuners have succeeded in extracting a safe and reliable 400bhp from the Subaru flat-four. Going much above this level requires more serious attention, and that means uprating the engine internals. Various options exist but internal modifications are really the province of specialists.

The Subaru block itself is tough but there is some debate over which block is the best for high-power tuning. Early STi closed-deck blocks are often seen as the best choice for classic-shape Imprezas. The EJ20 engine is a very well-known quantity and many have successfully been tuned to extremely high levels (Roger Clark Motorsport's 'Gobstopper', for example, ran to well over 700bhp using the 2.0-litre block). Many tuners favour the larger-capacity EJ25 block which can offer more torque potential but the larger piston sizes mean the engine walls are in fact thinner.

Nitriding the crankshaft strengthens it, while if you intend to run to 8,000rpm or more, high-strength conrods are recommended. Stronger pistons are another important choice; STi supplies forged pistons that are pretty expensive, but there are other cheaper options out there, as well as many very high-spec items. If you're doing serious mods, always get the engine fully balanced afterwards. Polishing and porting the heads is another common improvement.

Hydraulic lifters on 1994–96 Model Year Imprezas are good for engine speeds up to 7,200rpm, while solid lifters can go up to 7,800rpm. Anything higher will require special valve springs and lightweight valves and retainers, which can be expensive.

Camshafts for later cars are not compatible with those for early hydraulic lifter cars. As for solid lifter models, more aggressive cams can make a

→ There are plenty of modifications available to enhance the turbocharging, including higher boost, balancing or replacing the turbo or fitting new dump valves (seen here with a fitting kit).

→ The effectiveness of the turbocharger can be improved by cooling it more efficiently, and what better way than fitting an intercooler water spray. The switch pictured on this dashboard is the standard STi spray, but other aftermarket examples are available.

big difference. Uprated fuel rails are unnecessary unless you are into high-tune territory and expect turbo boost to exceed 1.1 bar. You may also need a motorsport fuel pump at this level. Always ensure that electronics and turbocharger are capable of handling high boost pressures.

Perhaps the most radical modification available is to increase the capacity of your engine. Several tuning companies offer 'stroker' kits to lengthen the stroke of the pistons. Such kits typically expand the EJ20 engine to 2.1, 2.2 or 2.3 litres in capacity. Another popular route is simply to use the 2.5-litre EJ25 die-cast aluminium semi-closed deck block, which is now in plentiful supply, offering the possibility of high power outputs with strong reliability and less radical internal changes.

In normal use, always fit original equipment platinum-tipped spark plugs, which are proven to be reliable and were designed for the Impreza's engine. Some aftermarket plugs have been known to cause problems. The only exception is where

you are using the car in very high performance applications when a cooler-running plug may be required, in which case follow the advice of an experienced expert.

One last and very easy modification is to fit a performance air filter. There are essentially two different types. A panel filter replaces the paper element in the standard airbox with a free-flow foam element, or there is the full blown induction system which does away with the factory airbox altogether. The panel filter is a subtle mod which will give only a small improvement, while noise levels are barely affected. The full induction system is a different story: turbo spool up is much faster, reducing lag and complimenting the exhaust by allowing more air into the engine. The car breathes far better at the top end of the rev range and works perfectly with a free-flow exhaust system. The compromise for having an induction kit is the extra induction noise: roar under acceleration where the filter can be heard sucking in the air, and whooshes from the standard dump valve when the throttle is released.

Turbocharger

Upgrading the turbocharger on many cars is one of the first jobs on owners' lists, but that's not necessarily the case with the Impreza. Early Turbos had a TD05 turbocharger that can be made to work very effectively if you make the right changes in other areas. Getting it overhauled and more finely balanced may well be all you need to do. From the 1997MY, the Turbo engine used a smaller

TD04 turbocharger and altered air flow, which is more efficient but operates closer to its limits in standard tune.

If you're going for serious horsepower gains, you may well decide to change the turbo. There is a good selection of bolt-on turbochargers from original equipment manufacturer IHI, which Subaru Tecnica International modifies and markets in various stages. VF24 is the Group N turbo, which is noted for its quick spool-up. Very popular is the VF23, which boosts mid and top-end power thanks to its larger size. The VF22 is ideal for top-end power gains but suffers from glacial lag and needs to be accompanied by some serious engine management mods. You will find lots of other IHI turbos out there, including the VF28 (similar to the VF23) and VF29 (almost identical to the VF24).

Offering almost as much in power gain terms as the VF22 but less lag is the VF30, a very popular choice. The VF34 has the same exhaust housing and compressor but uses a ball bearing design, which achieves full boost at lower revs. The VF37 is a twin-scroll turbo with very good spool-up characteristics and is capable of around 400bhp. The VF38 has a titanium turbine and shaft for even better spool-up but less top-end power. The VF42 was used on the Impreza S203 and S204, a twin-scroll roller-bearing turbo offering an excellent spread of power and usability.

There are many other turbochargers on the market. One of the best known is the Garrett-built HKS GT roller needle bearing turbine. These tend to be more expensive options but can be suitable for cars with very high power outputs.

The intercooler is another very common item to change. It's especially useful for earlier cars whose smaller intercooler is not as proficient as later cars. Fitting a larger intercooler is normally a simple operation, and there are many aftermarket ones to choose from but buying a good quality item is the key. Efficiency can also be improved by fitting a water spray, as on the Japanese-market STi, and various aftermarket kits are available at reasonable prices. Another modification to reduce intercooler temperature is to add in a splitter in the bonnet scoop. Normally the scoop directs air more to the rear half of the intercooler, so creating a splitter to share the incoming air more equally can reduce input-to-output intercooler temperature by as much as 3 degrees centigrade.

Fundamentally, the Impreza's top-mount intercooler is not in the best position to remain cool. Many owners opt to follow World Rally Car practice and move the intercooler to the front of the engine bay, behind the bumper. This not only improves air flow but insulates it from engine heat. While that has benefits for engine power, there are a couple of downsides: it's a costly option and the longer pipe lengths lead to more turbo lag.

The blow-off valve on early (1994–96) cars was quite small, while the 1997 and 1998 versions had a problem with leakage (fixed by new design valves), and the 1999 and 2000 cars mounted the valve directly on to the intercooler assembly. Fitting an aftermarket blow-off valve should increase flow capacity and also allow for adjustability.

Exhaust

As with most cars these days, the Impreza's standard exhaust system is pretty restrictive to ensure that it passes emissions and noise regulations. Upgrading the exhaust system can have a huge impact on the driveability of the Impreza and is one of the most worthwhile first modifications.

There are three parts to the exhaust system, the downpipe which contains the most restrictive primary catalytic converter, the centre section which contains a secondary catalyst and the rear silencer. Most cars should still be able to easily pass emissions tests with the secondary catalyst removed. This will make the car rev much more freely, but ultimately most owners also choose to replace the original downpipe with a straight-through downpipe unleashing more power. However, a car running with

← Replacing the back box with an upgraded item can produce immediate effects: higher power output, a more rorty noise and a meatier-looking tailpipe.

→ The variety of exhaust systems available is huge but if you want the ultimate, consider an equal-length manifold, as pictured here.

↓ A quickshift for the gear lever (as on the 22B pictured here) can transform the action and rapidity of gearchanges quite dramatically, and need not cost very much to install.

neither of the two cats will not pass the UK MoT emissions test or roadside emission check.

Replacing the rear silencer instantly boosts power, the sound emitting from it improves and you have a better-looking tailpipe under your rear bumper. The variety of systems available – and their variable quality – means that you should ask around for other owners' experiences to try to tailor your choice to match what you want from it.

Prodrive's exhaust system comes as part of its Performance Package, works well and sounds just right, but there are lots of good aftermarket exhaust choices out there. A very popular one comes from Scoobysport, whose system is manufactured by Hayward and Scott (suppliers to Ralliart), and is simple to fit. In Australia, another well-known supplier is Boost Performance Motorsport (BPM), while MRT also supplies various packages.

You could also consider the wide variety of Japanese aftermarket exhausts from the likes of Blitz and HKS – typically high quality but rather noisy. Exhaust manifolds from STi add extra exhaust tuning, while there are even equal-length stainless steel WRC-type manifolds available (at enormous cost but unbeatable street cred).

Transmission

The Impreza's gearchange is sometimes criticised as being rather slow and imprecise, perhaps not surprising given that the transmission basically dates back some 30 years. It should come as little surprise therefore that one of the most

immediately beneficial modifications for the Impreza is a quickshift gearchange mechanism. Essentially this changes the pivot point of the gear lever, which increases the effort required to change gear but improves shift quality noticeably. Easily the best-known in Britain is Prodrive's quickshift, consisting of a completely new linkage to shorten lever travel. This brings a new level of precision to the shift action, which is far quicker and has a vastly improved feel. Best of all, it doesn't cost very much for such a dramatic improvement in driving enjoyment.

Model Year 1997 cars have a shorter throw lever, while post-1998 cars have an improved linkage but neither of these is a quickshift, and even recent cars will benefit from the genuine article. Note that earlier (pre-1997) cars have a single synchro gearbox which can be 'beaten' by the quickshift.

The gearbox itself is a pretty tough unit that can handle up to 300bhp quite easily. However radical options exist if you want to get serious. For example, respected transmission experts Quaife Engineering offer a five-speed sequential synchro gearbox and Prodrive offer a six-speed rally-type 'dog' racing transmission. Competition gear sets offer close-set ratios and gears manufactured to much higher tolerances, at a price, while STi produces heavy-duty gears and shafts. Group N users fit cryogenically treated gear sets but these cost over £2,000 for the cogs alone!

Pre-1997 Model Year Imprezas used a smaller, 225mm clutch (upgraded for 1997 to 230mm), and the earlier version was barely enough for the standard 208bhp. The STi RA clutch transforms the feel of the clutch in early cars and is a popular item when it comes to replacement. Clutches on later UK cars can cope with all but the most serious of mods. Heavy-duty steel-back clutches are available as aftermarket items. More exotically, you can buy a ceramic clutch, which is very sharp-acting and noisy, but minimises slip, and is really for serious users only.

Lightening the cast-iron flywheel will give improved engine response but there is a limit to what can safely be removed. An alternative is to fit a steel billet flywheel, which saves much more weight and improves responsiveness substantially. If you have increased power output, consider switching to synthetic gear oil to improve lubrication and extend life expectancy.

As for the differentials, it is possible to upgrade but the costs are substantial. STi offers heavy-duty diffs (its centre diff is twice as strong as the standard item) that improve traction and stability out of corners. Perhaps the most worthwhile change is to ditch the open front diff for a clutch-type limited slip diff, which with careful setting up, improves bite substantially. However, you will lose ABS.

The New Age Impreza STi has a six-speed gearbox as standard which works much better than the original five-speed.

Wheels

In its original form the Impreza came with 15in alloy wheels that left a lot to be desired on the cosmetic side. Additionally the 6in rim was hardly sufficient to cope with the standard choice of 205/55 tyres, whose relatively low performance characteristics are often criticised by owners.

All this means that changing wheels and tyres on cars supplied before October 1998 has become one of the very first modifications for many owners. 1999 Model Year cars got 7 x 16in rims with 205/50 tyres as standard. Which wheel/tyre combination to go for is first and foremost a matter of cost, secondly a matter of what level of performance you are after and thirdly a matter of aesthetics. The popularity of big brake kits is another reason to switch to larger wheels.

On classic-shape Imprezas, the basic choice is between 16 or 17in wheels (18-inchers are

↑ While clutches on late-model European spec cars are able to cope with very high power outputs, heavy-duty clutches are popular, as are STi Type RA clutches.

possible but are a much more specialised fitment). Prodrive's view is that 16in wheels offer the best compromise between ride comfort, performance and cost, and 7in rims allow the tyres to sit flatter on the road. But there is no doubting that 17in wheel and tyre combinations look better and provide superior ultimate performance, especially if you're doing track days. On the minus side, 17in wheels increase the unsprung weight substantially, with negative consequences for ride quality and handling. However most owners fitting 17in wheels will also include uprated suspension, hopefully counteracting any negative effects. 7 x 18in wheels have been fitted to Imprezas (for example the Prodrive P1 WR) but these are even heavier and require ultra-low profile 35-section tyres which adversely affect ride quality.

Your first option when upgrading from 15in wheels is simply to find a set of five-spoke 16in wheels as fitted to post-October 1998 cars. This wheel design is the same as Japanese standard wheels fitted from October 1994 and comes in silver or gold. If you want to keep an 'original equipment' patina, consider fitting Prodrive-supplied Speedline wheels. These are available in 16, 17 and 18in sizes, either as wheels only, or fitted with high performance Pirelli P Zeros. A popular 16in choice is the 6.5 x 16 eight-spoke Safari, as used on the Series McRae special edition, offered in silver or gold finishes and with 205/50 tyres. This style can also be ordered as 6 x 15in, but it's much better to upgrade to 16in. It's not just about cosmetics though – the tough Safari wheel was widely used in Group N rallying (before 4-pot brakes became legal for Group N, when

↑ If you have 15in wheels, you should consider upgrading to either 16 or 17in wheels, of which there is a huge choice. The RB5 special edition has Speedline 17in six-spokers fitted with Pirelli P Zero 205/45 ZR17 tyres.

→ A rarer choice is 18in wheels. Prodrive used this 18in design for the P1 WR, but these have been criticised as too heavy and leading to a sizeable deterioration in ride quality.

most Group N cars switched to Raceline 6 x 15 wheels designed to fit over the 4-pot callipers).

Also from Prodrive comes an extremely popular double six-spoke design known as the Supertourismo, in 7 x 16in or 7 x 17in sizes, and in either silver or gold. The recommended tyre size for the 17in wheel is 205/45 ZR17, although 215/40 ZR17 tyres can also be used. As the Supertourismo does not fit over the STi four-pot callipers on 1999 Model Year and later cars, you can choose a Supertourismo 2 wheel type (17in) that does fit. Other Speedline designs include the five-spoke Mistral (7 x 17in) and the gold six-spoke Competition 2 (7 x 16in), which has been homologated for Group N Imprezas. Prodrive also selected another design, the ten-spoke OZ Racing 7 x 17in wheel, for the P1 (alternatively available in 8 x 18in size). Prodrive sizes for the new-shape Impreza hatchback now extend up to 19in.

Of course you don't have to stick with 'official' choices. The range available to fit Imprezas has become vast in recent years, in all sorts of diameters, widths, styles and colours, to suit all kinds of budgets and tastes.

Tyres

When fitting larger wheels, you need to keep the rolling circumference the same to avoid having to recalibrate the speedometer, therefore the corollary of larger wheels is lower profile tyres. These mean less spring and flex and therefore reduced body roll in corners, but on the other hand, the ride quality suffers as there is less suspension effect from the tyres. Additionally, you will get a noticeable improvement in steering response but there can be more of a 'tramlining' effect in ruts and grooves, unless you have the geometry modified as well.

The effect of tyres on the driving experience is often vastly underestimated. A quality tyre that is correctly specified for the wheel size and type of use you put the car to is absolutely essential. If you have 15in wheels, the standard 205/55 VR15 Bridgestone Potenza RE71/RE-010 tyres seem to last well but are rather hard. Grippier tyres (such as Pirelli and Yokohama) can improve grip but may be less long-lived. You have a great deal of choice at this size.

For 16in wheels the choice is more limited. The recommended tyre size is 205/50 VR16 or ZR16 and the standard choice is again Bridgestone Potenza. Other favourably regarded tyres include Bridgestone S-02, Goodyear Eagle F1 and Toyo T1-S.

With 17in wheels you are into rarefied territory. At the recommended size of 205/45 ZR17, you have Pirelli P Zero Asymmetrico (Prodrive's choice for the P1), Yokohama A520 and Dunlop SP9000, but more are available at 215/40 ZR17. The tyre choice for the Prodrive P1 8 x 18in wheel is 225/35 ZR18 Pirelli P Zero. Always ensure the speed rating matches the performance of your car. And always ask as many people as possible about tyre choices – their performance varies greatly according to the car they're fitted on.

The standard tyre on 2005 Model Year STi

cars switched to very sticky Bridgestone Potenzas which work very well, but do seem to produce more road noise.

Suspension

Compared to most other cars in the Impreza's price bracket, the handling and grip engendered by the suspension is a vast leap ahead. But there is plenty of scope to make things even better. While the Impreza's grip is universally praised, sometimes its handling is viewed as having room for improvement.

The cheapest modification is to get the wheels aligned properly. Identical cars can feel very different, simply because the geometry is improperly set up. Even new cars suffer from this, let alone cars with miles on the clock. The front suspension should have zero toe-in and a small amount (0.5–1.2) of negative camber. At the rear there should between 1.0 and 1.5mm of toe-out each side, while there is no standard camber adjustment.

Altering the anti-roll (also known as stabiliser or anti-sway) bars can have a dramatic effect on the understeer/oversteer balance. However, uprating these bars can leave the car under-damped and makes the progression from grip to slide much more violent (race drivers often disconnect roll bars in the wet to make the handling more controllable).

As the standard anti-roll bar link is a pretty cheap plastic-and-rubber device, some sources recommend steel and polyurethane bushed links. But the standard flexible links provide initial progression in the anti-roll bar's action, and once loaded probably match any steel link.

Beyond these simple changes, many owners find that the Impreza's suspension, while brilliantly balanced for most uses, can feel rather soft when driving more seriously, particularly on track days. Complete suspension kits can transform the cornering capacities of the Impreza substantially and, while they may not be cheap, they are one of the most effective ways of making your car go faster, for the simple reason that corners can be taken more quickly, more safely.

Once again, Prodrive's suspension kit is probably the best-known and one of the most highly respected, and for a long time it was the only kit available in Britain. Prodrive specified special Bilstein dampers and Eibach springs, both of which are much firmer than standard and lower the car by 25mm (1in) overall.

Apart from lowered and uprated suspension, STi produces a whole range of fast road/competition suspension mods. Among these are rose-jointed rear lateral links with solid rear anti-roll bar links, adjustable trailing arms, front and rear strut braces and uprated bushes. There are plenty of other independent brands with a huge choice of suspension parts for Imprezas, notably Australian company Whiteline. Its range of polyurethane bushes and drop-links, for example, is extremely popular.

You might opt for camber adjusters in the top of the struts and/or adjustable rear arms. Stiffer and shorter springs are popular – especially on earlier cars that were rather soft – but be aware that reducing ride height by more than around 25–30mm will limit the car's practicality for road use and have dubious effects on handling. Uprated dampers are the perfect accompaniment to different springs, ideally adjustable dampers that are matched to your spring choice. Usually new dampers will require the struts to be cut and drilled, meaning that you are really stuck with your choice, short of getting new struts fitted, so make sure you've selected the right dampers to start with.

At the most developed end of the spectrum, and one that is becoming increasingly popular with owners of highly tuned cars and track day enthusiasts, is a full coilover suspension set-up. Coilover systems open up the possibility of adjustment, which can be as tunable as you wish. In their simplest form, you have single-way adjustment, with others adjustable for ride height, bump and rebound. The more adjustability you have, the more you can fine-tune the understeer/oversteer balance of your car, tweaking parameters such as turn-in, straight-line stability and predictability at or beyond the limits of grip. There are many options out there from brands such as Tein, KW, Spax, Apex and D2. Overall, the subject of suspension set-up is a very complex one and it's something of a black art. Frankly, it's best left to professionals who have had experience in specifying and setting up suspension systems.

↑ **Leda suspension units are specifically tuned to the Impreza, and are fully adjustable to allow fine-tuning of the handling balance, grip and turn-in.**

You might also consider installing a strut brace between the suspension towers – after all, STi Imprezas from Japan have one. Opinion is split as to the benefits of strut braces, with many owners reporting big differences to the handling and feel. Reportedly some of the best strut braces on the market are the pink/aluminium STi competition spec ones and those from Cusco. A rear brace can work well on the five-door models (which do not benefit from a solid rear bulkhead). Other owners and specialists are dubious about the benefits as the Impreza's shell is already pretty tough (even the contemporary WRC car did not use one, although that was seam-welded and had a roll cage). The front brace has to be curved to clear the intercooler, impacting its strength, and it is sited rather close to the bulkhead in any case, and many on the market are more cosmetic than functional. If you do fit a strut brace, have the tracking checked just in case it has been affected.

Steering

The power assistance on the steering rack is often regarded as too powerful, leading to an over-light feeling that is typical of many Japanese cars. The standard steering rack with its 15:1 ratio can also feel a little slow for the performance available (it has 2.8 turns lock-to-lock). The Type R, Type RA and 22B versions come with a 13:1 ratio steering rack, and fitting one makes the steering much more direct and positive with none of the woolliness around the centre position associated with normal Imprezas. Although very expensive, this rack probably makes the greatest difference to steering and feel of all.

Subtle geometry changes can also make a very big difference. One easy way to improve the steering feel is to adopt the recommended toe and camber settings for Prodrive's suspension for standard cars (1mm total toe-in on the front and rear with equal negative camber on the front). This will result in sharper turn-in, enhanced steering response and more stable braking. However, the settings are outside the specifications listed in the handbook and your local Subaru dealer will probably refuse to make such changes for fear of invalidating the warranty.

A modification worth considering is to lower the steering rack using spacers, which has the effect of minimising bump steer, but the operation takes several hours. This work can be performed by Powerstation. Another popular change is to remove the standard 380mm airbag steering wheel and fit a smaller 350mm non-airbag wheel.

Brakes

This is one of the areas where great improvements can be made on the standard car, yet it is also one of the most overlooked. While perfectly safe and acceptable, the Impreza's standard disc brake package is not its strongest feature, and making a few simple changes can dramatically improve matters. Being able to brake just that little bit later, with equal confidence, makes your car effectively much quicker.

Pre-1999 MY UK Imprezas used 277mm front discs with twin-pot callipers and 264mm rear discs with a sliding pot calliper. This set-up was also used on Japanese models up to 1997, when STi versions gained upgraded four-pot front callipers with 294mm discs. In 1999, European and Japanese Imprezas were fitted with improved rear brakes when the rear discs became ventilated, while certain STi models (22B, Type R and Type RA) were all fitted with twin-pot rear callipers with 290mm vented discs as standard.

Therefore, brakes on pre-1999 MY cars are most in need of improvement. The European/Australian Turbo initially had 276mm ventilated discs with two-pot callipers up front and 230mm solid discs with single callipers at the rear. A significant upgrade arrived for the 1999 MY when STi-type brakes were standardised, including four-pot front brake callipers, larger diameters front discs and ventilated rear discs (four-pot callipers require 16in wheels as a minimum). This later set-up is pretty good for most applications and so may not need any improvement, although uprated pads are always a good idea.

Brake fade certainly is a problem, and the Impreza can consume pads with frightening alacrity. Uprated brake pads are a good first step, as they offer excellent fade resistance, longer pad life, do not need bedding in and they work well even when cold. The best-known are Mintex pads available in the UK from Prodrive via the Subaru dealer network. Pagid pads are also highly thought of and can be fitted with standard callipers.

While replacement discs do little to improve outright braking, the main problem with the standard brakes is the lack of cooling offered by the 24mm thick disc. Various alternative disc choices exist, including Tarrox, Pagid and Black Diamond. AP Racing produces a number of brake upgrade kits in several sizes and in the UK various companies sell an AP kit developed especially for the Impreza. The AP kit is available with either a 28mm × 305mm disc which fits under 16-inch wheels and four-pot callipers, or a 28mm × 330mm kit with either a four-pot or six-pot calliper. Scoobysport have exclusive rights to Brembo's well-regarded upgrade kit, with grooved and turbo-vented 28mm × 305mm discs, aluminium four-pot callipers, high-performance pads, steel-braided hoses and Silkolene Pro Race brake fluid. This kit is designed to fit under the later 16in wheels, which means you do not have to buy larger wheels and tyres. One of the most impressive braking systems is AP's six-pot calliper system (for 17in wheels only). Combined with 330mm discs, it is for extreme use such as track days. Indeed, Scoobysport recommends 17in slick tyres to use these brakes to their full potential. Prodrive's kit is a 330mm disc using an Alcon based four-pot calliper and will only fit under a 17in wheel.

It is also well established that hard braking can cause the Impreza's bulkhead to flex, making the pedal feel spongy. A special bracket can alleviate this for very little outlay, and is available from suppliers such as MRT, Scoobymania and Power Engineering.

Probably the most effective way to improve pedal feel is by fitting braided hoses and using high-quality brake fluid which will firm up the pedal, especially useful when hard pads are fitted. It is probably not worthwhile drilling brake discs, as the standard ventilated discs are quite satisfactory, and drilling holes can result in stress cracks developing.

The fluid must match the capabilities of your braking system. Certainly it must be at least Dot 4 rating (ideally Dot 5) and must be changed at least every 24 months or 30,000 miles (50,000km) – but ideally every 12 months if the car is driven hard. Fully synthetic fluid is superior but much more expensive, and it requires a full flush-out and regular changes. Many specialists recommend Silkolene Pro Race fluid, which is designed to last a minimum of 24 months in UK weather and exceeds the wet boiling point of all known Dot 5.1 fluids.

Bodywork

The original 'classic' Impreza revelled in its relatively low-key appearance. It gave little clue as to the performance that lay underneath, and the turbocharged Impreza ranks as one of the greatest Q-cars of all time. For many owners, drawing attention by adding cosmetic touches spoils the fun.

↖ **Braking is an area where great improvements can be made. These uprated Pagid discs are straight replacements for standard discs, but a huge range of options exists.**

↑ ↑ **Brembo aluminium four-pot callipers are extremely highly regarded. AP Racing even offers a six-pot calliper set for very serious applications.**

↑ **Perhaps the best way to improve what can be a rather spongy brake pedal feel is to fit steel-braided hoses. Together with high quality brake fluid, the pedal will firm up considerably.**

↑ Big WRC-style spoilers
are a popular cosmetic
addition, especially replicas
of the 22B's huge rear
aerofoil, as pictured here
on a 22B Type UK.

However, it can be tempting to tweak the
styling. The most common items are more
extreme versions of the standard pieces of
equipment – so larger spoilers, deeper air dams
and side skirts are the order of the day. Some
items are purely cosmetic, so always ask about
the aerodynamic credentials of any item you are
buying, especially front and rear spoilers.

Perhaps the most popular bodywork add-on
for the classic Impreza is the STi Group N rally-
style tall rear spoiler, fitted as standard from the
1999 Model Year. This is available from Prodrive
as well as from a variety of other sources, while
Scoobysport manufactures a carbon-fibre replica
WRC rear spoiler. Various other rear spoiler designs
are available, including some fairly extreme ones. It
is not only the saloon that benefits from larger rear
spoiler kits: for example Prodrive offers a double
upper and lower spoiler for the five-door version.

There is plenty of choice at the front end too.
STi makes many spoilers and front skirts, including
a three-piece front spoiler for pre-1999 cars and
a lip spoiler for 1999 and on. Prodrive offers a
front bumper lip spoiler that looks much more
aggressive, and markets various STi components.
But do check that any lip spoiler you are offered
is legal, as some jut out to such an extent that
pedestrian injuries become an issue. Complete
body kits are available from a variety of sources
– some from Japan are as wild as you can imagine
– while Revolution also offers all sorts of detail

→ Morette offers a twin
headlamp conversion
which not only enhances
the cosmetic appearance
but substantially improves
the spread of light available
at night.

items such as clear lenses, spotlamp covers and 22B
style bonnet vents.

As for the New Age Impreza, this became
more overt in its performance look, especially
the STi. Owners of the bug-eye headlamp WRX
often change the headlamps, while there is a vast
array of rear spoilers and various cosmetic items
to choose from. The latest Impreza hatchback
has courted controversy with its styling, and a
few body styling parts are now available for it.
Probably the most popular alteration is switching
the clear rear light lenses for red ones.

Lights

The standard Impreza is often criticised for having feeble headlamps that are not remotely in keeping with the level of performance available. Simply fitting higher wattage bulbs is not recommended, first because it is illegal in many countries and secondly, because neither the wiring nor the plastic reflectors are really up to the job.

A better alternative is to fit high-performance Xenon bulbs, which claim to provide 30 per cent more light on the same power. The light produced is much whiter and is particularly good off-beam for peripheral vision. Xenon bulbs are widely available. Even brighter, PIAA offer a range of high-efficiency 'super white' bulbs, such that their 80-watt bulb is claimed to produce the equivalent of a 130-watt conventional bulb, but these are very costly and in some countries are illegal.

Some owners fit twin headlamps, usually the Morette design which in the UK is supplied by Demon Tweeks. While the main effect is probably cosmetic – and opinion is sharply divided on whether it's positive or negative – you do get an extra throw of light on main beam, and the standard wiring need not be changed.

If you want to indulge in fast night-time driving you should consider a driving lamp conversion to replace the standard foglamps. (Driving lamps come on automatically when high beam is switched on, in contrast to foglamps which have a separate switch.) Prodrive offers a 120-watt PIAA high intensity driving lamp conversion which is very high quality but highly priced and has its own special loom to cope. A cheaper and popular high quality conversion kit comes from Scoobysport, consisting of two Cibie Oscar Plus driving lamps, 130-watt bulbs, mounting brackets, wiring, connectors, relay and fitting instructions. In Australia, MRT also offers a high quality driving lamp conversion. Of course, if you want to look like Colin McRae at the expense of any extra light at all, you can always fit STi foglamp covers, or even some bonnet-mounted light pods. Scoobysport also supplies a driving light kit that uses Hella gas discharge units, whose staggeringly good performance is matched by their price.

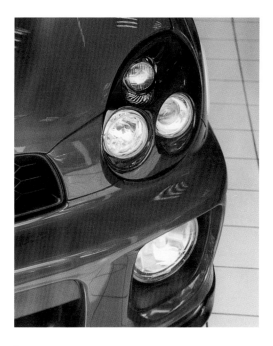

← Already the New Age Impreza is getting the tuning and modification treatment. This headlamp set – as seen on the UK300 special edition – transforms the controversial ovoid shape of the lights.

Interior

Possibly the weakest link in the Impreza's chain mail of strengths is its interior. The quality of the plastic used, the rather dull design, the scattered switchgear layout and the decidedly unsporty nature of the seats in early cars all conspire to leave you underwhelmed.

Things did improve with age. High-backed seats arrived for the 1997 Model Year but the really significant changes came one year later when the Impreza was given a new dashboard, white dials,

↓ The standard early Impreza's lacklustre interior treatment makes it the number one area for improvements, especially in seating. STi and Prodrive-badged packages are the most highly sought after.

↑ Sets of drilled pedals are another area of popular modification, as this UK car shows. In Japan, Subaru Tecnica International offers STi-branded pedal sets.

↗ Dashtop-mounted triple gauge sets are extremely popular, adding information on oil temperature, exhaust temperature and inlet air temperature, for example.

leather-trimmed Momo wheel and rearranged switchgear.

Leather trim was a dealer-fit option in the UK, with the standard seats retrimmed locally to variable levels of quality. One of the most appealing interior packages is Prodrive's offering, which includes Recaro front seats (with the rear seats and door panels trimmed in the same material), various gear knobs and Prodrive branded mats. However, this package works out pretty expensive as a percentage of the car's overall value.

You will certainly want to change the seats if you have a standard pre-1997 MY Impreza. Your options are manifold but most owners aspire to Recaros, although they are unlikely to match the trim in the rest of the interior (unless you go to Prodrive for a matched set, that is). Expense is likely to be the major consideration here.

Probably the most popular addition as far as instruments are concerned is a boost gauge. Ideally find one that matches the dial faces and you can locate it either on top of the dash or in the gap between the dash and the A-pillar. A boost gauge enables you to identify too much or too little boost and avoid damage to the engine. You can now buy

three-gauge centre pods (sited where the dash top box goes on post-1998 cars) to put gauges for oil temperature, exhaust temperature and inlet air temperature. Several companies offer carbon-fibre dash kits. STi meanwhile offered STi pedal sets and a range of STi gear knobs, plus gauge packs featuring various dials, including oil temperature, oil pressure, turbo pressure and voltage.

Audio

Subaru's standard audio systems are not much to write home about – for example, later cars may have had what looked like tweeters but in fact they are just grilles with nothing behind! There is certainly a case for upgrading and adding decent speakers, although the Impreza is not the quietest beast and therefore spending huge sums on audio equipment may not be entirely apropos.

If you are looking to mount a CD player, it usually goes in one of the recesses in the side of the boot, or it can go under the rear parcel shelf on the saloon, under the front passenger seat or, if the unit is small enough, inside the glove box.

Modifying an Impreza for track use

A standard road Impreza makes fabulous track day car. Even in standard form, its capabilities far outstrip the limits imposed by safe use on public roads. Track days allow you to explore the Impreza's performance in a relatively safe and controlled environment, far from Gatso speed cameras. For sheer adrenaline rush and enjoyment, not much can beat a track day.

These days there are plenty of circuits offering time for owners to bring their cars along and experience the thrill of driving more spiritedly than you can anywhere else. The phenomenon has increased in popularity at the same rate as traffic congestion and speed trap enforcement has strangled enjoyment on the roads. For details of how to enjoy track days and remain safe, please see the section in the chapter on ownership and maintenance.

Here we will consider how to make your Impreza a better track day car. Since the Impreza is not a single-seater racing machine, it's not perfect. There are plenty of changes open to you that will increase your enjoyment on the circuit, but what improvements should you consider, and at what cost?

Pete Croney of Scoobysport advised of the first modifications to make. 'First of all, don't go for increased horsepower. Going quickly on the track is not about power, it's about the speed you can carry through corners. I have a standard UK Impreza with modified suspension, brakes and exhaust and yet it's 3–4 seconds quicker a lap than an STi.

'So the first things to consider are the suspension and brakes. We recommend a specially developed Leda fully adjustable suspension set-up, which costs £1,200+VAT fitted with full geometry set-up. It improves road driving yet it only takes one minute to dial the dampers up to track settings and it makes a huge difference.

'As for brakes, that depends on your budget. If you're serious, there is no substitute for bigger brakes. Any change should advance the brake fade point (usually four to five laps for a standard car) but if you fit a Brembo or AP kit, you will get tired before the brakes fade.

'What a lot of people do is buy a second set of wheels and fit slick tyres for track use. If you go for 16-inch wheels, you can find second-hand slicks used once in, say, the Renault Sport Spider series and they cost just £40 each. These will last three or four track days, compared to road tyres that wear unevenly and rapidly if you're serious. A Brembo brake kit for 16in wheels costs £1,300+VAT. One stage up, 17in slicks are available for Imprezas but they're harder to find and cost up to £150 each second-hand. But this means you can fit the new AP six-pot brake kit. Braking is so violent with these kits that you really want to be on slicks to maintain grip.

'Power is not the crucial factor with Imprezas, but a safe and effective way to get more horsepower is to fit an uprated full exhaust system for around £650+VAT, which should give you 20–25bhp extra. Engine modifications are not worth doing unless you upgrade the chassis first though.

'Otherwise, always check your fluids, bearing in mind it's as important not to be overfilled as underfilled. Track days are hard on brake parts, so check pads regularly on the day. It's often worth fitting more expensive pads because they last longer. Also consider fitting four-point harnesses and pedal extensions for heel-and-toeing. Having said all this, you can take a standard, unmodified car to a track day and still have huge fun – even in the wet, when other cars are pussy-footing it around, you can have safe fun in an Impreza.'

And this is what modifications are all about – improving the driving experience. Whether you're on a budget or want the full works, the Impreza is readily adaptable and the benefits should be immediately apparent.

Specifications

IMPREZA 1st GENERATION (GC)

IMPREZA TURBO 2000
(GT or GT Turbo in Europe, WRX in Australia)
Mar 1994–Sep 1996

Engine	EJ20 1,994cc four-cylinder horizontally opposed at an angle of 52°, mounted longitudinally at the front, aluminium head and block, IHI turbocharger and air-to-air intercooler, oil cooler
Bore/stroke	92/75mm
Compression ratio	8.0:1
Valves	Four per cylinder, double overhead camshafts on each bank
Ignition	Electronic
Induction	Multipoint fuel injection
Power output	211PS (208bhp) @ 6,000rpm
Torque	270Nm (201lb ft) @ 4,800rpm
Specific output	104bhp per litre
Power-to-weight ratio	171bhp per tonne
Transmission	Permanent four-wheel-drive, front differential, centre viscous coupling, rear viscous coupling
Gearbox	Five-speed manual
Ratios/mph per 1,000rpm	1st 3.454/4.8 2nd 1.947/8.6 3rd 1.366/12.2 4th 0.972/17.2 5th 0.738/22.5
Final drive	3.545:1, 3.900:1 or 4.111:1
Suspension (front)	MacPherson struts, coil springs, transverse link, anti-roll bar
Suspension (rear)	MacPherson struts, coil springs, transverse link, trailing arms, anti-roll bar
Steering	Rack-and-pinion, power-assisted
Turns lock-to-lock	2.8
Turning circle	10.4m
Brakes (front)	276mm ventilated disc
Brakes (rear)	230mm solid disc
ABS system fitted	
Wheels	6 x 15-inch alloy (Series McRae 6.5 x 16-inch)
Tyres	205/55 R15 Michelin Pilot HX (Series McRae Pirelli P Zero 205/50 ZR16)
Weight	1,235kg (saloon), 1,270kg (estate)
Weight distribution	54 per cent front, 46 per cent rear
Wheelbase	2,520mm
Length	4,340mm
Width	1,690mm
Height	1,400mm (saloon), 1,435mm (estate)
Front track	1,460mm
Rear track	1,455mm (saloon), 1,450mm (estate)
Boot volume (VDA)	Saloon: 353 litres (seats folded 600 litres) Estate: 356 litres (seats folded 1,276 litres)
Fuel tank	60 litres (13.2gal)

Oct 1996–Aug 1998
As 1994–1996 except:

Compression ratio	9.7:1
Power output	211PS (208bhp) @ 5,600rpm
Torque	290Nm (214lb ft) @ 4,000rpm
Boot volume (VDA)	374 litres (saloon), 376 litres (estate)

In Australia:

Transmission	Four-speed automatic optional from 1997

Sep/Oct 1998–Sep 2000
As 1996–1998 except:

Power output	218PS (215bhp) @ 5,600rpm
Specific output	104bhp per litre
Power-to-weight ratio	174bhp per tonne (saloon), 159bhp per tonne (estate)
Ratios/mph per 1,000rpm	1st 3.454/5.1 2nd 1.947/9.1 3rd 1.366/12.9 4th 0.972/18.3 5th 0.738/24.0
Final drive	3.545:1
Brakes (front)	294mm ventilated disc
Brakes (rear)	ventilated disc
Wheels	6 x 16-inch alloy
Tyres	205/50 R16
Weight	1,235kg (estate 1,306kg)

Prodrive Performance Package (1996–1998)
As Turbo 1996–1998 except:

Power output	240PS (238bhp) @ 5,600rpm
Torque	325Nm (240lb ft) @ 2,400rpm
Specific output	120bhp per litre
Power-to-weight ratio	198bhp per tonne

Prodrive Performance Package/WR Sport (1999–2000)
As Turbo 1998–2000 except:

Power output	240PS (238bhp) @ 6,000rpm
Torque	350Nm (258lb ft) @ 3,500rpm
Power-to-weight ratio	194bhp per tonne

Prodrive P1 (1999–2000)
As Turbo 1998–2000 except:

Power output	280PS (276bhp) @ 6,500rpm
Torque	352Nm (260lb ft) @ 4,000rpm
Specific output	140bhp per litre
Power-to-weight ratio	219bhp per tonne
Gear ratios/mph per 1,000rpm	1st 3.166/5.1 2nd 1.882/8.6 3rd 1.296/12.4 4th 0.972/16.6 5th 0.738/21.8
Final drive	4.444:1
Brakes (front)	280mm ventilated disc (four-pot callipers), 330mm optional
Brakes (rear)	245mm ventilated disc (two-pot callipers)
Wheels	7 x 17-inch OZ Racing alloys (8 x 18-inch optional)
Tyres	205/45 ZR17 Pirelli P Zero (225/35 ZR18 Pirelli P Zero optional)
Weight	1,275kg

JAPANESE IMPREZA WRX AND STI

Impreza WRX Saloon Nov 1992–Sep 1994

Engine	EJ20 1,994cc four-cylinder horizontally opposed at an angle of 52°, mounted longitudinally at the front, aluminium head and block, IHI turbocharger and air-to-air intercooler, oil cooler
Bore/stroke	92/75mm
Compression ratio	8.5:1
Valves	Four per cylinder, double overhead camshafts on each bank
Ignition	Electronic
Induction	Multipoint fuel injection
Power output	240PS @ 6,000rpm
Torque	304Nm (224lb ft) @ 5,000rpm
Specific output	120PS per litre
Power-to-weight ratio	195PS per tonne
Transmission	Permanent four-wheel-drive, front differential, centre viscous coupling, rear viscous coupling
Gearbox	Five-speed manual
Gearbox ratios	1st 3.454 2nd 2.062
	3rd 1.448 4th 1.088
	5th 0.825
Final drive	4.111:1
Brakes (front)	Ventilated disc
Brakes (rear)	Solid disc
ABS system fitted	
Suspension (front)	MacPherson struts, coil springs, transverse link, anti-roll bar
Suspension (rear)	MacPherson struts, coil springs, transverse link, trailing arms, anti-roll bar
Steering	Rack-and-pinion, power-assisted
Turns lock-to-lock	2.8
Wheels	6 × 15-inch alloy
Tyres	205/55 R15
Weight	1,200kg
Weight distribution	54 per cent front, 46 per cent rear
Wheelbase	2,520mm
Length	4,340mm
Width	1,690mm
Height	1,405mm
Front track	1,460mm
Rear track	1,455mm
Boot volume (VDA)	353 litres (seats do not fold)
Fuel tank	60 litres (13.2gal)

Impreza WRX Saloon Oct 1994–Aug 1996

As 1992–94 except:

Power output	260PS @ 6,500rpm
Torque	309Nm (227lb ft) @ 5,000rpm
Specific output	130PS per litre
Power-to-weight ratio	211PS per tonne
Brakes (rear)	Ventilated disc
Wheels	6 × 16-inch
Tyres	205/50 R16
Weight	1,230kg

Impreza WRX Saloon Sep 1996–Aug 1998

As 1994–96 except:

Compression ratio	8.0:1
Power output	280PS @ 6,500rpm
Torque	328Nm (242lb ft) @ 4,000rpm
Specific output	140PS per litre
Power-to-weight ratio	227PS per tonne
Final drive	4.444:1

Impreza WRX Saloon Sep 1998–Aug 2000

As 1996–98 except:

Torque	338Nm (249lb ft) @ 4,000rpm

Impreza WRX Sports Wagon Sep 1993–Aug 1996

As WRX saloon except:

Power output	220PS @ 6,000rpm
Torque	280Nm (206lb ft) @ 5,000rpm
Specific output	110PS per litre
Power-to-weight ratio	171PS per tonne
	(SA version 178PS per tonne)
Transmission	Optional four-speed automatic
Gearbox ratios (automatic)	1st 2.785 2nd 1.545
	3rd 1.000 4th 0.694
ABS optional	
Weight	1,280kg (SA version 1,230kg)

Impreza WRX Sports Wagon Sep 1996–Aug 1997

As 1993–96 except:

Power output	240PS @ 6,000rpm
Torque	304Nm (224lb ft) @ 3,000rpm
Specific output	120PS per litre
Power-to-weight ratio	184PS per tonne
Weight	1,300kg

Impreza WRX Sports Wagon Sep 1997–Aug 1998

As 1996–97 except:

Compression ratio	9.0:1
Power output	250PS @ 6,000rpm
	(240PS with automatic)
Torque	306Nm (225lb ft) @ 4,000rpm
Specific output	125PS per litre
Power-to-weight ratio	192PS per tonne

Impreza WRX Sports Wagon Sep 1998–Jun 2000

As 1997–98 except:

Power output	240PS @ 6,000rpm
Torque	309Nm (227lb ft) @ 4,000rpm
Specific output	120PS per litre
Power-to-weight ratio	184PS per tonne

Impreza WRX Type RA Nov 1992–Sep 1994

As WRX saloon 1992–94 except:

Power-to-weight ratio	205PS per tonne
Transmission	Front viscous coupling, manually adjustable centre diff, rear mechanical limited slip diff
Gearbox ratios	1st 3.454 2nd 2.333
	3rd 1.750 4th 1.354
	5th 0.972

Final drive	4.111:1
No ABS fitted	
Turns lock-to-lock	2.6
Wheels	6 x 15-inch alloy
Tyres	205/55 R15
Height	1,405mm
Weight	1,170kg

Impreza WRX Type RA Oct 1994–Aug 1996

As WRX Type RA 1992–94 except:

Power output	260PS @ 6,500rpm
Torque	309Nm (227lb ft) @ 5,000rpm
Specific output	130PS per litre
Power-to-weight ratio	220PS per tonne
Final drive	3.900:1
	(3.545:1 from Aug 1995)
Brakes (rear)	Ventilated disc
Wheels	6 x 16-inch
Tyres	205/50 R16
Weight	1,180kg

Impreza WRX Type RA Sep 1996–Aug 1998

As WRX Type RA 1994–96 except:

Power output	280PS @ 6,500rpm
Torque	328Nm (242lb ft) @ 4,000rpm
Specific output	140PS per litre
Power-to-weight ratio	237PS per tonne

Impreza WRX Type RA Sep 1998–Jun 2000

As WRX Type RA 1996–98 except:

Torque	338Nm (249lb ft) @ 4,000rpm
Power-to-weight ratio	231PS per tonne
Weight	1,210kg

Impreza WRX STi Version I Jan 1994–Sep 1994

As WRX saloon except:

Compression ratio	8.5:1
Power output	250PS @ 6,500rpm
Torque	309Nm (228lb ft) @ 3,500rpm
Specific output	125PS per litre
Power-to-weight ratio	203PS per tonne
	(Sports Wagon 192PS per tonne)
Gearbox	Five-speed close-ratio manual

Gearbox ratios/		
mph per 1,000rpm	1st 3.17/5.1	2nd 1.89/8.6
	3rd 1.30/12.4	4th 0.97/16.6
	5th 0.740/21.8	

Final drive	4.444:1
Brakes (rear)	Ventilated disc
Height	1,405mm
Weight	1,230kg (saloon),
	1,300kg (Sports Wagon)

Impreza WRX STi RA Version I Oct 1994–Jul 1995

As Version I 1994 except:

Power output	275PS @ 6,500rpm
Torque	319Nm (235lb ft) @ 4,000rpm
Specific output	138PS per litre
Power-to-weight ratio	229PS per tonne

No ABS system fitted		
Gearbox ratios	1st 3.454	2nd 2.333
	3rd 1.750	4th 1.354
	5th 0.972	
Wheels	6 x 16-inch alloy	
Tyres	205/50 R16 Bridgestone Expedia S-01	
Weight	1,200kg	

Impreza WRX STi Version II Aug 1995–Aug 1996

As Version I except:

Power output	260PS at 6,500rpm (Sports Wagon)
Torque	309Nm (228lb ft) at 5,000rpm (Sports Wagon)
Specific output	130PS per litre
Power-to-weight ratio	200PS per tonne (Sports Wagon)
ABS system fitted only on non-RA models	
Wheels	7 x 16-inch alloy

Impreza WRX STi Version III Sep 1996–Aug 1997

As Version II except:

Compression ratio	8.0:1
Power output	280PS at 6,500rpm (all models)
Torque	343Nm (253lb ft) at 4,000rpm (all models)
Specific output	140PS per litre
Power-to-weight ratio	227PS per tonne
	(RA 233PS per tonne)

Impreza WRX STi Version IV Sep 1997–Aug 1998

As Version III except:

Torque	352Nm (260lb ft) @ 4,000rpm
Power-to-weight ratio	220PS per tonne
(RA 225PS per tonne)	
Brakes (front)	280mm ventilated disc
Brakes (rear)	245mm ventilated disc
Tyres	205/50 VR16 Bridgestone Potenza S-01
Front track	1,465mm
Rear track	1,450mm
Weight	1,275kg (saloon),
	1,340kg (Sports Wagon), 1,245kg (RA)

Impreza WRX STi Version V/VI
Sep 1998–Aug 1999/Sep 1999–Jun 2000

As Version IV except:

Power-to-weight ratio	215PS per tonne
	(RA 220PS per tonne)
Brakes (front)	298mm ventilated disc
Weight	1,300kg (saloon),
	1,370kg (Sports Wagon), 1,270kg (RA)

Impreza WRX STi S201

As STi Version VI except:

Power output	300PS @ 6,500rpm
Torque	352Nm (260lb ft) @ 4,000rpm
Specific output	150PS per litre
Power-to-weight ratio	235PS per tonne
Gearbox ratios	1st 3.083	2nd 2.062
	3rd 1.545	4th 1.151
	5th 0.825	

Final drive	4.444:1
Weight	1,275kg
Length	4,375mm
Width	1,690mm
Height	1,405mm

Impreza WRX STi Type R Jan 1997–Aug 1997

As STi Version III except:

Power-to-weight ratio	225PS per tonne
Gearbox ratios/	
mph per 1,000rpm	1st 3.083/5.6 2nd 2.062/8.3
	3rd 1.545/11.1 4th 1.151/14.9
	5th 0.825/20.8
Final drive	4.444:1
No ABS system fitted	
Wheels	7 x 16-inch alloy
Tyres	205/60 R16 Bridgestone Potenza RE10
Weight	1,240kg

Impreza WRX STi Type R Version IV/V/VI
Sep 1997– Aug 1998/Sep 1998–Aug 1999/ Sep 1999–Jun 2000

As Type R 1997 except:

Torque	352Nm (260lb ft) @ 4,000rpm

Impreza WRX STi Type R 22B Mar 1998–Aug 1998

Engine	Type EJ22 2,212cc four-cylinder horizontally opposed at an angle of 52°, mounted longitudinally at the front, aluminium head and block
Bore/stroke	96.9/75.0mm
Compression ratio	8.0
Valves	Four per cylinder, double overhead camshafts on each bank
Ignition	Electronic
Induction	Multipoint fuel injection
Power output	280PS (276PS) @ 6,000rpm
Torque	360Nm (265lb ft) @ 3,200rpm
Specific output	126PS per litre
Power-to-weight ratio	220PS per tonne
Transmission	Permanent four-wheel-drive, front viscous coupling, manually adjustable centre diff, rear mechanical limited slip diff
Gearbox	Five-speed manual
Ratios	1st 3.083 2nd 2.062
	3rd 1.545 4th 1.151
	5th 0.825
Final drive	4.444:1 (3.900:1 for Type UK)
Suspension (front)	MacPherson struts, coil springs, transverse link
Suspension (rear)	MacPherson struts, coil springs, transverse link, trailing arms
Steering	Rack-and-pinion, power-assisted
Turns lock-to-lock	2.6
Turning circle	10.4m
Brakes (front)	Ventilated disc
Brakes (rear)	Ventilated disc
No ABS system fitted	
Wheels	8.5 x 17-inch BBS alloy
Tyres	235/40 ZR17

Weight	1,270kg
Wheelbase	2,520mm
Length	4,365mm
Width	1,770mm
Height	1,390mm
Front track	1,480mm
Rear track	1,500mm
Fuel tank	60 litres (13.2gal)

Impreza 2.5 RS (USA)

Engine	Type EJ25 2,457cc four-cylinder horizontally opposed at an angle of 52°, mounted longitudinally at the front, aluminium head and block
Bore/stroke	99.5/79mm
Compression ratio	9.5:1
Valves	Four per cylinder, double overhead camshafts on each bank
Ignition	Electronic
Induction	Multipoint fuel injection
Power output	167PS (165bhp) @ 5,600rpm
Torque	220Nm (162lb ft) @ 4,000rpm (1998), 225Nm (166lb ft) @ 4,000rpm (1999–2001)
Specific output	67bhp per litre
Power-to-weight ratio	128bhp per tonne
Transmission	Permanent four-wheel-drive, front free differential, centre viscous coupling, rear free differential (rear viscous coupling from 2000 MY)
Gearbox	Five-speed manual or four-speed automatic
Ratios (manual)	1st 3.545 2nd 2.111
	3rd 1.448 4th 1.088
	5th 0.825 (0.780 from 1999MY)
Ratios (automatic)	1st 3.027 2nd 1.619
	3rd 1.000 4th 0.694
Final drive	3.900:1 or 4.111:1 (manual), 4.444:1 (automatic)
Suspension (front)	MacPherson struts, coil springs, transverse link
Suspension (rear)	MacPherson struts, coil springs, transverse link, trailing arms
Steering	Rack-and-pinion, power-assisted
Turns lock-to-lock	3.2
Turning circle	10.4m
Brakes (front)	272mm ventilated disc
Brakes (rear)	267mm solid disc
ABS system fitted	
Wheels	7 x 16-inch alloy
Tyres	205/55 R16
Weight	1,280kg (coupé man), 1,300kg (coupé auto), 1,282kg (saloon man), 1,302kg (saloon auto)
Weight distribution	54 per cent front, 46 per cent rear
Wheelbase	2,520mm
Length	4,375mm
Width	1,705mm
Height	1,410mm
Front track	1,460mm
Rear track	1,450mm
Fuel tank	60 litres (13.2gal/15.9 US gal)

IMPREZA 2nd GENERATION (GD)

EUROPEAN/AUSTRALIAN WRX AND STI
Impreza WRX (Europe) Oct 2000–Dec 2002

Engine	EJ20 1,994cc four-cylinder horizontally opposed at an angle of 52°, mounted longitudinally at the front, aluminium head and block, turbocharger, air-to-air intercooler, oil cooler
Bore/stroke	92/75mm
Compression ratio	8.0:1
Valves	Four per cylinder, double overhead camshafts on each bank
Ignition	Electronic
Induction	Multipoint fuel injection
Power output	218PS (215bhp) @ 5,600rpm
Torque	292Nm (215lb ft) @ 3,600rpm
Specific output	107bhp per litre
Power-to-weight ratio	155bhp per tonne (saloon) 152bhp per tonne (estate)
Transmission	Permanent four-wheel drive, front differential, centre viscous coupling, rear viscous coupling
Gearbox	Five-speed manual
Ratios/mph per 1,000rpm	1st 3.454/5.3 2nd 1.947/9.4 3rd 1.366/13.4 4th 0.972/18.8 5th 0.738/24.7
Final drive	3.900:1
Suspension (front)	MacPherson struts, coil springs, transverse link, anti-roll bar
Suspension (rear)	MacPherson struts, coil springs, transverse link, trailing arms, anti-roll bar
Steering	Rack-and-pinion, power-assisted
Turns lock-to-lock	2.75
Turning circle	11.0m
Brakes (front)	294mm ventilated disc
Brakes (rear)	266mm ventilated disc 4-channel ABS system fitted
Wheels	7 x 17-inch alloy
Tyres	215/45 ZR17 Bridgestone Potenza RE 011
Weight	1,385kg (saloon) 1,410kg (estate)
Weight distribution	60 per cent front, 40 per cent rear
Wheelbase	2,525mm
Length	4,405mm
Width	1,730mm (saloon) 1,695mm (estate)
Height	1,440mm (saloon) 1,485mm (estate)
Front track	1,485mm (saloon) 1,465mm (estate)
Rear track	1,480mm (saloon) 1,455mm (estate)
Boot volume (VDA)	Saloon: 311 litres Estate: 349 litres
Fuel tank	60 litres (13.2 gal)

Impreza WRX (Europe) Jan 2003–Oct 2005
As Impreza WRX Oct 2000–Dec 2002 except:

Power output	225PS @ 5,600rpm
Torque	300Nm (221lb ft) @ 4,000rpm
Specific output	113PS per litre
Power-to-weight ratio	162PS per tonne

Prodrive Performance Package WRX (May 2001-Oct 2005)
As Impreza WRX except:

Power output	245PS @ 5,600rpm (May 2001–Feb 2003) 265PS @ 5,600rpm (Feb 2003–Oct 2005)
Torque	354Nm (261lb ft) @ 4,000rpm (May 2001–Feb 2003) 349Nm (257lb ft) @ 3,500rpm (Feb 2003–Oct 2005)
Power-to-weight ratio	177PS per tonne (May 2001–Feb 2003) 191PS per tonne (Feb 2003– Oct 2005)

Impreza WRX (Australia)
As WRX (Europe) except:

Gearbox	Five-speed manual (and four-speed automatic option from 2001)	
Gearbox ratios (manual from 2001)	1st 3.166	2nd 1.882
	3rd 1.296	4th 0.972
	5th 0.738	
Gearbox ratios (automatic)	1st 2.785	2nd 1.545
	3rd 1.000	4th 0.694
Final drive	3.900:1 (4.444:1 from 2001)	

Impreza WRX STi (Europe/Australia) (Jan 2002-Oct 2005)
As Impreza WRX except:

Power output	265PS (262bhp) @ 6,000rpm	
Torque	343Nm (253lb ft) @ 4,000rpm	
Specific output	132PS per litre	
Gearbox	Six-speed manual/driver control centre differential, yaw control sensor from September 2004	
Gearbox ratios/mph per 1,000rpm (Europe)	1st 3.636/5.2	2nd 2.375/8.0
	3rd 1.761/10.8	4th 1.346/14.1
	5th 0.971/19.5	6th 0.756/23.9
Gearbox ratios/mph per 1,000rpm (Australia)	1st 3.636/5.2	2nd 2.375/8.0
	3rd 1.761/10.8	4th 1.346/14.1
	5th 1.062/18.0	6th 0.842/22.7
Brakes (front)	330mm ventilated disc	
Brakes (rear)	305mm ventilated disc	
Wheels	7.5 x 17-inch alloy/8x17 inch alloy from Sep 2004	
Tyres	225/45 R17	
Wheelbase	2540mm from Sep 2004	
Rear track	1495mm from Sep 2004	
Weight	1,470kg	

Prodrive Performance Package STi (Oct 2002–Oct 2005)
As Impreza WRX STi except:

Power output	305PS @ 6,000rpm
Torque	406Nm (299lb ft) @ 4,000rpm
Specific output	152PS per litre
Power-to-weight ratio	207PS per tonne

Impreza WRX STi WR1 (2004)
As Impreza WRX STi except:

Power output	320PS @ 5,800rpm
Torque	420Nm (310lb ft) @ 4,000rpm
Specific output	160PS per litre
Power-to-weight ratio	217PS per tonne
Wheels	18-inch diameter
Tyres	225/45 R18

Impreza WRX (Oct 2005-Sep 2007)
As Impreza WRX Jan 2003-Oct 2005 except:

Engine	EJ25 2457cc
Bore/stroke	99.5/79mm
Compression ratio	8.0:1
Power output	230PS @ 5600rpm
Torque	319Nm (235lb ft) @ 3600rpm
Specific output	93PS per litre
Power to weight ratio	163PS per tonne (saloon), 161PS per tonne (estate)
Length	4465mm
Weight	1410kg (saloon), 1425kg (estate)

Impreza WRX STi (Oct 2005-Sep 2007)
As Impreza WRX Oct 2005-Sep 2007 except:

Power output	280PS @ 5600rpm
Torque	392Nm (289lb ft) @ 4000rpm
Specific output	114PS per litre
Power to weight ratio	187PS per tonne
Transmission	6-speed manual, driver control centre differential

Gearbox ratios/mph per 1000rpm		
	1st 3.636	2nd 2.235
	3rd 1.521	4th 1.137
	5th 0.891	6th 0.707:1/26.2

Final drive	3.900:1
Wheelbase	2540mm
Weight	1495kg

Prodrive Performance Package WRX (Apr 2006-Sep 2007)
As Impreza WRX (Oct 2005-Sep 2007) except:

Power output	270PS @ 5700rpm
Torque	420Nm (310lb ft) @ 3000rpm
Specific output	109PS per litre
Power to weight ratio	191PS per tonne

Prodrive Performance Package WRX STi (Apr 2006-Sep 2007)
As Impreza WRX STi (Oct 2005-Sep 2007) except:

Power output	320PS @ 6000rpm
Torque	450Nm (332lb ft) @ 3700rpm
Specific output	130PS per litre
Power to weight ratio	214PS per tonne

JAPANESE IMPREZA WRX NB, 20K AND STI
Impreza WRX NB and 20K (Aug 2000- Aug 2007)

Engine	EJ20 1,994cc four-cylinder horizontally opposed at an angle of 52°, mounted longitudinally at the front, aluminium head and block, turbocharger, air-to-air intercooler, oil cooler
Bore/stroke	92/75mm
Compression ratio	9.0:1
Valves	Four per cylinder, double overhead camshafts on each bank
Ignition	Electronic
Induction	Multipoint fuel injection
Power output	250PS @ 6,000rpm
Torque	333Nm (245lb ft) @ 3,600rpm
Specific output	125PS per litre
Power-to-weight ratio	186PS per tonne
Transmission	Permanent four-wheel drive, front differential, centre viscous coupling, rear viscous coupling
Gearbox	Five-speed manual or four-speed automatic

Gearbox ratios (manual)		
	1st 3.166	2nd 1.882
	3rd 1.296	4th 0.972
	5th 0.738	

Gearbox ratios (automatic)		
	1st 2.785	2nd 1.545
	3rd 1.000	4th 0.694

Final drive	4.444:1 (manual and automatic from Sep 2001) 4.111:1 (automatic until Sep 2001)
Suspension (front)	MacPherson struts, coil springs, transverse link, anti-roll bar
Suspension (rear)	MacPherson struts, coil springs, transverse link, trailing arms, anti-roll bar
Steering	Rack-and-pinion, power-assisted
Turns lock-to-lock	2.75
Turning circle	11.0m
Brakes (front)	294mm ventilated disc
Brakes (rear)	266mm ventilated disc
4-channel ABS system fitted	
Wheels	6.5 x 16-inch alloy (7 x 17-inch optional)
Tyres	205/55 R16 Bridgestone Potenza (215/45 R17 optional)
Weight	1,340kg (saloon man) 1,370kg (saloon auto) 1,370kg (estate man) 1,400kg (estate auto)
Weight distribution	60 per cent front, 40 per cent rear
Wheelbase	2,525mm
Length	4,405mm (4465mm from Oct 2005)
Width	1,730mm (saloon) 1,695mm (estate)
Height	1,440mm (saloon) 1,485mm (estate)
Front track	1,485mm (saloon) 1,465mm (estate)
Rear track	1,480mm (saloon) 1,455mm (estate)

Boot volume (VDA)	Saloon: 311 litres		
	Estate: 349 litres		
Fuel tank	60 litres (13.2 gal)		

Impreza WRX STi (Oct 2000–Aug 2007)
As WRX NB & 20K except:

Compression ratio	8.0:1		
Power output	280PS @ 6,400rpm		
Torque	373Nm (275lb ft) @ 4,000rpm (STi Limited		
385Nm/283lb ft)	393Nm (290 lb ft) @ 4,400rpm from Nov		
2002			
Specific output	140PS per litre		
Power-to-weight ratio	200PS per tonne		
Ratios/mph per			
1,000rpm	1st 3.636/5.2	2nd 2.375/8.0	
	3rd 1.761/10.8	4th 1.346/14.1	
	5th 1.062/18.0	6th 0.842/22.7	
Final drive	3.900:1		
Wheels	7 x 17-inch alloy / 8x17 inch alloy		
	from Sep 2004		
Tyres	225/45 ZR17 Bridgestone RE040 (saloon)		
	215/45 ZR17 (estate)		
	235/45 ZR 17 from Sep 2004		
Weight	1,400kg (saloon) 1,430kg (estate);		
	from Oct 2005: 1460kg (saloon only, estate		
	ceases production)		
Height	1,435mm (saloon) 1,460mm (estate)		
Rear track	1,495mm from Sep 2004		

Impreza WRX STi RA (Japan) (Oct 2000-Aug 2007)
As WRX STi (Japan) except:

Power-to-weight ratio	207PS per tonne
Turns lock-to-lock	2.6
Wheels	(optional) 7 x 16-inch alloys
Tyres	(optional) 205/50 R16
Weight	1,350–1,370kg

Impreza WRX STi RA Spec C (Oct 2000-Aug 2007)
As WRX STi RA except:

Torque	385Nm (283lb ft) @ 4,400rpm
	412Nm (304lb ft) from Sep 2004
Power-to-weight ratio	214PS per tonne
Wheels	8 x 17-inch from Sep 2004
Tyres	235/45 R17 from Sep 2004
Height	1,425mm
Weight	1,310–1,350kg

Impreza WRX STi RA S202 (May 2002)
As WRX STi RA Spec C except:

Power output	320PS @ 6,400rpm
Specific output	160PS per litre
Power-to-weight ratio	240PS per tonne
Weight	1,330kg

Impreza WRX STi S203 (Dec 2004-Feb 2005)
As WRX STi except:

Power output	320PS @ 6400rpm
Torque	420Nm (310lb ft) @ 4400rpm
Specific output	160PS per litre

Power to weight ratio	221PS per tonne
Wheels	18in BBS alloy
Tyres	Pirelli PZero Corsa 235/40 ZR18
Weight	1445kg

Impreza WRX STi S204 (Dec 2005)
As S203 except:

Torque	432Nm (318lb ft) @ 4400rpm

Impreza WRX STi Spec C Type RA-R (Oct 2006)
As S204 except:

Power to weight ratio	230PS per tonne
Brakes (front)	Brembo monoblock six-piston callipers
	and grooved discs
Wheels	8.5 x 18 Enkei alloys
Tyres	Bridgestone Potenza RE070 235/40 ZR18
Weight	1390kg

USA IMPREZA WRX AND STI
Impreza WRX (USA)
As WRX (Europe) except:

Power output	227bhp @ 6,000rpm		
Torque	294Nm (217lb ft) @ 4,000rpm		
Specific output	114bhp per litre		
Power-to-weight ratio	162bhp per tonne (saloon) to		
	155bhp per tonne (wagon auto)		
Gearbox	Five-speed manual or four-speed automatic		
Gearbox ratios/mph			
per 1,000rpm			
(manual)	1st 3.454/5.3	2nd 1.947/9.4	
	3rd 1.366/13.4	4th 0.972/18.8	
	5th 0.738/24.7		
Gearbox ratios			
(automatic)	1st 2.785	2nd 1.545	
	3rd 1.000	4th 0.694	
Final drive	3.900:1 (automatic 4.111:1)		
Turns lock-to-lock	3.0		
Turning circle	10.7m		
Brakes (front)	290mm ventilated disc		
Brakes (rear)	260mm solid disc		
Wheels	6.5 x 16-inch alloy (7 x 17-inch BBS		
	optional)		
Tyres	205/55 R16 Bridgestone Potenza		
	(215/45 R17 optional)		
Weight	1,400kg (saloon man)		
	1,430kg (saloon auto)		
	1,435kg (estate man)		
	1,460kg (estate auto)		

Impreza WRX STi (USA)
As WRX (USA) except:

Engine	2,457cc
Bore/stroke	99.5/79mm
Power output	300bhp @ 6,000rpm
Torque	407Nm (300lb ft) @ 4,000rpm
Specific output	122bhp per litre
Power-to-weight ratio	202bhp per tonne
Transmission	Permanent four-wheel drive, front

differential, centre viscous coupling, rear viscous coupling

Gearbox	Six-speed manual
Gearbox ratios/mph per 1,000rpm	1st 3.636/5.2 2nd 2.375/8.0
	3rd 1.761/10.8 4th 1.346/14.1
	5th 0.971/19.5 6th 0.756/23.9
Final drive	3.545:1 from 2006
Turns lock-to-lock	2.8
Brakes (front)	322mm ventilated disc
Brakes (rear)	312mm ventilated disc
Wheels	7.5 x 17-inch alloy
Tyres	225/45R17 90W
Weight	1,483kg

Saab 9-2X Aero (USA)

As WRX (USA) except:

Turns lock-to-lock	2.8
Wheels	7 x 17-inch alloy
Tyres	215/45R Bridgestone Potenza RE011
Weight	1,477kg

IMPREZA 3rd GENERATION (GE)

EUROPE

Impreza WRX Nov 2007-

Engine	EJ25 2,457cc 4-cylinder horizontally-opposed at an angle of 52 degrees, mounted longitudinally at the front, aluminium head and block, turbocharger, air-to-air intercooler, oil cooler
Bore/stroke	99.5/75mm
Compression ratio	8.4:1
Valves	4 per cylinder, double overhead camshafts on each bank
Ignition	Electronic
Induction	Multipoint fuel injection
Power output	230PS (226bhp) @ 5,200rpm / WRX-S: 255PS (251bhp) @ 5,400rpm
Torque	320Nm (236lb ft) @ 2,800rpm / WRX-S: 390Nm (287lb ft) @ 3,000rpm
Specific output	93PS per litre / WRX-S: 103PS per litre
Power to weight ratio	164PS per tonne / WRX-S: 182PS per tonne
Transmission	Permanent four-wheel drive, front differential, centre viscous coupling, rear mechanical coupling and limited slip differential, Vehicle Dynamics Control
Gearbox	5-speed manual
Ratios/mph per 1000rpm	1st 3.166/5.3 2nd 1.882/8.8
	3rd 1.296/12.8 4th 0.972/17.1
	5th 0.738/22.6
Final drive	4.444:1
Suspension (front)	MacPherson struts, coil springs, transverse link, anti-roll bar
Suspension (rear)	Multilink, coil springs, double wishbones, trailing arms, anti-roll bar

Steering	Rack-and-pinion, variable power-assisted
Turning circle	11.2m
Brakes (front)	Ventilated disc
Brakes (rear)	Solid disc
	4-channel ABS system with EBD fitted
Wheels	7x17 inch alloy / WRX-S: 7.5x18
Tyres	205/50 R17 / WRX-S: 225/40 R18
Weight	1,395kg
Wheelbase	2,620mm
Length	4,415mm
Width	1,740mm
Height	1,475mm
Front track	1,495mm
Rear track	1,500mm
Boot volume (VDA)	1,257 litres
Fuel tank	60 litres (13.2 gals)

Impreza WRX STi Jan 2008-

As WRX Nov 2007- except:

Compression ratio	8.2:1
Power output	300PS (296bhp) @ 6,000rpm / 330S: 330PS (325bhp) @ 5,400rpm
Torque	407Nm (300lb ft) @ 4,000rpm / 330S: 255Nm (346lb ft) @ 3,400rpm
Specific output	122PS per litre / 330S: 134PS per litre
Power to weight ratio	199PS per tonne / 330S: 219PS per tonne
Transmission	Driver control centre differential
Gearbox	6-speed manual
Gearbox ratios	1st 3.636/5.2 2nd 2.235/8.4
	3rd 1.590/11.8 4th 1.137/16.5
	5th 0.891/21.1 6th 0.707/26.6
Final drive	3.900:1
Turning circle	11.0m
Brakes (front)	330mm ventilated disc
Brakes (rear)	305mm ventilated disc
	4-channel ABS system with EBD fitted
Wheels	8x17 inch alloy / 330S: 8.5x18 inch
Tyres	Dunlop SP01 235/45 R17 / 330S: Dunlop SP600 245/40 R18
Weight	1,505kg
Width	1,795mm
Front track	1,530mm
Rear track	1,540mm

JAPAN S-GT/WRX/GT AND STI

S-GT/WRX (Jun 2007-)

Engine	EJ20 1994cc 4-cylinder horizontally opposed, mounted longitudinally at the front, aluminium head and block, turbocharger, intercooler, oil cooler
Bore/stroke	92/75mm
Compression ratio	9.4:1
Valves	Four per cylinder, double overhead camshafts on each bank
Ignition	Electronic
Induction	Multipoint fuel injection
Power output	250PS (246bhp) @ 6,000rpm

Torque	333Nm (245lb ft) @ 2,400rpm
Specific output	125PS per litre
Power to weight ratio	181PS per tonne
Transmission	Permanent four-wheel drive, front differential, centre viscous coupling, rear mechanical coupling and limited slip differential, Vehicle Dynamics Control
Gearbox	5-speed manual or 4-speed automatic
Gearbox Ratios (manual)	1st 3.166 2nd 1.882
	3rd 1.296 4th 0.972
	5th 0.738
Gearbox Ratios (auto)	1st 2.785 2nd 1.545
	3rd 1.000 4th 0.694
Final drive	4.111:1
Suspension (front)	MacPherson struts, coil springs, transverse link, anti-roll bar
Suspension (rear)	Multilink, coil springs, double wishbones, trailing arms, anti-roll bar
Steering	Rack-and-pinion, variable power-assisted
Turning circle	10.6m
Brakes (front)	Ventilated disc
Brakes (rear)	Solid disc
	4-channel ABS system with EBD fitted
Wheels	16- inch alloy; 17-inch optional
Tyres	205/55 R 16; 215/45R17 optional
Weight	1,380kg (manual), 1,410kg (auto)
Wheelbase	2,620mm
Length	4,415mm
Width	1,740mm
Height	1,475mm
Front track	1,495mm
Rear track	1,500mm
Boot volume (VDA)	1,257 litres
Fuel tank	60 litres (13.2 gals)

WRX STi (Oct 2007-)

As S-GT/WRX/GT (Jun 2007-) except:

Compression ratio	8.0:1
Power output	308PS (304bhp) @ 6,400rpm
Torque	422Nm (311lb ft) @ 4,400rpm
Specific output	154PS per litre
Power to weight ratio	208PS per tonne
Transmission	Driver control centre differential
Gearbox	6-speed manual
Gearbox ratios	1st 3.636 2nd 2.235
	3rd 1.761 4th 1.346
	5th 1.062 6th 0.842
Final drive	3.900:1
Turning circle	11.0m
Brakes (front)	330mm ventilated disc
Brakes (rear)	305mm ventilated disc
	4-channel ABS system with EBD fitted
Wheels	8.5x18 inch
Tyres	Bridgestone 245/40 18
Weight	1,480kg
Width	1,795mm
Front track	1,530mm
Rear track	1,540mm

WRX STi A-Line (Feb 2009-)

As WRX STi except:

Engine	EJ25 2457cc
Bore/stroke	99.5/75mm
Compression ratio	8.2:1
Power output	300PS (296bhp) @ 6,200rpm
Torque	350Nm (258lb ft) @ 2,800rpm
Specific output	122PS per litre
Power to weight ratio	201PS per tonne
Gearbox	5-speed automatic
Gearbox ratios	1st 3.540 2nd 2.264
	3rd 1.471 4th 1.000
	5th 0.834
Final drive	3.583:1
Weight	1,490kg

USA IMPREZA WRX AND STI

Impreza WRX (USA)

As WRX (Europe) except:

Power output	265bhp @ 6,000rpm
Torque	331Nm (244lb ft) @ 4,000rpm
Specific output	107bhp per litre
Power to weight ratio	184bhp per tonne
Tyres	225/45 R17
Weight	1,440kg
Length	Saloon: 4,580mm
Boot volume (VDA)	Saloon: 320 litres

Impreza WRX STi (USA)

As WRX STi (Europe) except:

Power output	305bhp @ 6,000rpm
Torque	393Nm (290lb ft) @ 4,000rpm
Specific output	124bhp per litre
Power to weight ratio	198bhp per tonne
Wheels	8.5x18 inch
Tyres	245/40 R18
Weight	1,540kg
Width	1,795mm
Front track	1,530mm
Rear track	1,540mm

Performance figures

Turbo 2000 (Mar 1994–Sep 1996)

Max speed	137mph (220kph)
0–60mph (96.5kph)	5.8sec
Standing 1/4 mile	14.7sec (97mph/156kph)
Standing kilometre	27.5sec (114mph/183kph)
50–70mph (80–113kph)	
in top	13.4sec
30–70mph (48–113kph)	
through gears	6.6sec
Average fuel consumption	18.7mpg (15l/100km)
EC fuel consumption	Urban 24.8mpg (11.4l/100km)
	56mph (90kph) 39.8mpg (7.1l/100km)
	75mph (121kph) 30.1mpg (9.4l/100km)

Source: *Autocar* 6/4/1994

Turbo 2000 (Oct 1996–Sep 1998)

Max speed	143mph (230kph)
0–60mph (96.5kph)	5.5sec
Standing 1/4 mile	14.2sec (87mph/140kph)
Standing kilometre	26.7sec (120mph/193kph)
50–70mph (80–113kph)	
in top	8.5sec
30–70mph (48–113kph)	
through gears	5.6sec
Average fuel consumption	19.5mpg (14.5l/100km)
EC fuel consumption	Urban 20.5mpg (13.8l/100km)
	Extra-Urban 34.9mpg (8.1l/100km)
	Combined 27.7mpg (10.2l/100km)

Source: *Autocar* 4/2/1998

Turbo 2000 (Oct 1998–Sep 2000)

Max speed	143mph (230kph)
0–60mph (96.5kph)	5.6sec
Standing 1/4 mile	14.3sec (96mph/154kph)
Standing kilometre	26.5sec (119mph/191kph)
50–70mph (80–113kph)	
in top	9.1sec
30–70mph (48–113kph)	
through gears	5.7sec
Average fuel consumption	22.3mpg (12.7l/100km)
EC fuel consumption	Urban 20.5mpg 13.8l/100km)
	Extra-Urban 34.9mpg (8.1l/100km)
	Combined 27.7mpg (10.2l/100km)

Source: *Autocar* 3/3/1999

STi Type R 22B

Max speed	149mph (240kph)
0–60mph (96.5kph)	5.0sec
Standing 1/4 mile	13.7sec (102mph/164kph)
Standing kilometre	24.7sec (127mph/204kph)
50–70mph (80–113kph)	
in top	5.8sec
30–70mph (48–113kph)	
through gears	5.0sec
Average fuel consumption	20mpg (14l/100km)

Source: Autocar 9/12/1998

P1

Max speed	155mph (249kph)
0–60mph (96.5kph)	4.7sec
Standing 1/4 mile	13.9sec (105mph/169kph)
Standing kilometre	24.6sec (127mph/204kph)
50–70mph (80–113kph)	
in top	6.8sec
30–70mph (48–113kph)	
through gears	4.8sec
Average fuel consumption	19.5mpg
(14.5l/100km)	
EC fuel consumption	Urban 19.2mpg (14.7l/100km)
	Extra-Urban 31.0mpg (9.1l/100km)
	Combined 25.2mpg (11.2l/100km)

Source: *Autocar* 5/4/2000

WRX STi Version III

Max speed	150mph (241kph)
0–60mph (96.5kph)	4.6sec
Standing 1/4 mile	13.3sec (104mph/167kph)
Standing kilometre	24.1 secs (129mph/208kph)
50–70mph (80–113kph)	
in top	6.5sec
30–70mph (48–113kph)	
through gears	4.8sec
Average fuel consumption	19.9mpg (14.2l/100km)

Source: *Autocar* 13/5/1998

2.5 RS (USA)

Max speed	124mph (199kph)
0–60mph (96.5kph)	7.9sec
Standing 1/4 mile	16sec
(85.9mph/138kph)	
Fuel consumption	EPA city 22mpg (12.8l/100km)
	Highway 28mpg (10.1l/100km)
	Average 27mpg (10.5l/100km)

Source: *Edmunds*

New Impreza WRX 2000 (Europe/Australia)

Max speed	141mph (227kph)
0–60mph (96.5kph)	5.7sec
Standing 1/4 mile	14.5sec (95mph/153kph)
Standing kilometre	27.9sec (120mph/193kph)
50–70mph (80–113kph)	
in top	9.6sec
30–70mph (48–113kph)	
through gears	5.8sec
Average fuel consumption	18.7mpg (15.1l/100km)

Source: *Autocar* 25/10/2000

WRX 2003 5-door

Max speed	140mph (225kph)
0–60mph (96.5kph)	5.5sec
Standing 1/4 mile	14.3sec (95mph/153kph)
Standing kilometre	27.0sec (121mph/195kph)
50–70mph (80–113kph)	
in top	9.5sec
30–70mph (48–113kph)	
through gears	5.8sec
Average fuel consumption	23.0mpg (12.3 l/100km)
Source: *Autocar* 29/1/2003	

WRX STi 2003 with Prodrive Performance Pack

Max speed	155mph (250kph)
0–62mph (100kph)	4.6sec
Source: *Autocar* 29/1/2003	

New Impreza WRX STi (Japan)

Max speed	155mph/249kph (est)
0–60mph (96.5kph)	4.6sec (est)
Average fuel consumption	19.6mpg (14.4l/100km)
Source: *Autocar* 14/2/2001	

New Impreza WRX (USA)

Max speed	140mph (225kph)
	(automatic limited to 130mph/209kph)
0–60mph (96.5kph)	5.8sec (automatic 6.5sec)
Standing 1/4 mile	14.7sec (automatic 15.2sec)
Average fuel consumption	20.3mpg (13.9l/100km)
Source: *Car & Driver*	

WRX STi 2008

Max speed	155mph (250kph)
0-60mph (96.5kph)	5.2sec
Standing kilometre	25.1sec (130mph/209kph)
50-70mph (80-113kph)	
in 5th	5.1sec
Average fuel consumption	18.1mpg (15.6 l/100km)
Source: *Autocar* 5/3/2008	

Production evolution and production totals

PRODUCTION EVOLUTION

Nov 1992 Subaru's all-new Impreza makes its debut in Japan, including 240PS WRX and WRX RA versions.

Mar 1993 The non-turbo Impreza range for Europe is launched at the Geneva Motor Show. Sales begin in the UK in May 1993.

Oct 1993 The 1994 MY WRX goes on sale in Japan boasting revised spring and damper rates, reprogrammed engine management and improved electrics. The WRX range is expanded to include a 220PS five-door – also available with automatic transmission.

Jan 1994 The fabled STi-tuned WRX makes its production debut, offering 250PS, a close-ratio gearbox, uprated suspension and brakes and bodywork enhancements.

Mar 1994 After a Geneva show debut, the Swiss and British markets are the first to receive the new 211PS (208PS) turbocharged Impreza. The Australian market also receives the turbo model (called WRX but not the same as the Japanese version) this month.

Oct 1994 The 1995 MY WRX is launched in Japan, with the WRX and WRX RA now having 260PS engines; the STi Type RA (the only STi model sold this year) responds with 275PS.

Apr 1995 The turbocharged Impreza GT finally makes it to the French market but Germany does not follow until a year later. Jun 1995 To celebrate Colin McRae's victory in the RAC Rally, Subaru UK launches a Series McRae special edition with larger wheels, special paint, unique trim and decals.

Aug 1995 The 1996 MY WRX and STi Version II are launched in Japan, alongside a range of special editions called 555 and V-Limited. The STi saloon has 275PS but the new STi wagon has only 260PS.

Sep 1996 The 1997 MY WRX and STi Version III arrive on the Japanese market, together with two special editions (555 Individual and V-Limited). The two-door STi Type R also appears for the first time (also with a special edition, the yellow-painted Signature). All WRX Imprezas now have 280PS, with the exception of the WRX wagon (240PS).

Oct 1996 The European 1997 MY Turbo arrives, sporting a front and rear facelift, better interiors with sports seats, extra refinement, better gearchange and extra torque for the engine. The Australian version has an automatic transmission option for 1997.

Mar 1997 The Catalunya special edition in the UK has gold wheels, black paint, air conditioning and red-and-black interior trim.

Apr 1997 A turbo-lookalike Impreza is launched in the USA, called the 2.5 RS and fitted with a non-turbo 2.5-litre boxer engine.

Sep 1997 The 1998 MY WRX and STi Version IV make their debut in Japan, alongside more V-Limited editions. More torque for the STi and the WRX wagon gets an extra 10PS.

Oct 1997 The 1998 MY European Turbo arrives, boasting a much-improved interior, 16-inch wheels and a smoother engine.

Mar 1998 Celebrating 40 years of Subaru car production, the STi Type R 22B limited edition offers the closest roadgoing equivalent to Colin McRae's WRC; its 2.2-litre engine has more torque than any other Impreza.

Apr 1998 The Terzo edition in the UK has blue paint, gold wheels, special badging, grey Alcantara trim and air conditioning.

Aug 1998 Australia is the first country to see the 1999 MY turbocharged Impreza (the European debut is October), with its four-pot front callipers, bigger brakes including ventilated rear discs, taller rear wing and height-adjustable front seats, plus deeper single-vane bumper and new grille. The Phase 2 engine now boasts 218PS (215PS).

Sep 1998 The 1999 MY WRX and STi Version V arrive in Japan, as do various V-Limited editions. There is more torque for all standard WRX versions but the wagon's power output drops again to 240PS.

Oct 1998 The Birmingham Show sees the debut of the Prodrive-altered 22B Type UK, a limited run of only 16 cars, not actually on the road until January 1999.

Jan 1999 Australia receives its first official STi imports: modified Version V-Type R coupés to suit local conditions.

Mar 1999 The fourth and final UK special edition arrives in the form of the RB5, with its Japanese-spec bodyshell, 17-inch wheels, special paint, Alcantara trim, air conditioning, Prodrive quickshift gearchange and RB5 decals. Prodrive's WR Sport Performance Package was optional.

Aug 1999 Australia is again first to see the 2000 MY Turbo Impreza with its body-colour door mirrors and handles, new six-spoke alloy wheels and slightly revised interior.

Sep 1999 The 2000 MY and STi Version VI appear in Japan.

Oct 1999 The dramatic Prodrive P1 makes its debut at the London Earl's Court Motor Show (sales beginning in Spring 2000).

Nov 1999 Australia receives another limited batch of STi Imprezas, based on the four-door STi Version VI.

Apr 2000 Following the October 1999 Tokyo Show appearance of the pumped-up Electra One concept car, the limited-availability production version, called S201, goes on sale in Japan.

Jun 2000 Subaru ends production of the first generation Impreza after more than 700,000 cars have been sold.

Aug 2000 The 'New Age' Impreza range is launched in Japan, including 250PS versions (called WRX in saloon form and 20K in five-door form).

Oct 2000 An STi version of the WRX arrives in Japan, just one week after the debut of the European-spec 215PS WRX at the Birmingham Motor Show.

Jan 2001 The 227PS US version of the WRX – and the first-ever turbocharged Impreza sold there – goes on display at the Detroit Show ahead of an April on-sale date.

Feb 2001 STi Version S goes on sale in Japan.

May 2001 First UK New Age limited edition model is launched, the UK300. Prodrive's 245PS performance upgrade is launched at the same time.

Sep 2001 Range-wide Type B launched across the world with minor changes, including a deeper front air intake, strengthened front cross-member and EBD. STi Type RA briefly dropped while a new WRX NB-R version is launched in Japan. Australia has an automatic transmission option.

Oct 2001 STi Prodrive Style launched in Japan.

Dec 2001 STi RA Spec C launched in Japan, weighing 90kg less than the STi and boasting a higher torque output. Australia becomes the first market outside Japan to get the new STi.

Jan 2002 265PS STi goes on sale in many European markets. Porsche-designed Sports Wagon Type Euro launched in Japan.

May 2002 Limited edition S202 arrives in Japan.

Sep 2002 The Paris Motor Show is the world debut for the facelifted Impreza, featuring sculpted headlamps, new rear lights and larger air intakes, plus strengthened suspension. When the revised version goes on sale in December in Europe, the WRX also has a power boost to 225PS.

Oct 2002 Prodrive's 305PS performance upgrade for the STi goes on sale in the UK.

Nov 2002 Impreza facelift model goes on sale in Japan, at which time the domestic STi gets a torque boost.

Jan 2003 A 2.5-litre 300bhp turbocharged STi and facelifted WRX are launched in the USA. The facelifted Impreza goes on sale in Europe during January and February.

Feb 2003 Prodrive launches 265PS performance pack for the non-STi WRX.

Jan 2004 Special edition WR1 launched in UK.

Sep 2004 2005MY Impreza launched with chassis upgrades. STi has longer wheelbase and wider rear track, extended rear arches, driver-controlled centre diff, yaw sensor. WRX gets inverted strut suspension.

Dec 2004 S203 special edition launched in Japan

May 2005 Subaru UK launches WRX 300 special edition

Oct 2005 'Hawkeye' facelift launched with new front end design, new rear lights, 2.5-litre engine for WRX and STi in Europe (Japan retains 2.0 engine), revised gear ratios and DCCD

Nov 2005 Spec C Type RA 'Hawkeye' launched in Japan

Dec 2005 S204 special edition launched for Japanese market

Jan 2006 STi Spec D ('discreet') launched in UK, followed by A-Line in Japan

Apr 2006 Prodrive Performance Packs launched for 2.5-litre engines

Oct 2006 STi Spec C Type RA-R launched in Japan with very hardcore specification

Nov 2006 RB320 special edition arrives in UK

Apr 2007 All-new third-generation Impreza GE previewed at New York Auto Show, in hatchback and saloon forms. US receives 224PS 2.5-litre WRX

Jun 2007 New Impreza GE goes on sale in Japan, including 250PS turbocharged S-GT (in hatchback form only)

Jul 2007 Run-out GB270 editions launched in UK

Oct 2007 All-new Impreza STi launched in Japan featuring 280PS 2.0-litre engine and hatchback body shape, Si-Drive, upgraded DCCD, new multi-link rear suspension

Nov 2007 2.5-litre WRX with 230PS launched for UK market

Dec 2007 EU-spec 2.5-litre STi with 300PS previewed at Bologna Motor Show

Jul 2008 Two UK-market specials launched: 255PS WRX-S and 330PS STi 330S. WRX updated in US with retuned 2.5-litre engine and 265PS (224PS version remains on sale as 2.5GT)

Sep 2008 Impreza Boxer Diesel launched with 150PS flat-four diesel engine

Feb 2009 STi A-Line launched in Japan, with 2.5-litre single-scroll turbo engine, 300PS and Sportshift five-speed automatic transmission

Jul 2009 Spec C version of new-shape Impreza launched in Japan with ball bearing turbo, intercooler water spray, 308PS, reinforced suspension, mechanical rear limited-slip differential and lightweight items

Oct 2009 STi Carbon special edition launched in Japan with carbon-fibre roof and automatic transmission

Jan 2010 – STi R205 edition launched with hardcore spec in Japan

SUBARU IMPREZA PRODUCTION AND SALES

Production totals

	Saloon (domestic)	Saloon (export)	Sports Wagon (domestic)	Sports Wagon (export)	Total
1992	9,034	2,941	9,764	1,022	22,761
1993	18,830	48,063	18,271	30,060	115,224
1994	9,446	32,369	14,813	10,616	67,244
1995	16,428	19,719	33,308	16,387	85,842
1996	12,336	21,075	24,436	26,820	84,667
1997	12,207	22,816	27,202	30,229	92,454
1998	12,713	28,741	25,723	26,923	94,100
1999	10,267	32,293	17,260	26,924	86,744
2000	11,261	28,893	23,381	16,900	80,435
2001	48,553*		53,737*		102,290
2002	47,431*		47,960*		95,391
2003	9,250	46,280	14,386	29,106	99,022
2004	11,155	41,450	15,988	33,076	101,669
2005	10,837	45,794	18,505	26,987	102,123
2006	8,144	52,953	17,080	31,377	115,554
2007	2,798	46,065	34,464	73,875	157,202
2008	1,914	35,903	21,245	67,898	126,690
TOTAL	757,959 (all saloons)		871,723 (all Sports Wagons)		1,629,682

* No separate figures for domestic and export sales were available for 2001 and 2002

Sales Totals

	Domestic sales Annual	Cumulative	Exports	Knockdown*	Total sales Annual	Cumulative
	7,118	7,118	1,790		8,908	8,908
1993	31,319	38,437	73,915		105,234	114,142
1994	35,916	74,353	46,419		82,335	196,477
1995	44,986	119,339	35,844		80,830	277,307
1996	40,722	160,061	49,114		89,836	367,143
1997	38,986	199,047	53,480	1,800	94,266	459,609
1998	36,844	235,891	55,178	2,088	92,022	551,631
1999	29,934	265,825	58,122	2,232	90,288	639,687
2000	28,217	294,042	49,371	3,189	80,777	720,464
2001	28,069	322,111	76,302	1,356	105,727	826,191
2002	24,673	346,784	74,568		99,241	925,432
2003	23,589	370,373	74,934	-	98,523	1,023,955
2004	26,760	397,133	74,438	-	101,198	1,125,153
2005	28,937	426,070	72,386	-	101,323	1,226,476
2006	26,039	452,109	89,894	-	115,933	1,342,409
2007	34,013	486,122	111,489	-	145,502	1,487,911
2008	24,737	510,859	113,324	-	138,061	1,625,972

*Knockdown production in Taiwan

As ever with statistics, the respective figures for production and sales provided by Fuji Heavy Industries do not always agree with each other. Unfortunately, no separate figures are available for WRX and Turbo models.

Impreza's Best Sales Markets (to 2000)

Japan	277,910	UK	23,806	Switzerland	17,459
USA	172,885	Israel	23,541	Benelux	10,704
Australia	30,905	Germany	21,315	Canada	9,849

Specialists, clubs and websites

CLUBS

Great Britain
Subaru Impreza Drivers Club www.sidc.co.uk
The Subaru Impreza Drivers Club claims to be the largest Impreza Club in Europe. It has a Club Magazine (True Grip) and an active web forum. It runs lots of activities, from WRC trips and regional events to track days. Discounts are available on parts, insurance and breakdown services.

Other clubs:
Impreza Web Owners Club www.iwoc.co.uk
Scoobycity www.scoobycity.co.uk
Scoobynet www.scoobynet.co.uk

Australia & New Zealand
WRX Owners Club www.wrx.com.au www.wrx.com.au
NSW WRX Owners Club www.wrx.org.au
ClubSub www.clubsub.org.nz
WRX STi Club New Zealand www.wrxsticlub.co.nz

Europe
Subaru Club Netherlands www.cometo.555club.nl
    www.subaruclub.nl

USA
I Club www.i-club.com
New England Subaru Impreza Club www.drive.to/yourlimits
North American Subaru Impreza Owners Club www.nasioc.com

TUNING, PARTS & MODIFICATION

AFP, 07720 888610, www.andyforrestperformance.co.uk
API, 01926 614333, www.apiengines.com www.apiengines.com
Blue Print, www.blueprint-adl.co.uk www.blueprint-adl.co.uk
BR Developments, www.brdevelopments.com
Collins Performance Engineering, 01260 298500,
    www.mongooseexhausts.com
Demon Tweeks, 0844 815 8630 www.demon-tweeks.co.uk
Graham Goode Racing, 0844 3911 780 www.grahamgoode.com
Japarts, www.japarts.co.uk
Lateral Performance, 01923 238477, www.lateralperformance.co.uk
Litchfield Imports, 01684 850999, www.litchfieldimports.co.uk
Power Engineering, 01895 255699 www.powerengineering.co.uk
PowerStation, 01684 296675 www.powerstation.org.uk
Prodrive, 01295 273355 www.prodrive.com
Revolution Motorstore, 0845 002 3009, www.revolution247.com
Roger Clark Motorsport, 01455 828610,
    www.rogerclarkmotorsport.co.uk
Scoobyclinic, 01246 590807, www.scoobyclinic.com
Scoobymania, www.scoobymania.co.uk
Scoobyparts, 01234 300630, scoobyparts.com
Scoobysport, www.scoobysport.co.uk
Scoobyworld, 01509 266400, www.scoobyworld.co.uk

SW Motorsport, 07956 119962 www.sw-motorsport.co.uk
TDI Power Tuning, 0800 107 3250 www.tdi-plc.com
Turbo Technics, 01604 705050 www.turbotechnics.com
Zen Performance, 0845 055 9366, www.zenperformance.co.uk

INSURANCE

A-Plan 0845 071 1234
Adrian Flux 0800 505 3000, www.adrianflux.co.uk
Advance Insurance 0800 970 2566, www.advanceinsurance.co.uk
Footman James 0845 330 8410, www.footmanjames.co.uk
Insurance Factory 0800 440 2044, www.insurancefactory.co.uk
HWG 0845 130 4151
Keith Michaels 0845 618 5355, www.keithmichaels.co.uk
Mark Richard 01275 792270
Osborne & Sons 0845 330 6001, www.osborneandsons.co.uk
Performance Insurance 0844 4935 731,
    www.performanceinsurance.co.uk
Privilege 0800 051 6989, www.privilege.com
Swinton Specialist 0800 072 6620, swintonspecialist.co.uk

TRACK DAYS

Club MSV, www.clubmsv.com
Easytrack, www.easytrack.co.uk
Gold Track Driving Club, www.goldtrack.co.uk
Javelin Trackdays, www.javelin-motorsport.co.uk
RMA, www.rma-limited.com
Tracksense, www.tracksense.co.uk

BOOKS
Training WRX by Nick Warne. Very thorough work, mainly on tuning and modifying the Impreza Turbo (WRX in Australia). Written by an Australian in conjunction with MRT Performance.

High-Performance Subaru Builder's Guide by Jeff Zurschmeide. How to modify Subarus for performance on the street and track.

Selected official Subaru websites
Japan	www.subaru.co.jp
UK	www.subaru.co.uk
Australia	www.subaru.com.au
New Zealand	www.subaru.co.nz
USA	www.subaru.com
Canada	www.subaru.ca

Index